Elgar: The Man

MICHAEL DE-LA-NOY

ALLEN LANE

ALLEN LANE

Penguin Books Ltd

536 King's Road

London SW10 0UH

First published 1983

British Library Cataloguing in Publication Data

De-la-Noy, Michael
Elgar: The Man
1. Elgar, Edward   2. Composers –
England – Biography
I. Title
780'.92'4   ML410.E41

ISBN 0 7139 1532 3

Filmset in Monophoto Photina by
Northumberland Press Ltd, Gateshead
Printed in Great Britain by
Richard Clay (The Chaucer Press) Ltd,
Bungay, Suffolk

212397

For Bruce

Contents

List of Plates

Preface

No one is likely to embark on a life of Elgar without consulting the research and scholarship accumulated by three acknowledged experts in the field, and my debt to the pioneering industry of Percy Young, Michael Kennedy and Jerrold Northrop Moore will be perfectly apparent. In particular I am obliged to Dr Moore for his courteous interest in my own work and for his generous encouragement.

Practically everything that has been written about Elgar in the past has been written by musicians, professional or amateur. I am not a musician, and anyone whose concern is to read a detailed analysis of Elgar's music will be well advised to consult appropriate books by Diana McVeagh, Percy Young, Michael Kennedy and William Reed. My primary aim has been to try to understand the personality of the artist and to unravel the complexity of his many and varied relationships rather than to discuss in detail once again the nature of his creative achievement. Nevertheless it was my admiration for the artistic achievements of a man so racked as Elgar was by emotional problems that inspired me to attempt a biography for the general reader.

Elgar's personality and conduct are open to any number of interpretations, and accounts of him given by eye-witnesses differ widely. Part of the explanation seems to be that Elgar displayed quite different aspects of his character to different people. It also seems to have been the case that much of his conduct was so bizarre and unpleasant, and certain aspects of his personality so unnerving, that out of respect and affection for the agreeable side of his nature, and in order perhaps to protect the reputation of his music, a rather defensive approach has been adopted by some who are able to recall meeting him. In other words, there has been a serious temptation to over-protect Elgar, just as there has been a temptation to lampoon him and criticize him unfairly. In addition, an amazing growth of mythology has risen up around the man, many of the seeds of which were sown by Elgar himself. In trying to weed my way through the maze of myth and fantasy, contradictory opinions and sly innuendo, I have relied upon two primary sources of information:

Elgar's letters and the published reminiscences of those who knew him.

In weighing up the value of the evidence left by those who did know Elgar I have had to bear in mind that practically everything written about him until as recently as 1967 was written with the active assistance or blessing of his daughter, Carice Blake, whose life, like her mother's, was largely spent in fostering an image of Elgar as a happy-go-lucky, affectionate family man. This is in no way to cast aspersions on the integrity of Elgar's more recent biographers; out of common decency it cannot have been easy for anyone prior to Carice Blake's death in 1970 to have discussed perhaps as frankly as they would have wished the characters of Edward and Alice Elgar, their relationship with their daughter, and the most controversial aspect of Elgar's domestic life, his marriage. The one book written by a contemporary of Elgar which goes some way towards redressing the balance, *Edward Elgar: The Record of a Friendship*, by Rosa Burley in collaboration with Frank Carruthers, was actually withheld from publication until after Mrs Blake's death; without being salacious it quite simply contains comments and judgements upon Elgar and his relations with his wife that no daughter would have wanted to read.

William Reed's two books on Elgar, *Elgar* and *Elgar As I Knew Him*, while useful as source material and valuable at a musical level, go far beyond the call of duty in their reticence on personal matters. In a perceptive essay in the second edition of *Elgar*, published after Reed's death, Eric Blom, editor of the Master Musicians series, writes, 'There is no harm in saying that Dr Reed thought all criticism of the great presumptuous, and he was incapable of anything that looked to him even remotely like disloyalty.' Dorabella of the *Enigma Variations* – Dora Penny, who wrote her reminiscences, *Edward Elgar: Memories of a Variation*, under her married name of Mrs Richard Powell – has contributed perhaps the most fascinating personal account of life in the Elgar household, a book which seems to a surprising extent to have been accepted until now at face value. With its picture of Elgar in the role of amusing, hearty genius, Dorabella as his capable and sympathetic Girl Friday, and Alice as Elgar's simpering, incompetent little wife, I find this, because officially sanctioned by Carice Blake, the most revealing personal account of all.

There are now of course very few people left who knew Elgar, and they fall into two categories: those who are very old, who in order to recall anything of Elgar's middle years need to throw their minds back at least sixty years, and those who were merely children or at best very young when they knew Elgar in old age. With the greatest respect – and this goes for the first-hand testimony of all eye-witnesses when examined after any lapse of time – their evidence has to be treated with caution. I was, for example, categorically assured by someone who knew Elgar for a number of years that he and his wife were 'deeply in love' (whatever precisely that may mean) all their lives. This information was offered as first-hand evidence. My informant, however, turns out to have been not much more than ten years of age when Lady Elgar died. Someone with a rather different view of Elgar's marriage described it to me as 'a disaster', adding that Elgar had kept an apartment in London – he thought it might have been in Albany – in order to get away from Alice, the implication being that in this apartment he was in the habit of carrying on clandestine relationships with other women. Elgar never had an apartment in Albany, and there is no evidence to suggest that the rented flats that Elgar did have in London while Alice was alive, prior to their move to London in 1912, were anything other than necessary business *pieds à terre*. Elgar's marriage, no doubt complex and private like everybody else's, is the most conspicuous area of his life on which contradictory opinions have been offered, often without a shred of evidence. Rosa Burley speculates that after Lady Elgar's death 'an over-mastering sense of guilt towards Alice led him to shun the society of those who had been allowed to look behind the façade of happiness and who were thus regarded as having in some measure connived at his disloyalty to her'. Miss Burley knew Elgar and his wife, off and on, for nearly thirty years but she has left it to her successors in the biographical field to discover for themselves what she meant by disloyalty and guilt.

A good deal of mythology has also grown up on the subject of Elgar's alleged abilities outside the sphere of music, which may be accounted for by an inclination to romanticize the stories of poor boys who clambered up the social ladder in the nineteenth century, as Elgar did. Thanks to his mother's influence, for example, Elgar's literary knowledge and taste is supposed to have been such that – and I quote again from someone who knew him – he could 'as easily have made a name for himself as a man of letters as a musician'. There is however no evidence to show that Elgar had literary gifts of any description; his extensive knowledge of literature is of course another matter. In testing evidence about Elgar's life and habits it needs to be remembered that many of the myths were sown in Elgar's own lifetime, by people who knew him personally, and that Elgar and his daughter often ignored the opportunity to correct basic errors of fact. Writing in *Elgar: His Life and Works*, a book published in 1933, the year before Elgar died, Basil Maine, a music critic and a friend of Elgar, asks us to believe that 'Books that he found in the stable-loft stirred his imagination. Especially favoured were Baker's *Chronicles*, Drayton's *Polyolbion* and Sir Philip Sidney's *Arcadia*.' The only stable Elgar's parents ever possessed was a brand-new one at the cottage in Lower Broadheath where Elgar was born, which they left when he was only two years old. 'After his eldest sister, Mary, married he went to lodge with her,' Maine tells us. The sister in question was his second sister. Maine also asserts that it was Alfred Rodewald who attempted to effect the reconciliation between Elgar and his estranged friend Stanford. The attempt was in fact made by Granville Bantock in 1922, nineteen years after Rodewald's death. Even more absurd is Maine's notion that Alice Elgar's father, Major-General Sir Henry Roberts, 'could have been proud of a son-in-law with so upright and soldier-like a figure as Edward's'. General Roberts died in 1860, when his prospective son-in-law was three.

The more one explores Elgar's personality the more diverse and complicated it seems to have been, and no definitive explanation for his character or his actions can ever, one hopes, be attempted. There will always remain room for speculation and personal interpretation. In supplying my own, I have tried to bear in mind Sir Adrian Boult's admonition: 'An awful lot of rubbish has been written about Elgar,' he told me. I can only hope that I have not added too greatly to the pile.

I have to record my special thanks to Sir Adrian, whose services to Elgar's music have been outstanding, for sharing with me his recollections of Elgar and some opinions on his work. Mr Edgar Day, for fifty years assistant organist at Worcester Cathedral, has also been good enough to recall his first-hand memories. Lady Dudley, whose father rented a house to Elgar in 1923, and who spent her childhood as Elgar's next-door neighbour, has given her youthful recollections; so, too, has Elgar's godson, Mr Wulstan Atkins. And Lady Barbirolli has kindly passed on to me her late husband's memories of his last meeting with Elgar.

I am grateful to Mr Humphrey Burton, former Head of Music and Arts, BBC Television, for up-to-date information about the BBC's plans to perform the unfinished Third Symphony. The Earl of Dudley has provided historical information about his family's connections with Witley Court. Sir Robin Mackworth-Young, the librarian at Windsor Castle, has been good enough to unearth correspondence between Elgar and the Court, and Miss Jane Langton, registrar of the Royal Archives, has prevented me from falling on occasion into error. Sir Edward Fox, secretary and registrar of the Order of Merit, has furnished information about the sovereign's prerogatives relating to the Order. Mr Jack McKenzie, curator of Elgar's Birthplace, has answered innumerable queries with friendliness and patience. The Reverend David Owen, vicar of St John the Baptist, Claines, has identified for me the graves of Elgar's maternal grandparents. The Reverend John Mahoney, sj, has confirmed that the Last Rites were almost certainly administered to Lady Elgar. Mr Eric Willats, principal reference librarian at Islington Library, helped me solve the riddle of William Elgar's temporary domicile in London in 1848, and Miss Alison

Hennegan has drawn my attention to sources relating to Arthur Benson, and to Elgar's row with Sir Charles Stanford. Sir Thomas Armstrong, principal of the Royal Academy of Music from 1955 to 1968, has shared with me his views on Elgar and his extensive knowledge and understanding of Elgar's music and associates. Mr H. Montgomery Hyde put me on the trail of two previously unpublished photographs of Elgar, and Mr Michael Parkin has been generous with suggestions, information and the supply of photographic material. Dame Felicitus Corrigan, osb, has also been kind and helpful. I am especially grateful to the Dean of Westminster, the Very Reverend Edward Carpenter, and to the Keeper of the Muniments at Westminster Abbey, Mr Nicholas MacMichael, for providing previously unpublished information about attempts to have Elgar buried in the Abbey.

The Dean of Worcester, the Very Reverend Thomas Baker, Lord Bruntisfield, Lt-Colonel G. A. L. Chetwynd-Talbot, Dr Eric Fenby, Mr Christopher Hibbert, Lady Susan Hussey, the Hon. Richard Lamb, the late Lady Mary Lygon, Sir Oliver Miller, the Marquess of Northampton, the prime minister's secretary for appointments, Mr Colin Peterson, Major-General Desmond Rice, the Earl of Shaftesbury, Mr C. Tagholm of British Rail, Mr Ronald Taylor, editor of the *Elgar Society Journal*, and Sir Osmond Williams, Bart, have all responded to requests for help and information. Mr Nigel Edwards, music critic of the *Malvern Gazette*, has generously provided interesting new evidence about a holiday the Elgars enjoyed in Malvern in 1889. I have received help from the County of Hereford and Worcester Record Office, the British Museum, the Reference Library and the Written Archives Centre of the BBC, and valued assistance from staff at Westminster Reference Library, Somerset House and the excellent music and research libraries at Swiss Cottage. Miss Sally Cavender of Boosey & Hawkes, Mr Bernard Axcell of Novello and Mr G. M. Neighbour, secretary of the Performing Right Society, have gone out of their way to be helpful. So too have the current inhabitants of some of the houses once occupied by Elgar, who have received me without appointment, sometimes at unearthly hours, made me welcome and shown me, with justifiable pride, over their homes. To the composer, Robert Walker, who has restored and lives in Brinkwells, I am particularly grateful for hospitality and information.

Michael Jacob went to the trouble of reading the manuscript and has offered valuable suggestions, but any errors of fact and misinterpretation of data remain entirely my own responsibility. I am grateful to Miss Jill Trudgill for retyping the manuscript.

I have the honour to acknowledge the gracious permission of Her Majesty the Queen to make use of extracts from papers in the Royal Archives. I am indebted to the Sir Edward Elgar Will Trust and the Elgar Birthplace Trust for permission to quote from Elgar's letters, and to the latter also for the majority of photographs reproduced in this book. I am grateful to Michael Parkin for two photographs of Elgar at The Hut (Plates 26 and 27) and to the Sir Barry Jackson Trust for the photograph of Elgar with George Bernard Shaw (Plate 29). Victor Gollancz Ltd have generously consented to my quoting at length from *Elgar As I Knew Him* by William H. Reed, and I am greatly indebted to Mr George Sassoon for permission to reproduce Siegfried Sassoon's poem written on hearing Elgar's Violin Concerto and four lines from his *Afterthoughts on the Opening of the British Empire Exhibition*. Letters from Sir Adrian Boult are reproduced by kind permission of Sir Adrian. I have also quoted from *Edward Elgar: Memories of a Variation* by Mrs Richard Powell, by permission of Methuen & Co. Ltd, and from *Edward Elgar: The Record of a Friendship* by Rosa Burley and Frank C. Carruthers, by permission of Barrie & Jenkins Ltd.

The help I have received from John Denny of Allen Lane has been incalculable.

Michael De-la-Noy
London NW6

CHAPTER ONE

'A Most Miserable Looking Lad'

The Elgars came from Kent; the Greenings and Apperlys, Elgar's maternal relations, came from the West Country. Elgar's mother, Anne, was the daughter of Joseph Greening, a yeoman farmer, and of Esther Apperly, who had distinguished herself at the age of seven, in 1796, by working a sampler which survives in the cottage where her grandson was born. Anne was born in 1822 on a farm at Weston-under-Penyard in the Forest of Dean. As a young woman she moved to Claines, a village three miles north of Worcester where she took a job at an inn called The Shades, in Mealcheapen Street in the centre of the city. She was later to make four of her homes within walking distance of the inn. Today she would have some difficulty finding her way about for although the streets remain, The Shades, and the shop round the corner at No. 10 High Street, where she lived and worked with her husband and family for the larger part of her life, have both been demolished.

Elgar's father, William, was born in 1821 in Dover. He served an apprentice-ship in Soho with the musical firm of Coventry & Hollier, and when he was only nineteen he decided to move to Worcester, where the Three Choirs Festival, founded in 1724 and destined to remain throughout the Victorian age the most important musical event of the year outside London, had created the kind of environment likely to provide regular work for a young piano-tuner. Within two years he had an amazing stroke of luck. In 1843 William IV's widow, Queen Adelaide, who cared little for Court life and whose carriage had been mobbed in London on account of her antagonism to the 1832 Reform Bill, decided she would like a rural retreat as an alternative to Marlborough House. She settled on Witley Court, near Abberley, twelve miles north-west of Worcester, an enormous mansion with formal Italian gardens designed by William Nesfield, which she rented from the trustees of Lord Ward, then a young boy in his minority. Like any fashionable lady of the time, the queen had a piano in her drawing-room, and one of the tasks facing the comptroller of the new royal residence, Sir Andrew Barnard, was to find a piano-tuner in Worcester. He probably knew his way around the city as little as Queen

Adelaide herself, so he turned for advice and help to William Elgar's former London employers. They remembered that young Elgar had moved to Worcester and gave him a recommendation.

So, at the age of twenty-two, William was in receipt of the following note: 'Sir A. Barnard requests that Mr Elgar will come as soon as he receives this to tune the pianoforte of Her Majesty.' He was clearly regarded as respectable, and he must have done his work well, for within a few months of first presenting himself at Witley Court, William had received an official appointment. He was told by Sir Andrew that he might 'advertise himself tuner of pianoforte to Her Majesty the Queen Dowager'. What could have been better for business? What could have been a more auspicious foretaste of royal favours in store for his second son?

The young and energetic William was not merely a piano-tuner; although this was the basis of his livelihood, later to be expanded by selling music and instruments, he also played the organ and the violin and he was eventually to play in the Three Choirs Festival Orchestra. He came from a family whose formal education lacked a certain polish (in the matter of letter-writing he himself was semi-literate and remained so all his life) but whose inventiveness and initiative were clearly out of the ordinary, even for an age when people were automatically thrown back on their own resources for entertainment and communication. In 1851 William's eldest brother, Thomas, dispatched an astonishing amount of family news from Kent to Worcester in the form of the 'Dover News', a lively home-made tabloid conveying stories about family and local events written as a pastiche of the journalistic style of the day. One item, headed 'Look Here!', may offer an explanation for the frequent use of the expression 'look here' in later years in his nephew Edward's letters. It must have been some kind of family catch-phrase. In the 'Dover News' it appears alongside a drawing of a fierce-looking dog, discovered to be 'The celebrated British Bull Terrier Trap, the property of T. Elgar', and the report goes on to announce that Trap 'will have a set to at the Clay-Pits on Sunday next during Divine Worship'. Enjoying opportunities to nip out of church in the middle of services seems to have been something of a family tradition, too; during his time as organist at St George's Roman Catholic Church in Worcester, a post he gained within a year of settling in the city, William was reputed always to refresh himself at a nearby public house while the sermon was being delivered.[1]

1. *Notes on Catholic Worcester* by Hubert Leicester (published in Worcester in 1928). However, writing to Dr C. W. Buck in 1884, Elgar reported that just before Christmas, i.e., in 1883, the younger generation at St George's had taken exception to his father and had had him turned out of the organist's post he had held 'for 37 years'. If Leicester is correct, it would appear that William had actually held the post for forty-one years; if Elgar is correct, he could not have been appointed until 1846.

Although the few existing photographs of William in old age depict him as a relaxed and benign old man, with the face of a retired schoolmaster or perhaps a head gardener, there is little doubt that as a young man he combined a natural charm with a brisk, hedonistic interest in life, in which music and the enjoyment of food went hand in hand with a cheerful disregard for spelling and grammar. In 1843 he wrote home to report on his activities in a re-assuring letter which gives an authentic impression of a robust, slightly hearty young man living on his own in a busy city and thoroughly enjoying himself.

'Tomorrow Monday,' he announced, 'I am going to Mr d'Egville's to practice some Quartetts, some of Correlli's music, good *stuff* ... I off course tune the Piano and in a short time our next Harmonic Concert takes Place – in about 3 weeks.'[2] He goes on to describe an excursion to Kidderminster, a journey of fifteen miles each way: 'We started for Kidder at about 10 o'clock on Tuesday about 18 in number and a fine swell we cut I assure you. We started from the Punch Bowl Inn[3] a Stage coach for the occasion with four horses and two postillions, in the Top of the coach were most of the Instruments. Double Basses, Violoncellos Fiddles and the Devil knows what – I was stuck on the Boot with that old Monkey-Coat that I used to wear in Dover with my Cap – and some with Great Coats Mackintoshes and a pretty lot we was. We sang all the way their and all the way Back – and a good spree we had – we reached our journey end at ½ past 12 and returned home at 11 and got to bed at 2 o'clock – buy the buy we had a good dinner at ½ past two – *rehearsal* at 4 Tea at ½ past 5 Concert at 7 – Supper at ½ past 10. The concert went off pretty well ... I almost forgot to say that it was second fiddled by Mr W. H. Elgar.'

The carefully noted time-table of events, both musical and gastronomic, indicates a well-organized young man. He had found convenient and no doubt convivial lodgings with a Mrs Greening out at Claines – convivial because he seems to have divided his time between Mrs Greening's house and her daughter Anne's place of work, The Shades. Anxious as ever to keep his family fully in the picture, in 1845 he drew a sketch map of 'The Environs of Worcester – From Worcester Cross to Mrs Greenings'. The Cross stood at the west end of Mealcheapen Street, and in typical Elgar family style the sketch map informed the Dover recipients that it had been published at 'The Shades Tavern' and entered at Stationers' Hall.

Presumably William kept up an enticing correspondence with his amusing brother, for Tom arrived in Worcester in 1845 to have a look at the attractions of the place for himself and it was not long before the two of them were joined

2. Mr d'Egville ran a dancing academy at 32 Britannia Square, Worcester. William was later to send his son Edward to a Dame School at 11 Britannia Square.
3. In College Street, very near the cathedral; the inn no longer stands.

by one of their sisters, Susannah, who also found The Shades to her liking. Under the guise of being chaperoned by her brothers she set up a liaison with the landlord, Francis Simmonds.

William joined the Worcester Instrumental Society, an organization not averse to slipping a song called *Flora Gave Me Fairest Flowers* between the second and third movements of a Mozart symphony. Connivance at a commonplace lapse of taste of that sort apart, it would be reasonable to assume that a respectful appreciation of the classical composers would have been instilled in William by the organist at St Mary's Church in Dover, himself a pupil of Beethoven. The family were strangely fortunate in their friendships: another Dover acquaintance, William Salter, had been a pupil of Mozart's friend Michael Kelly.

William made good use of his royal appointment, for by the time Queen Adelaide left Witley Court in 1846 he had, on the strength of it, built up a smart county clientele. He earned £90 a year from his post as organist at St George's, and local concert engagements brought in additional income. At the age of twenty-six he further justified his adventurous move to Worcester by getting married to a local girl. He chose Anne Greening.

Anne's home-spun accomplishments tuned in well with William's artistic nature. She never strove to appear more clever than she was, and her verses and the tight little pencil sketches she drew were modest, effective tributes to her own small talent and sympathetic nature. Like her mother, she worked a sampler. When her five surviving children were aged between twelve and twenty-two she devised an affectionate and succinct couplet to describe each one's character. In the manner of Wagner and his *Siegfried Idyll*, she even presented a poem to her husband on the birth of their first daughter, and later on corresponded by verse with a nephew in the United States. Her love of the countryside and of literature became a part of the Elgar family saga. In so far as it is possible to piece together anything like a comprehensive picture of Anne from the fragments of evidence, including photographs, one gets the impression of a simple, kindly woman drawing comfort from religion, content with her role in life and sensitive to the aims and potential of others.

William and Anne were married in London on 19 January 1848, at St Mary's Church, Islington. Rumour has always had it that Anne's parents disapproved of the match, which would account for the clandestine circumstances of the marriage. In the register William gave his address as 6 High Street, Islington, though there was no such place. Had '6 High Street' existed it would in fact have been the Peacock Tavern,[4] one of the most famous coaching inns in north London, mentioned by Charles Dickens in *Boots at the*

4. *Robson's Commercial Directory*, 1843.

Cherry Tree Inn and noted too for having given hospitality to Tom Brown on his way to Rugby School. (After becoming officially 11 High Street, The Peacock was eventually demolished in 1962.) William evidently took up temporary residence here in order to establish a connection with the parish of St Mary; it is a reasonable assumption that Anne joined William at The Peacock prior to the marriage ceremony, and that to spare her blushes he filled in a street number in the register rather than the name of an inn. In the register William also described himself as a music-master, so presumably he was earning money giving violin lessons. The bridegroom's father was described as a builder, the bride's as a gentleman – here perhaps is the clue to Mr Greening's disapproval – and although William had left home six years before and was firmly settled in Worcester, he gave Dover as his home.

Not to be outdone by Tom's 'Dover News', the newly married Elgars sent reports of life in the West Country to Kent by means of the 'Worcester Papers'. The flooding of the Avon, sanitation in the city and capital punishment – a public execution took place in Worcester in 1849 – were among the hotly debated local issues of the day. On the subject of music, William noted how very few English composers there were, comparatively speaking, compared to 'the superior number of foreign'. He hoped the time was not very far distant when England 'in all her glory will stand pre-eminent, at least in Musical Affairs'. The country was still recovering from the rule of a sadly deranged monarch, the loss of his American colonies, and from the unprecedented unpopularity of his appalling sons. No doubt William's patriotic fervour had been kindled by his own parent's pride in the feats of Nelson and Wellington (the battle of Waterloo had been fought only twelve years before William went to school). It was not surprising that living in Worcester generated in such interested minds as the Elgars' an appreciation of national trends and events as well as purely parochial ones. Even allowing for the fact that the Three Choirs Festival had by then been in existence for more than a century, Worcester was culturally a more lively place in the early nineteenth century than might be supposed. Jenny Lind, who sang at the festival, had made her home only eight miles away in Malvern (she is buried in Great Malvern Cemetery); Paganini played in Worcester, Constable went there to lecture and Queen Victoria's blustering uncle, the Duke of Cambridge, attended the festival. There were natural history, literary and scientific societies; and madrigal, glee and harmonic societies supplemented the choral music to be heard every week in the cathedral where Boyce had been a conductor and Thomas Tomkins had played the organ.

The church where Edward Elgar was one day to follow his father as organist, St George's, on the corner of Sansome Street and Sansome Place, looks from the outside as much like a small town hall as an ecclesiastical edifice. It stands on the site of an older chapel where, much to the embarrassment of the mayor and corporation, James II attended Mass in 1687. It is unusual for an Anglican to be offered a post in a Roman Catholic church, and it says much for William's musical gifts that he was appointed organist there. Anne, too, was a member of the Church of England at the time of her marriage. A likely explanation for her conversion to Roman Catholicism in 1852, two years after the birth of her first child, Harry, and the same year as Lucy, the first of three girls, was born, may be simply that having gone along to church with her husband on Sundays, more or less to keep him company, she had been so influenced by the services as to be led to ask for instruction. William followed her into the Roman Catholic Church at a much later date.

The Elgars' third child and second daughter, Polly, was born in 1855, and perhaps by that time their lodgings in the College Precincts, off College Street at the east end of the cathedral, were getting crowded. In any case Anne, having been brought up on a farm, hankered to live in the country again, so in 1856 she and William moved to a charming red-brick cottage in the hamlet of Lower Broadheath, four miles to the north-west of the city.[5] Here, on 2 June the following year, their second son and fourth child, Edward, was born in a tiny bedroom at the back of the house.[6]

Writing fifty-five years later, when her brother was famous, Lucy, who was only five when Elgar was born, remembered the day quite well. The air, she said, was sweet with the perfume of flowers, bees were humming and all the air was lovely – though of course all great men are born on days like this. When Lucy adds that there seemed to be a lot of unnecessary running about in the house, her father tearing up the drive in a carriage with a strange man (obviously the doctor), and that she and Harry (by then an inquisitive seven-year-old) were taken to scamper across the heath to be out of the way, the scene will be instantly recognizable to families with members old enough to recall the days when babies were born at home.

At Broadheath, Anne had the best of all worlds. With pony and trap it was easy to get into the city, and she could walk at will down the country lanes. Her home had views of the cathedral and the Malvern Hills. If she wanted to explore the county she had only to accompany William on his piano-tuning jaunts to country houses. In an age of cheap and plentiful labour (according

5. The address is now Elgar's Birthplace, Crown East Lane, Lower Broadheath, Worcestershire. The cottage was opened as a museum in 1938, having been purchased by Worcester Corporation, and is administered by the Elgar Foundation and the Elgar Birthplace Trust. Visitors are welcome, and the cottage is signposted off the A443 Worcester–Tenbury Road.

6. Elgar apparently identified the room late in life to Herbert Howells; it should be remembered, however, that Elgar left Broadheath when he was two, so presumably the room now officially designated as the one in which he was born was pointed out to him by his parents on a return visit, after they had moved back to Worcester.

to the 1841 census, almost one in sixteen of the population was in domestic service) the Elgars' lower-middle-class status was assured of leisure, even with four children to bring up; they acquired an out-of-work actor as a servant, a nurse for the children and a maid called Matilda Knott. She was known as Kit and in the manner of the times she stayed with the family for more than thirty years. The cottage had two floors, with shutters on the downstairs windows (the shutters have since been removed) and a wooden porch. Roses climbed over the trellis set across the garden path, and the grounds were treated, as they still are today, in the style of an old-fashioned English cottage garden. All that was lacking was a coach house, so William's younger brother, Henry, who went into business with him at about this time, put to use what building skills he had acquired from his father in Dover and set to work erecting one.

The family seem to have been fortunate in having as a friend a competent professional painter by the name of Buckler, who produced a delightful watercolour of the cottage the year they moved in (Plate 1), with tiny figures said to be William and Anne on the garden path, accompanied by Lucy (then aged four), and with Polly (just a baby) and the nurse in the porch. Uncle Henry stands outside the new coach house, and the pony is poking its head out of what today is the gentlemen's lavatory. The same artist made a series of drawings of the interior of Worcester Cathedral in about 1840, and the painting of Broadheath was a rare possession for such a family. Except that a large tree that once sheltered the lawn has since come down, nearly everything is as it was in the Elgars' time, and the mystery is where, with four young children and three servants to house, they all slept. Idyllic though the cottage appears today, it must have lacked some of the space and amenities Anne would have been used to in the farm house of her childhood. At most there could not have been more than four small rooms downstairs, including the kitchen, and four small rooms upstairs. By 1859, with four children already and a fifth on the way, and with relations from Dover no doubt wanting to come to stay, a move back into Worcester became inevitable.

A new house was found at 1 Edgar Street, by the east entrance of the cathedral. It is now demolished, but it was once pointed out by Elgar to Edgar Day, for fifty years assistant organist at Worcester Cathedral, as the house in which he had lived as a small boy, Elgar saying to Mr Day, who happened to live at 13 Edgar Street, 'At least they've named a street after you. That's more than they ever did for me!'[7] Joe was born there in 1859, and in 1861, the year that Frank was born, the family moved again, a few yards round the corner, into 2 College Yard, on the north side of the cathedral. Here Elgar had a toy drum to play with, and from here he was packed off each day to a Dame School

7. Mr Edgar Day, in conversation with the author.

a mile away at 11 Britannia Square, a spacious and elegant grouping of Regency town houses in a prosperous residential area of the city, an environment that may conceivably have fired his ambition one day to own such a house himself.

By 1860, while the Elgars were still lodging in Edgar Street, William and his brother Henry had aquired business premises at 10 High Street, with living accommodation over the shop, and by the time William and Anne had six children to feed it must have occurred to them that it would make sense to pay one rent instead of two. And so, in 1863, when Edward was six, the family moved yet again.

The High Street building (Plate 4) was quite a stylish affair, with four floors and a hanging sign as well as large lettering across the two first-floor windows to advertise the firm. Here Edward Elgar lived until he was twenty-two. Every time he stepped out of the front door on to the cobbled street he would have seen to his left the great fourteenth-century tower of the cathedral looming over his head, and as he made his way the short distance to the end of the High Street the whole length of the nave would have unfolded before him. It was an apposite spot for a young musician to live, above a music shop and next door to one of the Three Choirs cathedrals. And it seems he was not the only budding musician in the family: his elder brother Harry showed early signs of musical promise, and later in life Lucy recalled that Joe had actually been referred to as 'the Beethoven of the family', having 'a very remarkable aptitude for music from the time he could sit up in his chair'.

Within a year of the move to the High Street, however, tragedy struck. Harry contracted scarlet fever and died, at the age of thirteen. Edward was seven, just at an age when he would have been looking up with admiration to an older brother on the brink of puberty. For Anne, the death of her first child must have been a shattering blow; Harry died, in fact, the year that Anne gave birth to her seventh and last child, Helen, whom she therefore had to nurse while grieving for her first-born.

Suddenly, Edward found himself the eldest son. It has been said that Joe, two years younger than Edward, was Edward's inseparable companion, and a photograph was taken of the two boys together when they were seven and five showing Edward gently resting his arm on little Joe's shoulder (Plate 2). When Joe himself was seven, and Edward nine, Joe also died. In the light of much of Edward Elgar's subsequent conduct, it seems unlikely that he ever came to terms with this second devastating shock.

There is a strong tradition that as a schoolboy Elgar used to take musical scores from his father's shop to study them in the churchyard of St John the Baptist at Claines, the red sandstone fifteenth-century church where his mother's parents are buried a few yards from the gate on the north-west side of the tower. As a result of the loss of two brothers, and in the light of his behaviour in adult life when faced with bereavement, it is not difficult to imagine Elgar acquiring in youth a morbid obsession with death, a fashionable enough trait in Victorian England anyway. His pilgrimage would have entailed a three-mile trek each way, presumably carried out at weekends or on summer evenings after school. Not many boys walk six miles when they need walk only one, but in Elgar's case the story has a convincing ring of truth. It should be remembered, however, that since both Anne's parents died before he was born (her father in 1848, her mother in 1852), Elgar never knew his maternal grandparents, so that if the pilgrimage did take place it was a strictly senti- mental or romantic one. Many children who for one reason or another feel rootless often do try to make contact with predecessors they have never met, and Elgar already had a strongly developed sense of history.

There are no known photographs of Elgar that show him smiling or looking happy, though few people in Victorian England ever did have their photograph taken smiling. This had nothing to do with having to pose during a protracted exposure; it was just considered undignified. They wanted to set up a record of themselves looking, as they thought, at their best, dressed in their best clothes, responsible and imposing. The often gloomy-looking photographs of Queen Victoria led to the myth that she never smiled, but there are far too many contemporary accounts of the girlish laugh and charming smile that animated her conversation in old age to doubt that the photographs give a completely misleading impression. We should not therefore assume that Elgar never smiled or laughed. A rather smudgy photograph taken of the five sur- viving children together, when Elgar was about eleven, shows him to have been a pleasant-looking boy, neatly dressed and, even allowing for the presence of a camera, rather serious. A better picture of him on his own and at the same age has him seated in a smart chair, obviously a studio prop, his finger marking a place in a book which rests on his knee (Plate 3). He is looking away from the camera, and the pose, together with the book, is clearly intended to convey the impression of a studious lad, self-possessed and hard- working. None of the family could really be described as good-looking. Anne had rather a moon-shaped face, and seems in a photograph taken with Edward on her knee when he was two years old to have been a woman with a large bone structure and big hands. Harry had been a boy with an interesting but slightly disquieting face; Lucy, who married but had no children, and lived to be seventy-three and stone deaf, seems to have inherited her mother's large build, sharing Harry's severe outline. Polly, who became the mother of six children and had a longer life than any of her siblings, dying at the age of eighty-one, was the gayest and prettiest of the family. Little Joe just stands with his mouth open. Frank, who had one son and died at the age of sixty-seven after taking over his father's business, shared in later life his brother Edward's hawk-like nose. A photograph of Helen at about the age of seventeen suggests the self-possessed nun of the Dominican Order she was destined to become; she rose to be Mother Superior, and living to the age of seventy-five she was the last of the children to be born and the last to die.

The photograph of the five children together may well have been the one that Anne sent to a nephew in America, accompanied by a sad little poem recalling his two dead cousins, full of the kind of rationalizing religious sentiment mothers sometimes summon up to comfort themselves over the loss of children, but free of cloying sentimentality:

> *Aunty's picture of the jewels*
> *In her earthly diadem,*
> *Two have been removed for safety*
> *So she cannot send you them.*
> *If perchance across the photo*
> *Shines a ray of lustre bright*
> *Think it is a bit of sunshine*
> *From the others out of sight.*

It was in 1874, when Elgar was seventeen and his character more or less formed, that Anne penned her couplets on each surviving child. Of Lucy she wrote, 'Dainty, dainty little girl, Fit to sit in gold or pearl'. Polly's went, with a touch of northern rhyming, 'Mirthful, saucy singing lass, Greets you gaily as you pass'. Of Frank, then thirteen, she wrote with confidence, 'As a graceful, strong young tree, He will live on joyously'. Helen's affectionate tribute was: 'Slender, thoughtful, timid maid, Like a young fawn in the shade'. She paid her most extravagant compliment to Edward: 'Nervous, sensitive and kind, Displays no vulgar frame of mind'.

Another picture of Elgar as a boy, and not a particularly flattering one, has been left us by his closest schoolfriend, Hubert Leicester, who lived two doors away and who in later life was to become mayor of Worcester. Looking back quite clinically, he recalled Elgar as 'a most miserable looking lad, with legs like drumsticks and nothing of a boy about him'. 'Nothing of a boy about him' implies that, as a worthy upright burgher, Leicester entertained the conventional view that boys should be seen to be overtly athletic and virile, and that on this score the young Elgar fell down somewhat, tending perhaps to mooch around, not much interested in the games boys are supposed to play or in ostentatiously chasing the local girls. No doubt Elgar was unaware of Leicester's views about his legs, for at the age of twenty-two he dedicated to him an Andante for wind quintet. Twenty-nine years later, the second *Wand*

of Youth suite, in itself a recollection of childhood, was also dedicated to
Leicester, who had played the flute in a wind quintet formed when the two
of them were twenty, and in which Elgar played the bassoon. Leicester alleged
that Elgar had stayed away from school 'about a third of the time', which must
have been the kind of exaggeration of childhood exploits in which men often
indulge in later life, but he did add, 'it was not merely to play truant'. Whatever
reason Elgar may have had for failing to attend school, his absence would have
amounted to truancy, but Leicester was trying to imply that in Elgar's case
there was a valid excuse, Elgar being a genius, and that far from wasting his
time he was out in the countryside reading scores, trying to gain inspiration
to write music of his own. Elgar himself much later declared that he was 'still
at heart the dreamy child who used to be found in the reeds by the Severn,
with a sheet of paper, trying to fix the sounds, and longing for something very
great'.[8] He has also left a highly romanticized account of his walks to school
with Hubert Leicester, 'always to the brightly-lit west ... two pence were
"allowed" for the ferry ... at our backs "the unthrift sun shot vital gold", filling
Payne's Meadows with glory and illuminating for two small boys a world to
conquer and to love'.[9]

Boys do not on the whole set out to conquer or to love the world, nor are
they aware, every morning, of the west being brightly lit. On the way to school,
boys talk about the homework they have failed to complete, their dread of
sitting through a class with a master they do not like, and how rotten their
mother was to give them only one boiled egg for breakfast. It is the fate of many
romantics to create much of the myth that comes to be believed about their
lives simply by trying too hard to recapture and understand the sources of their
own inspiration. In so doing, they often create a lot of trite and scarcely
believable fairy-tales.

Far from coming to love the world, in many ways Elgar came to hate it. Why
this was no one will ever know for certain, but on the assumption that the
characteristics of most of our adult behaviour are formed in childhood, it is
reasonable to deduce that Elgar's early years were not entirely happy. It is
worth considering that his father may have felt so keenly the death of his eldest
son that he failed to accept Elgar as a satisfactory substitute, and if Elgar was
rejected by his father he would have had that to cope with as well as the death
of two brothers. William Elgar was always said to be in a muddle over his
business affairs, and a man who is a poor manager is generally seen by his
children as a weak man, and by his sons in particular as an ineffectual father-
figure. If Elgar did not gain from his father a concept of the role a man is meant

8. Letter to Sir Sidney Colvin written in 1921.
9. Elgar's foreword to *Forgotten Worcester* by Hubert Leicester (Trinity Press, Worcester, 1930).

to play, that might account for his almost non-existent sexual interest in women before his marriage, at the age of thirty-two and then to a woman eight years older than himself. Even after marriage Elgar confined his female flirtations to the pages of letters, thus keeping his emotional involvements with women at bay; the same device was employed – to brilliant literary effect – by Bernard Shaw, another virtually, if not totally, celibate married man, with whom Elgar was in due course to form a warm friendship.

Also to be contended with was the relative intellectual and social predominance of Anne over her husband. William remained semi-literate all his life while his wife set about improving herself, and she was certainly the parent who encouraged the children to read, although it is stretching credulity too far to believe, as Siegfried Sassoon was apparently informed in 1922 by Frank Schuster, the man who was to become Elgar's most important patron, that Anne 'used to sit up half the night reading Greek and Latin with him when a boy'.[10] Anne was the daughter of a yeoman farmer, she had worked as a barmaid, and she was only just literate in English; whence was she supposed to have acquired a knowledge of Greek and Latin, and to what use is Elgar supposed to have put this astonishing extra-curricular education? However, despite his over-reliance for musical purposes on Longfellow, Edward did become well read, and while it can be claimed that to some extent he achieved an unusual degree of social mobility by dint of ambition, he was also destined to educate himself out of the class of his birth by virtue of intellectual ability. Few boys more clever than their parents feel entirely at ease with them; in Elgar's case it would have been surprising had he not built up a sense of resentment against his father for failing to be rich enough – and that meant smart enough – to purchase for him a formal musical education.

Men with moderate musical gifts, like Leopold Mozart, who have fathered a musical genius have often coped with the situation well, rejoicing in their sons' talents and helping to foster their careers. There is no direct evidence to suggest that William Elgar was consciously jealous of Edward but it is a possibility worth bearing in mind; in any event, it could have been embarrassing for a boy who was 'nervous, sensitive and kind', and who nursed secret social ambitions, to have realized early in life that musically as well as intellectually he was going to overtake his father. William had turned his back on the relative security of the building trade in Dover for a far more uncertain future in the musical profession. He had had the initiative to take an apprenticeship in London and the courage to seek his fortune in a strange city. He had been hired at the age of twenty-two by a queen, and engaged, as an Anglican, by a church of another denomination. He had housed his family in

10. Entry for 24 August 1922, *Siegfried Sassoon Diaries: 1920–22* (Faber, 1981).

pleasant homes. By his own lights, and in view of his expectations and background, he had really done rather well, so that to have been unable to outshine his elder son – indeed, to have realized from very early on that the boy was going to outshine him – may have caused a certain withdrawal.

Resentment came to play a major part in Elgar's emotional life. As a young man, he came to resent what he believed to have been a lack of recognition for his work; when middle-aged and famous, he was capable of resenting what he took to be a social slight. Rosa Burley, headmistress of The Mount, a school in Malvern where for many years Elgar was to teach the violin, tells us that by about 1891 he had built up what seems to have been an entirely imaginary resentment on the grounds that 'his career had been hampered by his Catholicism'. It is true he failed to secure employment in London through an advertisement placed in the *Tablet* when he was twenty-one, but that advertisement had been directed expressly at potential Roman Catholic employers, and his failure on that occasion could not have been through religious prejudice; there is in fact no recorded instance of a job of any kind being denied to Elgar because he was a Roman Catholic, yet he apparently told Miss Burley of 'post after post which would have been open to him but for the prejudice against his religion, of golden opportunities snatched from his grasp by inferior men of more acceptable views'. It was, she tells us, a subject on which he evidently felt very bitter for he embroidered it at great length.[11] And all his life, while living in an elegant and gracious style, Elgar resented what he regarded as a chronic shortage of money. In any consideration of his childhood these factors need to be taken into account, for resentment usually indicates an early deprivation. For all of us the possession of money to some extent spells emotional as well as material security; a man who constantly complains that he has no money, even though he clearly has enough to live on very comfortably, as Elgar had from the age of thirty-two, is surely complaining that no one loves him.

If we take at face value Elgar's memory of himself as a schoolboy 'longing for something very great' we have to accept that at a young age he had both concrete musical ambitions and a considerable self-assurance about his abilities. But this self-assurance went hand in hand with a lack of any coherently planned campaign, and his boyhood saw no achievement remotely equivalent to Bizet's youthful symphony, for instance. It took Elgar a long time to accept that great music does not write itself but has to be struggled for, and as a child he may well have felt he had musical gifts trapped within him which he was somehow unable to express. If so, a sense of failure as well as frustration would have been building up.

11. *Edward Elgar: The Record of a Friendship* by Rosa Burley and Frank C. Carruthers.

Throughout Elgar's childhood and adolescence his mother had her hands full with the care and nursing of young children; Helen was still only fifteen when Elgar left home at the age of twenty-two. With a younger son no doubt claiming a major portion of Anne's affection, for elder boys are always thought, for some reason, to be more self-reliant than younger ones, there is no reason to suppose that Elgar received an undue amount of attention from his mother, and it is quite possible that he received rather less than his due. The larger the family the more difficult it is for parents to distribute attention and love in equal measure, and in big families siblings inevitably become more dependent upon one another for support than upon their parents. In this situation Elgar was playing a number of taxing roles: younger brother to two sisters, elder brother to another boy, surrogate eldest son, and middle child. All this needs to be remembered when one considers the state of near hysteria into which he slipped from time to time during the course of his often desperately un-satisfactory life. One has to remember too that as a child he carried an extra burden which most of us are spared – the germ within him, even if it had not begun to develop as early as in Mozart or Mendelssohn, of that decidedly mixed blessing, genius.

When Elgar outgrew the Dame School in Britannia Square he moved to Littleton House School, out on the Powick Road. With one brief change of scene to attend a Roman Catholic school, Elgar completed his formal education at Littleton House, leaving when he was fifteen (five years, in fact, after the usual school-leaving age). He had won a prize when he was eleven, but unless in adult life he had discarded a once legible hand the school did nothing to equip him with an even passable form of hand-writing. It was music-paper that in-terested him, not writing-paper, and only about a year after winning his book prize he and his brother and sisters were setting up an entertainment depicting the universal child's concept of the perfect world, one, of course, from which all ill-natured adults are excluded. Elgar's lifetime habit of hoarding sketchbooks dates from this earliest period; a number of tunes he wrote for this play were kept until, years later, they became the basis for the *Wand of Youth* suites.

Elgar had received piano lessons at the Dame School, but he never attempted to play the instrument professionally. Under the influence of his father, who played both the organ and the violin, and of Uncle Henry, a competent organist and all-round musician, and with instruments to hand in the family music shop, Elgar learned to play one instrument after another: the organ, the violin, the cello, the viola, the trombone and the bassoon.[12] Passing through the shop

12. In *Edward Elgar: Memories of a Variation*, Dorabella recalls Elgar playing passages from the score of *The Dream of Gerontius* on a trombone while correcting the proofs in 1899, but she says, 'He didn't do it very well and often played a note higher or lower than the one he wanted, in fact anywhere but in the "middle of the note".'

every time he went in or out of doors, he had permanent access to musical scores which he learned to read as other boys read books. His formal musical education in both composition and playing was non-existent, yet six weeks after his fifteenth birthday he was playing the organ at Mass at St George's for the first time.

There was however no reason for his parents to believe that music would provide their son with an income. Like most other boys of his age, with no prospect of further education, he had to take seriously the search for a job, preferably in keeping with his father's respectable status as a provincial shopkeeper with musical talent and a royal crest on his business paper, which meant a job in a profession. Mr William Allen, treasurer of the local Law Society, was a fellow Roman Catholic, with offices in Sansome Place almost next door to St George's. What Mr Allen thought young Elgar's qualifications might have been for a life in the law we shall never know, although with hindsight it is not too difficult to conjure up an image of the adult Elgar swaying a jury with his imposing appearance, or even dressing up (a habit he came to enjoy to a remarkable degree) as a judge. But without a private income to support him in chambers for the first ten years without a brief, Elgar could never have had any serious hope of being called to the Bar, and presumably the plan was for him to sit the law examinations as a solicitor. At the time the opportunity to work in a solicitor's office must have seemed, if not to the boy, at least to his parents, an attractive proposition, and Elgar entered the world of dusty ledgers, tiresome lawsuits, legal verbiage and immaculate attire. Perhaps sartorial fastidiousness was Elgar's most conspicuous qualification for the life of a lawyer, for notwithstanding a partiality for spats and well-cut jackets he left the offices of Mr Allen in less than a year. He was to make other mistakes later in life, but he never extricated himself from one so quickly.

Looking back in 1930 on his formative years, Elgar wrote, in his foreword to Hubert Leicester's *Forgotten Worcester*, 'I am said to have left the humdrum atmosphere of Worcester for etc. I object to this. I deny that any atmosphere could be humdrum while Hubert Leicester and myself were of it and in it; it might well have been disagreeable but that is another matter.' In *Elgar: OM*, Percy Young says that these words were an answer to the following observation by Neville Cardus: 'I can think of no greater composer who took his rise from an environment as unpromising to his art as Elgar's when he was a young man ... Elgar lived for long in his formative years in the narrowest of holes and corners of culture – Worcester and the West Country, not amongst the yokels thereof but in the presence day by day of the dull middle classes.' Elgar could not have been replying to Cardus, who wrote these words in *Ten Composers*, published in 1945, eleven years after Elgar's death; but with the exception of the Cello Concerto it is interesting to note that all Elgar's great works were in fact written 'in the narrowest of holes and corners', and that both his attempts to live in London were artistic failures. In saying the atmosphere of Worcester had been disagreeable, Elgar might have had in mind his brief spell at a desk in a solicitor's office, but not too much should be read into the remark, for when he made it, at the age of seventy-three, he had lost almost all capacity for resting on his laurels or for believing his life had been anything but a failure.

How did Elgar, or his parents, think he was going to earn his living after he had left the employment of Mr Allen? A glance at his juvenile output more than justifies the original decision to seek a secure position. Sketches for a family entertainment at the age of twelve were all very well, but they hardly rivalled Mozart's precocious operetta *Bastien und Bastienne*. He had attempted a Fugue in G Minor for organ, but had left it unfinished. At fifteen, the year he left school, he had presented his sister Lucy with an original gift for her twentieth birthday, a song called *The Language of Flowers*, but this was never published. In the same year he also wrote a piece for piano called *Chantant*. He was seventeen and two years out of school before his work received a public performance; this was an anthem, arranged for strings with an original introduction, sung at All Saints' Church in Worcester some time in 1874. Altogether it was hardly an output to suggest that an original or prolific composer was about to burst upon the world.

At the time that Elgar boldly cut himself off from a legal apprenticeship he had become a boy with what any employer would have regarded as a 'clean and honest countenance', with what a novelist might perhaps have described as 'clear and well-set eyes, a broad forehead and a full, slightly sensuous mouth'; his hair was swept back to the left in a natty quiff, and a faintly haughty air seems to have crept into his sixteen-year-old face. There is a look, too, of determination. However, no employer seems to have presented himself or been sought, and no doubt Elgar made himself useful in his father's shop. For a time he stood in as deputy ringer of the curfew bell at St Helen's Church in Fish Street,[13] just across from his home, though his duties there would not have brought in more than a few pence pocket money; in any case, Elgar was eventually sacked for making unauthorized and unorthodox experiments in campanology.[14] He was not appointed organist and choirmaster at St George's

13. Now deconsecrated and the headquarters of the County of Hereford and Worcester Record Office.

14. Writing in 1916 to William Starmer, organist at St Mark's Church, Tunbridge Wells, and an authority on campanology, Elgar explained, 'At St Helen's in Worcester I rang the curfew for a long time by favour of the parish clerk – a favour churlishly withdrawn because in a moment of enthusiasm I gave out the day of the month. This was done by "clappering" the seventh bell after the curfew bell proper was silent – as the thirty-seventh; parishioners who counted reflected on the supposed convivial habits of the P.C. [Parish Clerk] and my services were dispensed with.'

until 1885, so even though he was playing the organ in church when still a boy it was in the capacity of understudy to his father, and it is unlikely that for these duties he was paid anything more than nominal pocket money. What little wages he did earn over the next few years came from a haphazard series of musical engagements, but even these were interspersed with appearances for charity. His philanthropic enterprises included accepting in 1877 the leadership of the Worcester Amateur Instrumental Society, and typical of concerts for which he gave his services free between 1876 and 1880 were a performance to raise funds to enlarge the organ at St Michael's, another in support of the Stourport Cricket Club, and one organized in favour of the Royal Albert Orphan Asylum Saturday Fund.

These early years were not just spent dithering between amateur and professional status. Elgar's problem lay in not knowing how to plan a professional career because he had no real means of knowing whether he was destined to play the violin for a living, become a teacher, or end up as a composer. The fact that he branched out in all three directions at once gave him a broadly based and in many respects invaluable musical education, but he came to resent bitterly the emotional conflicts this way of life induced, and Miss Burley was surely correct when she said that he hated teaching because he was not in the least interested in technique.

In 1877 he managed to scrape together sufficient money – £7 15s. 4½d. to be precise – to enrol for violin lessons in London with Adolphe Pollitzer, leader of the New Philharmonic Orchestra. Pollitzer, a Hungarian who as a boy had played Mendelssohn's Violin Concerto in the presence of the composer, had settled in England in 1851 at the age of nineteen and went on to become leader of the Royal Choral Society. Not surprisingly, Elgar made use of his trips to the capital to attend symphony concerts, and in later life he spoke with reverence to Billy Reed, for many years leader of the London Symphony Orchestra, of the performances he had heard at that time under August Manns, a German bandmaster who had settled in England in 1854 and the following year had instituted the Crystal Palace Saturday Concerts. Elgar gave Reed to understand that it was hearing Manns conduct works by Beethoven, Schubert, Mendelssohn, Schumann, Liszt and Wagner that fired his ambition to become a serious composer.[15]

Having achieved little in the way of composition during 1877 besides arranging five pieces, including one by Mozart, as studies for the violin, Elgar devoted 1878, the year of his twenty-first birthday, to the task of teaching himself to be a serious composer. Again taking his inspiration from Mozart, he used the G Minor Symphony as a model on which to compose a symphony

15. *Elgar As I Knew Him* by William H. Reed.

of his own. Unlike Prokofiev's First Symphony, a deliberate tribute to the classical masters, Elgar's effort was more in the nature of an examination exercise, and it is most unlikely that it was ever intended for performance. Only the first movement survives. The year 1878 also saw abandoned one attempt after another at writing chamber works: a Fantasia for violin and piano, two String Quartets, a String Trio, a Trio for two violins and piano and an Allegro for oboe, violin, viola and cello were all left unfinished. But appropriately, the year in which Elgar came of age did see the completion of a work that was eventually to become his Opus 1; this was a Romance for violin and piano, which had to wait seven years for its first performance and publication in 1885. Elgar was also able to celebrate his majority by conducting a perform-ance in Worcester of an *Introductory Overture for Christy Minstrels*.

All this was however hardly likely to provide an immediate income, so an attempt was made, possibly by one of the priests at St George's, to find Elgar a job in London. An advertisement was placed in the *Tablet*, the Roman Catholic weekly review. It was addressed to 'Musical Catholic Noblemen, Gentlemen, Priests, Heads of Colleges etc or Professors of Music', stating that 'a friend of a young man, possessed of great musical talent', was anxious to obtain partial employment for him, thus giving the unfortunate impression that the young man in question had not the initiative to apply on his own behalf. The advertisement went on to spread the options about as wide as possible, suggesting Elgar's suitability as 'Organist or Teacher of Piano, Organ, or Violin, to young boys, sons of gentlemen, or as Musical Amanuensis to Composers or Professors of Music'. Just in case none of these openings happened to be vacant, a suggestion was made that the young man 'Could combine Organist and Teacher of Choir, with Musical Tutor to sons of noble-men etc'. Elgar's potential employers were informed that he was 'of quiet, studious habits, and gentlemanly bearing', and that he had also been 'used to good society'. The neighbourhood of London was preferred, but the continent was not objected to, and the young man would be 'disengaged' in September. The advertisement appeared in June.

With its rash of capital letters, muddled punctuation, and general tone of pomposity smacking more of the eighteenth century than the nineteenth, the advertisement failed to achieve its objective, which can have done nothing for Elgar's morale. But at least there was a good reason why he would not have been 'disengaged' until September: he was due to play for the first time at the Three Choirs Festival, among the second violins.

His first attempt to move to London having failed, Elgar continued with his three-dimensional musical life in Worcester, playing, teaching and writing. It was a life which kept him busy, which taught him at first hand, by playing for a living in orchestras, the demands of orchestral writing, and which was not in any case entirely rooted in provincial life. In conjunction with visits to Pollitzer for violin lessons, Elgar still enjoyed opportunities to go to concerts, and relatively poor though he may have been (a room for the night at the Grand Hotel in Northumberland Avenue could be had for five shillings, so that life in the metropolis was not exactly expensive), he still managed to fit in visits to the Vaudeville Theatre in the Strand to see a musical comedy, to the Globe for other light entertainment and to Alexandra Palace to hear a military band. Before long he would be paying his first visit to the continent, and friendships with people living in other parts of the country, entailing visits to the Yorkshire Dales for instance, were also on the horizon. Nevertheless, money was a problem and, the advertisement in the *Tablet* having failed to provide offers of employment in London, Elgar settled upon a source of income in Worcester as pathetic as it seems improbable. Far from finding himself 'Musical Tutor to sons of noblemen', he landed the job of bandmaster at the Worcester City and County Pauper Lunatic Asylum, surely one of the most bizarre appointments ever held by a major composer.

The asylum lay – indeed, it still does lie – four miles south of Worcester at Powick, just off the road that Elgar had travelled as a boy on his way each day to Littleton House School. He was to take that road again once a week for the next five years, to conduct the Attendants' Orchestra for the princely sum of £32 a year. The existence of the orchestra and their weekly concerts for the inmates indicates that the asylum was a relatively progressive and enlightened place. In appearance it has hardly changed at all (it is now simply called Powick Hospital), and Elgar's heart must have sunk each time he approached that bleak and hopeless complex of red-brick buildings with their barred windows. As often as possible he had a new composition under his arm, for the tiny annual salary was supplemented by a fee of five shillings for every polka or quadrille he wrote for the orchestra. His mother had described him, not so long before, as nervous and shy. He was a creative artist, even if a very uncertain and struggling one, and it is unnerving today to visit the place and imagine the man who was to become one of his country's greatest composers scraping a living conducting here for the benefit of a mentally disturbed audience. For Elgar, it must have been a searing experience.

In the first year, 1879, he composed a set of five Quadrilles which he dedicated to the Asylum Clerk, another set of five dedicated to Miss J. Holloway, pianist and organist (Elgar early on acquired the habit of dedicating almost everything he wrote, however slight, to someone), and yet a third set of five, the fifth of which was rescued twenty-nine years later to make its appearance as 'The Wild Bears' in the second *Wand of Youth* suite. A Minuet received a performance in Worcester in January 1879 but has since been lost or destroyed. In an attempt to write chamber works, two Polonaises for violin and piano remained unfinished, but he did complete several pieces for his own wind quintet, including a set of five Intermezzos, a Minuetto, a Gavotte, a Sarabande, a Gigue, an Andante and an Adagio. Another work written at the same time, an Adagio Solemne, had to wait thirty-three years to be played at the Albert Hall, and then only after Elgar had scored the piece for small orchestra. Elgar's attempts at vocal works were more successful than his premature sortie into the enclosed, sophisticated world of chamber music, and the choir at St George's Church gave performances in 1871 of his *Domine Salvam Fac* and *Tantum Ergo*. In the following year the first performance of his *Salve Regina* was also given at St George's. One cannot be certain that these early liturgical works were necessarily inspired by any particular religious fervour; most composers wrote for the church at some time, local choirs at least provided a body of people on the look-out for new works, and Elgar's father was choirmaster at St George's.

In addition to accepting the post at the asylum Elgar made a second decision, a significant one in the life of any young person: he decided to leave home. By doing so, he may have felt able to relieve himself of the obligation to serve in the shop, a task that must have eaten into the time he set aside for composition, and for which he could hardly have expected to be paid; his mother, after all, was still feeding and housing him. But he made no attempt to set up a home of his own; he could not have afforded to, and he was in any case totally undomesticated. Like most men of his time, whether married or single, Elgar expected that throughout his life a woman of some sort, his wife, mother, sister or housekeeper, would sew, clean and cook for him. So, as soon as the opportunity to leave home presented itself, he moved in with his second sister, Polly, the minute she got married. Not many young women of twenty-four take their brother to live with them under such circumstances, but Polly did, and she, her husband William Grafton, and Elgar set up home together at 35 Chesnut Walk (since renumbered to 12), a neat little three-storey, semi-detached house on the corner of the Walk and Chesnut Street, only a minute or two from St George's Church and Elgar's musical and ecclesiastical duties. It was to be another eleven years before Elgar had a child of his own, and there is evidence of his affection in the meantime for children outside the family, an affection always easy to give without the burdens of parental responsibility. Polly was eventually to provide him with half a dozen nieces and nephews, and when she and William moved from Worcester, four years after their marriage, Elgar went to stay with them whenever he could.

During the next year, 1880, Elgar's horizons were to be expanded well beyond the cosy domesticity of Chesnut Walk. In the company of Charles Pipe, who next year was to become another brother-in-law (by marrying his eldest sister Lucy), he paid his first visit to Paris. The two young men shared a common interest in music and the theatre, and Charles also had a bit of a reputation as a ladies' man, so it seems inconceivable that a trip to Paris, reputedly the centre of gaiety and girls, would not have provided an irresistible opportunity for Charles to wink and nudge his rather staid companion in the general direction of female allurements. After all, what was the purpose of two young provincial blades saving up their money and risking the hazards of foreign travel if they were not to return with a rakish tale or two for the benefit of their stay-at-home friends? There were certain conventions to be observed on such visits, no doubt well understood by the other members of the Glee Club (Elgar became leader of their orchestra), who would be waiting at the Crown Hotel in Broad Street upon their return, and ogling can-can dancers was certainly one of them. Actually losing one's virginity in the naughty French capital was more of a voluntary matter, and stories related along those lines could be left to the imagination, modesty and veracity of each individual returning traveller. In a letter written fifty-three years later to Fred Gaisberg of the Gramophone Company in connection with a visit he was planning to make to Paris in 1933 (to conduct his Violin Concerto and to visit Delius), Elgar asked Gaisberg if they might travel together for, he said, he had not been to France for years, he had forgotten all the French he ever knew, and because 'Paris must have changed since 1880 (!)'. Whether the exclamation mark was intended to indicate an old man's natural aversion to change, or whether it was meant to convey a sly hint of daring escapades in his youth, we cannot be sure. Quite possibly it was the latter, for he seems to have deliberately overlooked the fact that he was also there in 1923.

During the summer, a Benedictine bishop descended on St George's to consecrate a new chancel, and Elgar led the orchestra. The *Salve Regina* he had composed in 1878 received its first performance and the *Domine Salvam Fac* and *Tantum Ergo*, both performed in the church the previous year, were repeated for the episcopal visit. Other works written for St George's in 1880 included arrangements of the Allegro from Mozart's Sonata in F (K547) as a Gloria and themes from three of Beethoven's symphonies as a Credo. His secular output for the year included more music for the asylum; a 'five-shilling polka', five Lancers and another set of five Quadrilles inspired by his visit to Paris and dedicated, once again, to Miss Holloway. The movements have such evocative titles as 'L'Hippodrome' and 'Café des Ambassadeurs'.

The twenty-three-year-old Elgar also spent a few idle moments during a charity concert jotting down and trying out signatures for future use, including Edward Wm Elgar (he had been given his father's name as a second Christian name), E. W. Elgar and Edward Elgar. In view of the rather grand image we gain from photographs of him in old age, it is amusing to recall that Elgar's mother called him Ed, and rather surprisingly, as late as 1904, we actually find him signing letters 'Ed Elgar'. His father and his sister Lucy called him Ted. Once he had been knighted he settled for Edward Elgar. Choosing names for people and places became something of a fixation with Elgar, for he was always experimenting with anagrams and combinations of letters. He liked the silly sounds some words made, and much of his correspondence is cluttered with home-made expressions. In choosing the name by which he was to be known professionally, Elgar was actually doing no more than any writer or musician is obliged to do early in their career, and on this occasion he had every excuse for occupying his mind: the concert programme included the Misses Reader Glover singing *Sister Fay*.

In 1881, when Elgar was twenty-four, his music lessons with Pollitzer paid off. He passed with honours in his Royal Academy of Music examinations in both violin and general musical knowledge, an achievement that could only enhance his prospects as a teacher. It was in the same year (again, no doubt, as a direct result of his academic attainments) that Elgar was promoted from the second to first violins in the Three Choirs Festival Orchestra, and it was probably shortly afterwards that he took part in one of the earliest performances in England of Verdi's *Requiem*, written in 1874.[16] Promotion in the Festival Orchestra did not however stimulate a corresponding success in the field of composition: a Fantasia on Irish Airs for violin and piano remained unfinished, though he did carry off another Polka to Powick.

Elgar's unfulfilled years as a composer could never be said to have been wasted. Earning his living as an orchestral player gave him a personal and invaluable insight into the potential of individual instruments and into the general requirements of a symphony orchestra; he said in later life that he knew exactly what his music would sound like before he heard it played and never found it necessary to alter his scoring. As a composer and conductor Elgar also came to enjoy a rare rapport with orchestral players. In his early life, too, his connection with orchestras resulted indirectly in performances of his work. His promotion to the first violins in the Festival Orchestra, for example, led to an invitation in 1882 to join W. C. Stockley's orchestra in

16. Writing in 1931 to Fred Gaisberg of the Gramophone Company to tell him he had just been revelling in records of Verdi's *Requiem*, Elgar said it was a work he had always worshipped since taking part in a performance as a first fiddle 'in one of the earliest performances in England 1880 about'. On looking back half a century, the year 1880 would have been a more rounded one upon which to fix than 1881, and in view of Elgar's seeming certainty that he took part as a first fiddle, but his approximation as to the exact year, it seems likely to have been 1881, the year of his promotion from the second fiddles.

Birmingham, also as a first violin, and before long Stockley (who was to figure again, disastrously, in Elgar's life in 1900) had offered to include in one of his concerts a movement from an orchestral suite Elgar had written that year. Stockley was impressed by Elgar's modesty in declining to conduct the Intermezzo himself, preferring to take part in the performance from his place in the orchestra, and the audience must have been surprised when they called for the composer and up stood one of the young violinists. A provincial 'critic', groping for appropriate expressions as local reporters so often do when assigned to tasks they do not understand, announced that Mr Elgar was not deficient in scholarship, but had 'plenty of fancy' and orchestrated with facility; he hoped, in fact, that Mr Elgar would 'go on in a path for which he possesses singular qualifications'.

The year of Elgar's twenty-fifth birthday probably marked the beginning of one of his most fruitful friendships. We know that Dr Charles Buck, who was five years his senior and whose home was at Giggleswick in Yorkshire, played the cello in an orchestra led by Elgar and assembled to perform at a soirée in Worcester on 16 August 1882. The friendship between Elgar and Buck is often dated from that occasion, though by the end of October that year Elgar was writing to Buck in terms of shared domestic knowledge that make it seem likely they had known each other and enjoyed mutual friends some time prior to August. A letter written by Elgar to Buck on 31 October contains interesting confirmation of Elgar's original ambitions to be a concert violinist, ambitions which probably first prompted his visits to Pollitzer and which collapsed in favour of becoming a serious composer when he attended the concerts conducted by Manns. 'I never was more alive & "kickinger" than just now,' he tells Buck, obviously in one of his exuberant moods. 'But I am so busy I really get no time to myself. This is, of course, all very nice from a commercial point of view, but oh! my fiddling; I never touch it now, save to give lessons or scrape at a concert.'

The year ended with another success for Elgar: he was elected by thirty-three votes to three as conductor of the Worcester Amateur Instrumental Society, of which he had previously been the leader. It was a satisfying victory considering that the other candidate, Herbert Wearing of Birmingham, possessed a musical doctorate.

New Year's Day 1883 found Elgar again sailing to the continent, this time to pay his first visit to Germany. He went to Leipzig (where he would have liked to study on leaving school) on a trip he was later to describe as 'adventurous'. In musical terms it was certainly so; he frequently went to the opera to hear the works of Wagner, and became enraptured by the music of Schumann, whom he enthusiastically described as 'my ideal!'. He was surprised by

Haydn's *Surprise* Symphony, however – 'I thought it strange to go so far to hear so little,' he reported to Buck.

Elgar's reference to having an adventurous journey may also refer to a minor flirtation. It seems that during his two-week stay in Germany he met a girl with whom he must have spent a great deal of time. 'They have a good opera in Leipzig & we went many times,' he tells Buck in one letter, and use of the word 'we' crops up again in a later letter, when he says, 'We used to attend the rehersals at the Gewandhaus.' The rehearsals, it should be noted, took place at nine o'clock in the morning. Not only was the young lady prepared to be dragged out of bed at crack of dawn, but after a fortnight it was arranged that she should come to England for six or seven weeks 'during the vacation in Leipzig', which indicates that she was a student. All this information is culled from a letter to Buck in which, however, it is also easy to see that Elgar had made up his mind even before the girl arrived in England that nothing serious would come of her visit. He says he will remain in Worcester until her departure, after which he will look forward to staying a day or two with Buck and playing chamber music with him; somewhat prematurely, he describes the condition he will then be in as 'brokenhearted' – less the tragic plight of a determined lover than a piece of conventional role-playing. He described the young lady as his 'Braut' – his fiancée – but he placed the word in inverted commas, thus indicating that although like most young men of twenty-six he was perfectly capable of hitting it off with a girl, a girl who was moreover prepared to spend her holiday with him in England, Buck must not assume the affair was to be of any lasting importance.

As well as a girlfriend, Elgar brought back from Germany an interesting observation on German orchestral practice: the violinists apparently played three to a desk, though how the two on the outside managed to read the music he does not say.

It was shortly after Elgar's return from Leipzig, and before his 'Braut' arrived for her holiday, that his sister Polly and her husband moved to Bromsgrove to be closer to William's place of work; he was a manager at the salt works at Stoke. So Elgar simply moved in with his eldest sister Lucy and her husband, the lively Charles Pipe, who was a partner in a grocery wholesale business. He and Lucy lived at 4 Field Terrace, a prosperous row of houses, described quite unfairly by Elgar in a letter to Buck as rather out of the way – the Terrace was only a short walk from the centre of the city, admittedly uphill, along the Bath Road, and the house had a good view of the cathedral. Even with Elgar installed, the Pipes had a spare bedroom, and Elgar lost no time in telling his new friend he would be only too delighted to see him and he was to arrange to stay 'a night at least'. Elgar's mode of address in letters to Buck at this time is interesting. In August 1882, when he hardly knew him at all and was fixing up his first journey to Yorkshire, he began 'My dear Sir' and ended his letter 'And from, Yours very truly, Edward Elgar'. It was altogether a very proper, well-mannered letter from a well-mannered young man who had just been asked to visit. Almost immediately afterwards he took to addressing him as 'My dear Doctor' (Buck was a physician), and this form of address, rather than the more intimate 'Dear Buck', let alone the condescension of using his Christian name (which he only got round to in 1888), persisted for six years through an increasingly intimate friendship. On the other hand the flourishes at the end of his letters are slightly embarrassing in their effusion of respect; an informal, chatty letter of 1883 closes 'With kind regards, I am, my dear Doctor, Faithfully yours, Edwd Wm Elgar'.

Elgar's formality broke down somewhat towards the end of the year. On his visits to Yorkshire he had clearly fallen in love with the doctor's dogs, and he ended a letter in November by sending a kiss to the animals '& one for yourself, if you like'. It is always difficult to decipher Elgar's 'familiarities', to disentangle his genuine affection from mere jocularity, and sometimes from a tiresome streak of facetiousness. By the time he was sending kisses to the dogs and their master, he was signing off 'Always yours', and soon he was to adopt on a fairly regular basis the unexceptionable 'Yours ever'. Buck married two years after he and Elgar first met and to begin with Elgar was always very correct in referring to Buck's wife as 'Mrs Buck'. Even when he gets round to sending his love to Buck he deliberately excludes Mrs Buck, though in quite a clever way. 'Please give my humble duty to Mrs Buck,' he writes in 1885. 'I believe "kind regards" are out at present, With much love, Believe me, Yrs ever sincerely, Edward Elgar.' (Elgar was still in the habit of sending love to his male friends and mere kind regards to their wives as late as 1913. 'My very dear Hans,' he began a letter to the great German conductor Hans Richter on 24 November that year, ending it, 'My wife and daughter join me in kindest regards to Madame Richter and with all love to you.') In their correspondence as well as their clothes, the Victorians were past masters at disguise. They wrapped their bodies in full-length swimming costumes, knickerbockers and plus-fours, never took their jackets off and wore wing-collars in the country. Elgar's farewells in letters to friends appear as an attempt to camouflage and excuse his true feelings; it is as though he could never quite bring himself to say good-bye.

Elgar complained to Buck in a letter written on 11 November 1883 that he had no time now for composition, but the year did see the completion of three pieces for violin and piano, as well as a Fugue for oboe and violin and yet another Polka for the asylum. No doubt inspired by his visits to the opera house at Leipzig, he also arranged music from *Tannhäuser* for the piano. When Elgar said he had no time for composition he was using the expression relatively; he really meant he had not as much time as he would have wished, for he was increasingly occupied with violin lessons in and around Malvern and with journeys to Hereford and Birmingham to play in concerts, as witness one surviving letter written in the refreshment room at Malvern station.

One might have hoped that Elgar's ambitions to become 'a serious composer' would have received some encouragement in the following year, for he did find time to write an orchestral piece he called *Sevillana*, a depiction of a Spanish fête. Dedicated to Stockley, no doubt in gratitude for the conductor's performance of the Intermezzo that had rounded off the previous year in Birmingham, it was later published as his Opus 7. Not only did *Sevillana* receive an almost immediate first performance, by the Worcester Philharmonic Society on 1 May 1884, but on 9 July it was actually conducted at the Crystal Palace by Elgar's hero, August Manns. Alas for Elgar, he was soon to allow this success to become soured. In September he went up to London – 'just to look round' as he wrote to Buck – and to try 'to get some things done at Covt. Garden, but their arrangements are (I fear) made too far ahead for this season. Did I tell you Manns has been playing one of my pieces through the summer? Joke, isn't it?'

Elgar's disappointment with the management of Covent Garden for not following the lead given by Manns coincided with a general attack of depression. On 14 January he had written to Buck complaining he had no money – 'not a cent' – and he feared he had no prospects of getting any. He added, 'I am disappointed, disheartened and sick of the world altogether.' These sentiments may not however have been entirely to do with artistic or financial matters; they may have had something to do with an affair of the heart, a few details of which can be gleaned from his correspondence with Buck. In a letter written on 25 February 1884 we discover that Elgar had just 'rushed up to London Friday afternoon & returned yesterday (Sunday) by a horribly slow train'. It was, he tells Buck, business that took him up; he is sorry to say he is bidden to some secrecy so will hold his peace, but he promises to tell Buck about it later on. Just to whet his appetite, however, he adds, 'I can tell you that it has some reference to my leaving Wor: & settling in London,' though he also says, somewhat pessimistically, 'but I do not think 'twill come off.' In March the following year Elgar recalled for Buck certain events of the previous summer. He wrote, 'After my Scots excursion – I got in a very desponding state last summer (you ken what happened) and it behoved me to do something out of the common to raise my spirits ... so I thought of Scotland and went there from here to Glasgow – thence to Rothesay – to Oban – to Inverness – Sterling

– Edinburgh and home – three weeks.' Earlier in that same letter Elgar had written, 'Now as to your queries as aforesaid – Miss E.E. at Inverness is nobody – that is to say that I shall ever see again. I wrote down the little air when I was there & dedicated it to her "with estimation the most profound" as a Frenchman would say, that's all.' But was that all? After a couple of paragraphs referring to plans for another visit to Yorkshire, and for Manns to conduct his Intermezzo, Elgar reverted to the subject of Scotland and surely also to 'Miss E.E.'. 'The lakes overture is done with,' he says. 'I am on the Scotish (with one t) lay just now & have a big work in tow. Of course all these things are of no account but they serve to divert me somewhat & hide a broken heart.'

This time it is just possible that his heart, having remained intact throughout his association with his German 'Braut', had indeed been broken by 'Miss E.E.'. The 'little air' that Elgar dedicated to 'Miss E.E. of Inverness' was written in 1883; it was in fact one of the three successfully completed chamber works of that year, one of the pieces for violin and piano. In order to disentangle Elgar's state of mind it is necessary to get his itinerary and the sequence of events quite clear. In 1883, having presumably only just said good-bye to his 'Braut', Elgar went to Inverness (no wonder he was writing to Buck the following January to complain he had no money), met 'Miss E.E.' and dedicated a composition to her. A few months later he is 'disappointed, disheartened and sick of the world altogether', when nothing in the musical line had occurred at that time to make him so depressed. In February 1884 he rushed up to London, ostensibly on business. Having failed to achieve whatever may have been the object of the visit, and feeling in a 'desponding state', he then took a second summer holiday in Scotland, again including Inverness in his tour. What, under the circumstances, are we to make of the visit to London? Elgar says it was a business trip, but business takes many forms. Assuming a conventional definition of the word – a trip to procure employment – it seems unlikely that normal plans to try to find accommodation and a regular job would have entailed a frenzied weekend train journey. Few potential employers hold interviews at the weekend, but even assuming that musical ones might, the whole tone of 'rushing' up to London on a Friday afternoon speaks of some sudden emergency or response to a telegram, rather than the calm acceptance of an invitation to an interview. Moreover this was a 'business' trip of such a delicate nature that Elgar had been sworn to secrecy and could disclose nothing even to a warm and sympathetic friend like Charles Buck. Even if Elgar was genuinely in search of some new musical post, the necessity to keep future plans quiet before they had been disclosed to pupils and the orchestras with whom he played hardly accounts for the air of cloak and dagger surrounding the episode. The expression 'settling in London' is ambiguous; it is true that if Elgar had been offered a job in London he would have had to settle there, but 'settling' in the sense of 'settling down' is usually synonymous with getting married. Elgar did not say that exactly, but did he mean it? Was the real purpose of his visit to London to discuss his future with Miss E.E.? Against this theory stand the words 'After my Scots excursion – I got in a very desponding state last summer (you ken what happened)' which place the onus of his unhappy state of mind on events in Inverness rather than London. Either the meeting with Miss E.E. in 1883 and the dash to London in February 1884 are intimately connected or they remain coincidental; if coincidental, then the dash to London was probably in pursuit of a job, which would have represented his second attempt at emancipation (the first when he tried to gain employment through an advertisement in the *Tablet*), and the second attempt to fail.

What we also do not know is whether Elgar met Miss E.E. in Inverness on his second visit, in the summer of 1884. Either he went back specifically to see her, or he was retracing his steps on a sentimental journey. While it is quite likely that a young man should dedicate a composition on impulse to a girl who has taken his fancy, Elgar was not in the habit of dedicating works to people he did not know reasonably well (and usually he knew them very well), and although he says in 1885 that Miss E.E. is nobody, she must have been somebody in 1883. He is answering queries about her after his second visit to Inverness, some eighteen months after first meeting her, but by that time he seems convinced that she is someone he will never see again, although had they wished to continue their acquaintance, Miss E.E. could presumably have been induced to pay a visit to Worcester; after all, his 'Braut' had come all the way from Germany. But his words, 'Miss E.E. at Inverness is nobody – that is to say that I shall ever see again', are precisely the kind a jilted lover would use, and on this occasion we can be reasonably sure that Elgar came as close as he ever would to having an unhappy love affair. The biggest mystery of all is why, if the first visit to Inverness had reduced him to a 'desponding state' and 'it behoved him to do something out of the common to raise his spirits', he chose to go back to the scene of the disaster. Unless, of course, by doing 'something out of the common to raise his spirits', Elgar had intended girding his armour and galloping back north to claim his maiden.

Not everything that happened in 1884 plunged Elgar into a desponding state. The year had one real excitement in store, a visit to Worcester by Dvořák to conduct his *Stabat Mater* and his Symphony in D Major at the Three Choirs Festival, with Elgar in the orchestra. Eighteen days after the concert Elgar wrote to Buck to say, 'I do wish you could hear Dvorak's music. It is simply ravishing, so tuneful & clever & the orchestration is wonderful; no matter how few instruments he uses he never sounds thin. I cannot describe it; it has to be heard.'

The year required something of an emotional readjustment in the Elgar household. William, who had held the post of organist at St George's Church since about 1846, had been ill the previous Christmas and had fallen victim to a youthful congregational plot to oust him from his job. He was then only sixty-two, no great age for a musician, and Elgar had told Buck, 'He thinks a great deal of this and I fear 'twill break him up.' Elgar junior had been in a somewhat delicate situation. In the event, he had allowed a decent interval of a year to elapse before slipping officially into his father's place in the organ loft, combining the post of organist with that of choirmaster. Although he held the choir in no great esteem, a paid job at the church was nevertheless an attractive proposition because it gave him an opportunity, which he lost no time in taking, of resigning from the asylum. Elgar did not attempt to compete with his father's term of office, giving up the post at St George's just as soon as he was able, in 1888. By 8 January 1886 he was already writing to Buck to complain of his lot: 'I am a fully fledged organist now – *hate* it. I expect another three months will end it; the choir is awful and no good to be done with them.'

A year after his second visit to Scotland, Elgar's broken heart seems to have mended sufficiently for him to put the journey to good use, in the manner of Mendelssohn, by writing a Scottish overture. In October 1885 he reported to Buck that the work was progressing favourably and that the score was beginning to look important. Seven weeks later the overture had been abandoned after he had shown the score to Stockley. The outcome, he reported to Buck, was that he would not bother further with it; 'Old Stockley is afraid of it. He says candidly he cannot read the score & would like to hear it first – I am sorely disappointed.' Elgar must have brooded upon this disappointment, for early in January 1886 he returned to the subject in another letter to Buck, having forgotten he had already told his friend all about the matter. He added one jot of new information, to the effect that Stockley had found the score 'disconnected'. Clearly down in the dumps, Elgar added a wry reminder of his recent chores on behalf of the asylum: 'I have retired into my shell,' he told Buck, '& live in hopes of writing a polka someday – failing that a single chant is probably my fate.'

This was Elgar in dispirited mood. It only required the company of a dog to cheer him up. For some reason, Buck was no longer able to keep his collie, Scap, and Elgar had become his new master in September 1885, fetching him home to Field Terrace first class by train from Leeds. In order to keep the dog

45

with him rather than put him in the guard's van, Elgar had to tip the enterprising guard. Scap rode a great part of the way with his head out of the window, and although he refused water at Sheffield, by Derby 'he was gasping' and devoured two glasses of milk. Elgar was out at half past seven the next morning with Scap, who immediately got into the river and fought with a Newfoundland. Apparently by lunch-time that day (in a letter to Buck reporting on Scap's adventures, Elgar slipped into the solecism of calling it dinner-time, a habit he was going to have to break before much longer) the dog knew the house and 'the turning' (instantly recognizable today – Field Terrace is a narrow passageway turning immediately off the main road), and by the second night Elgar had the dog sleeping in his room. Charles Pipe, fortunately, took to Scap at once.

Elgar was good at keeping Buck informed about his former pet. On 7 October he was writing to report that Scap had a new, expensive collar with his new address on it, had been to the vet but was quite well again, and had been introduced to the Graftons at their country home in Stoke, where he had a 'vagabond day' on the common, chasing rabbits. 'He has,' Elgar assured Buck, 'developed into a much more affectionate animal than I anticipated & loves me. When I am away he retires to my room & won't move ... 'till I return.' There can be no doubt that Elgar loved Scap. With no immediate family of his own to love, he was in any case exceptionally fond of dogs; it was to be over a quarter of a century before he was allowed to indulge his pleasure again.

CHAPTER TWO

'A Weird & Blackened Thing'

1885–98

By 1885 Elgar's character was formed. Like many aspiring children from the ranks of the lower middle class before and since, he had become a Tory, helping to campaign in November that year and catching a cold on election night for his pains. He took Scap with him to try to ensure that what he described as 'this Radical hole' did not fall prey to a Liberal, and 'owing to their exertions' got a Conservative in. Scap was even enlisted to the extent of having to wear the Tory colours on his collar, and seems to have been indoctrinated with some of his master's social values. In a letter to Buck, Elgar reported that they were getting on better now with the local hounds and never had a row, though there was 'one crossbred brute down the road' who always followed Scap and was anxious to fight. Elgar's remedy was to hurl a rock at the offending creature.

Electioneering in the rain not only gave Elgar a cold, but Scap too developed a cough and had to go to the vet again. In the same letter (written on 8 January 1886) Elgar recounts with glee another clout administered by him to some poor beast intent on molesting Scap; this time (on Christmas Eve, in fact) Elgar hit the animal with his walking-stick – so hard that he knocked the handle off. The incriminating missile, with Elgar's name engraved on it, went flying so far that Elgar could not find it; someone else did, however, which brought the 'owner of the cur', as Elgar described the man whose dog he had be-laboured, after him 'threatening police court etc etc'. Perhaps it was as well for Elgar that he had spent a few months in a solicitor's office. 'I talked to him like a man,' he assured Buck, '& came off with flying colours; my knowledge of the law, real and *pretended*, startled him (& well it might) – he touches his hat to me & keeps his dog tied up.'

Scap crops up again in a letter to Buck written on Whit Monday: he is enjoying his runs alongside Elgar's tricycle (forerunner of the bicycles on which he was later to explore the lanes of the West Country in company with two of the most liberated, unchaperoned young ladies of his day), and 'Every-body loves him, all my lady pupils kiss him, to my intense disgust.' We can be fairly sure there was one lady pupil Elgar began to teach later that year whose attentions to Scap would have caused him no such feelings. Her name was Alice Roberts.

For some time Elgar had been giving violin lessons ('advanced and elementary') in Malvern, advertising himself as a 'Pupil of Herr A. Pollitzer, London'; he also offered 'lessons in Accompaniment and Ensemble playing'. For 'Terms' prospective pupils were invited to 'address themselves' to 4 Field Terrace, Worcester. Malvern had something of a genteel musical atmosphere, nurtured and encouraged by its well-off, retired professional population and by a proliferation of girls' schools, all of them rating music high on the curriculum. In 1757 John Wall had analysed the waters at Great Malvern and the area had soon grown into a typical Victorian spa, respectable, affluent and rather dull.

Alice Roberts lived with her widowed mother some dozen miles south of Malvern on the borders of Worcestershire and Gloucestershire, in a large Georgian house called Hazeldine in the village of Redmarley d'Abitot. Her father, Henry Roberts, had been a major-general in the Indian Army; attached to the 13th Native Infantry, he had served in Gujarat, Sukkur and Schwan, and had gone round India using 'the influence acquired as a daring sportsman and a successful soldier to give to the wretched people about him their first example of power used for other purposes than tyranny and oppression', in the words of Sir Bartle Frere. By 1851, when he had achieved the rank of major, Roberts had covered himself in so much glory that he was said to be the best officer of his rank in the Bombay Army, and perhaps in India.

Roberts had taken time off from his army career in 1838, two months before his thirty-eighth birthday, to marry Julia Raikes, the daughter of a country parson and the granddaughter of Robert Raikes, a Gloucester publisher and founder of the Sunday Schools. In addition to Alice, the Roberts had three sons, one of whom, Albert, died in Poona at the age of four. In 1850, hoping to enjoy the leisured life of an English country gentleman on his eventual retirement, Roberts purchased Hazeldine, an enormous house the cost of which could not have come out of his army pay (when he died he left less that £3,000). Returning home in 1859, he received the thanks of parliament for his services to the British Empire, was awarded the medal and clasp of Central India, and retired to Hazeldine as a KCB. He enjoyed his home and his knighthood for only a year however, for in 1860, suffering from cancer of the throat, he died. Alice was twelve.

'Deserted' as a child by a flamboyant and famous father, with two elder brothers gone off to the army, leaving her at home with her widowed mother and no sisters with whom to share the burden, Alice's adolescence was spent in classic Victorian upper-middle-class boredom. Surrounded by servants, with no necessity for her to cook or sew, she had not enough to do and turned her attentions to music and literature, writing some abysmal poetry and a two-volume novel. Reviewing a narrative poem published by Alice in 1879 under the title *Isabel Trevithoe*, the *Scotsman* gave it the kind of notice from which many authors would take a decade to recover: 'As a rule the writer seldom rises above, if she does not sink below, the dead level of mediocrity ...' Undeterred, three years later Alice produced her work of fiction. This time the *Glasgow Herald* tackled her merits: 'We feel it very difficult,' its reviewer wrote, 'to do justice to the singular charm of *Marchcroft Manor*... The story is very slight, the characters few, there are no startling incidents and yet there is a quiet brightness and sunniness which are very attractive.' Under the almost intolerable weight of such patronizing encouragement, Alice's career as a novelist came to an end.

In the same year, 1882, another of her brothers, Frederick, died. Life at Hazeldine, for all its material comfort, must have been gloomier than ever. Alice consoled herself by taking an interest in Persian cats, expurgated editions of Shakespeare's plays and local amateur music-making. When she spotted Elgar's advertisement offering music lessons in Malvern she decided to see if the piano rather than literature was her forte, and off she went in her carriage through the narrow lanes of Worcestershire, arriving at Elgar's rented studio for the first time on 6 October 1886, three days before her thirty-eighth birthday.

Alice was already plump and she was never tall.[1] She had rather a pert, determined mouth, with a delicate, rounded chin and a severe bun of hair on the top of her head, perhaps to give the impression of extra height. Eight years Elgar's senior, and looking old for her age, her marital prospects were dim, though with a modest private income and the certainty of inheriting a large and valuable house she was relatively wealthy (Elgar had no money at all). Socially she was two rungs up the ladder from her music teacher. However, Elgar may have recognized something of his mother in this managing, though not very efficient, high-minded woman; and if at first sight these two seemed to have little in common, on closer acquaintance they must have come to realize they might both benefit by pooling their resources. This at any rate was the impression gained by the coachman who, according to a manuscript fragment of biography left by Elgar's daughter, Carice, was heard to say he thought there was more to Alice's visits to the studio than music. And before

1. In his autobiography, *My Own Trumpet* (Hamish Hamilton, 1973), Sir Adrian Boult has described Alice as 'very tiny indeed, with a quiet, intimate way of speaking', which 'caused her to come close up to anyone to whom she had anything to say'. Frank Schuster, one of Elgar's wealthy patrons, amusingly summed up this characteristic when he recalled to Boult 'the way dear Alice used to come up to one and confide in one's tummy'.

long Elgar was riding back to Hazeldine to be introduced to Lady Roberts. This was almost certainly his first experience of entering a large country house by the front door; as a boy he had been more accustomed to receiving hospitality in the servants' hall while waiting for his father to finish tuning the piano in the drawing-room.

Some months before meeting Alice, Elgar was writing to Buck to say he had been coming out of his shell, flirting during a picnic organized by his sister Lucy, taking up dancing and playing tennis again for the first time for three years.[2] In August he spent ten days in London and then had a holiday with the Bucks ('I shall be in paradise while it lasts,' he had told them while fixing up the dates), and on his return he had a second chance of playing, at Birmingham this time, under Dvořák's baton. 'We are on our mettle somewhat,' he had told Buck prior to the concert. (The soloist on this occasion was the young pianist Fanny Davies, for whom Elgar was later to write his *Concert Allegro*; she had been a pupil of Clara Schumann and her performances of Schumann's music, like those of her contemporary and fellow pupil, Adelina de Lara, were regarded as 'authentic' interpretations.)

Picnics, dancing and violin lessons, tennis and then visits to Hazeldine left little time for composing, and the year ended on a pleasantly boisterous note, with Scap stealing half a fried sole from Lucy's kitchen and a beef steak from Anne's.

In 1887 Alice Roberts's mother died, leaving £7,946 2s. 2d. A legacy of £500 to her surviving son Stanley had been reduced in a codicil to £300. Alice got £200 absolutely, her mother's jewellery and household effects, and a further £2,500 on trust. The Will was witnessed by a gardener. Alice had no inducement to remain on her own in Hazeldine, so she let the house and moved into furnished accommodation at Ripple Lodge in Malvern Link, presumably to be nearer to Elgar's studio.

The year had started in gloom for Elgar, with a letter in January to Buck regretting time wasted over the Christmas holidays, spent reading three novels by Walter Scott[3]; the outlook must have improved when he set up a Ladies' Orchestral Class, attracting sixteen pupils; and it ended, rather surprisingly, with a letter sent in December asserting that he had written 'a vast quantity of Music' that year – 'but *no money* in any of it' (Michael Kennedy's compilation of works for 1887 merely records a String Quartet and a Sonata for violin and

2. Elgar must have taken up lawn tennis very early in the history of the game; by his own rough reckoning he was playing in 1883, but he may have played before that, and the game was only patented in 1874.

3. Another of Elgar's favourite novelists was Kipling. At about this time he had also read Pepys's diaries, and evidence of the extent of his literary knowledge in later life is given by Sir Adrian Boult, who records in *My Own Trumpet* that one day, at tea in Severn House, the Elgars' London home from 1912 to 1921, Elgar and Ernest Newman, the music critic, spent some time capping each other's knowledge of out-of-the-way books, mainly novels.

piano, both of which were destroyed, and three religious vocal pieces[4]).

The engagement during 1887 of Elgar's younger brother, Frank, must have drawn Elgar's attention to his own bachelor status. His collaboration with Alice Roberts was progressing slowly, and in 1888 he set one of her poems to music and dedicated to her one of the most famous pieces of salon music ever written, his *Salut d'Amour*. Alice's first name was Caroline and Elgar had taken sufficient interest in his pupil to spot that by combining the first three letters of Caroline with the last three letters of Alice he could invent a new name, Carice. Perhaps he thought that by dedicating *Salut d'Amour* to 'Carice' he would successfully conceal from the world the true identity of the lady in question. But soon there was to be no need, for on 22 September 1888 he and Alice announced their engagement. One of her aunts promptly cut her out of her Will. Alice's father, after all, had been a major-general; Elgar's a piano-tuner. Alice had been brought up in a sprawling Georgian mansion, educated to a life of good works and county pursuits; Elgar had spent his childhood over a shop and taught the violin for a living. Instead of being gratified as they might have been today that, on the verge of forty, and with no great looks, Alice had found a man eight years younger than herself who wanted to marry her, a man who, however humble his origins may have been, dressed and behaved immaculately, all Alice's family could see was a liaison in which the sacred class barriers and conventions of the day were brought crashing down. There was also religious bias to be faced. Elgar was a Roman Catholic, Alice an Anglican, and she would be under an obligation to have her children brought up in the Catholic faith. Alice's aunts may have been praying that she had left it too late to have any children, but that apart, Rome was to many upper-middle-class provincial minds at that time the 'Scarlet Woman' and Roman Catholics belonged to a dangerous minority. The West Country also happened to be a particularly Evangelical part of England.

What did the marriage hold in store for Elgar? He was a romantic, but emotionally and artistically so, not sexually. There is no evidence of a con-summated affair prior to his marriage, and he was thirty-one when he got engaged. For the past decade he had been living with his sisters, with no settled home of his own and a career that was making no progress (in 1888 the *Musical Times* inadvertently rubbed in the point by referring to him as Mr Alger). His circle of friends was restricted to the local families he met through teaching and playing in ensembles. If he was ever to get on in the world, which meant achieving the leisure in which to compose and comfortable surround-ings in which to relax, he was going to need influential friends and a private income. Alice, through her social position and investments, offered the

4. *Portrait of Elgar* by Michael Kennedy.

gateway to both. She was by temperament unlikely to prove a demanding lover, which was just as well for a man who tended to place women on a pedestal, regarding them as objects to be adored, not made love to. They were both on the wrong side of youth and were unlikely to have entertained unrealistic expectations about marriage, and no one could have accused them or rushing into it; they had known one another for two years before they got engaged, and they were engaged seven months before they got married – at Brompton Oratory, at noon on 8 May 1889.

The choice of church (it had been enlarged the year before) was indicative of many decisions to come. Neither Alice nor Elgar lived in London, most of their friends and relations lived in the West Country, and yet they felt the need to get married not just in London but in one of London's most fashionable churches. Elgar's parents travelled up to Town for the ceremony and lunch was provided in Drayton Gardens by a loyal friend of Alice. A coy piece of local journalism had reported a rumour 'that a well-known and distinguished member of the musical profession in Worcester had gained the hand of a wealthy patroness'. To describe Alice as wealthy was an exaggeration: she enjoyed the rent from Hazeldine and the income from a trust fund of £2,500, but invested at ten per cent that would only have ensured the Elgars of a private income of £5 a week (admittedly at a time when many domestic servants worked for £15 a year). The capital sum of the trust fund was, however, increased in 1892 by the sale of Hazeldine and most of its contents. When the reporter went on to retail a second rumour to the effect that 'the wealthy patroness' had ordained that her fiancé was to give up all further musical engagements, he could hardly have been more misinformed. What he may have got wind of were plans for the newly married couple to live in London, but a move away from Worcester and a break with teaching were part of Alice's plan to further Elgar's musical career, not to put a stop to it.

To suggest, as Percy Young has in *Edward Elgar: OM*, that Alice was to make Elgar into a great composer is surely over-stating the case, but there seems little doubt that, before Elgar had provided a shred of concrete evidence of his genius, Alice pinned her faith on his musical gifts, and that for the rest of her life the furtherance of his career as a composer served as a more than adequate substitute for any frustrated literary ambitions she may have nursed for herself. She continued to pen bad verse, and no doubt that brought her satisfaction, but she was rationalizing when she wrote (in her diary in 1914) that the care of a genius was enough of a life's work for any woman. There is no question of her having sacrificed a literary career of her own in order to foster Elgar's musical one; after spending a quarter of a century looking after her widowed mother, with no obvious prospects of marriage or of leading a life of her own, she was fortunate to find an over-riding purpose to occupy the remainder of her life.

The weather at the time of the Elgars' wedding was apparently all too seasonable, for in April Elgar had told Charles Buck (who travelled down from Yorkshire to be with his friend at Brompton Oratory) that if it was fine and warm the honeymoon would be spent in the north, but if cold, in the Isle of Wight. They ended up at Ventnor, whence news about them was relayed to Worcester by means of a newspaper cutting which listed Mr and Mrs Edward Elgar among the 'fashionable' visitors. Elgar was on his way up. The only blight cast upon the wedding had been his wrench from Scap. It seems the irrepressible companion of Elgar's last bachelor years, who had recently fathered a puppy as badly behaved as himself, was not going to be made welcome in the matrimonial home. A letter written by Elgar to Buck before his wedding is rather pathetic: 'My only regret about leaving . . .' he says, 'is about my dear, dear companion, poor old Scap; he is lying at my feet now as he has done these $3\frac{1}{2}$ years: my sister Lucy will take great care of him & he knows her as well as he does me . . . but the parting will be bitter on my side.' Presumably Alice feared that Scap (who eventually died in 1892) might mess up the carpets at 3 Marloes Road, a house in Kensington that one of her more liberal cousins, William Raikes, had let them borrow for the first month following their return from the Isle of Wight. As they were packing up to move to Norwood from Marloes Road on 23 July, Elgar reported to Frank Webb, a member of the Amateur Instrumental Society in Worcester, that London suited him extremely well, and no doubt the news was broadcast among his other friends in Worcester. He had however been sampling the capital's charms for less than a month, and the impression given that all was well was soon to be dispelled.

In August Alice was recalling her duties as lady of the manor by sending two prizes, one of six shillings and one of four, to a local flower show held near her old home in Redmarley d'Abitot, and during a holiday in Malvern Elgar was shown off to some of Alice's smart friends, including the Hon. Mrs Roper-Curzon. 'Gosh,' wrote Elgar in his diary. Mrs Roper-Curzon lived at 5 The Lees, and had become a neighbour of Alice's after the lease on Ripple Lodge, the house where Alice was living at the time of her engagement, ran out in January and Alice had taken a short lease on a villa in The Lees called Saetermo (probably No. 7). (The Elgars were in fact already acquainted with both The Lees and the villa; in March, before his wedding, Elgar had lodged for a couple of nights at No. 3 when he was leading the orchestra for a Malvern Choral Society performance of the *Messiah*, dining with Alice at Saetermo on the night of the rehearsal.) It was here that she and Elgar stayed during their holiday, intending to remain until 25 September, the Quarter Day on which the lease on Saetermo was due to expire and when they were to move into a house called Oaklands, in Fountain Road, Upper Norwood – convenient for the Crystal Palace and the Saturday concerts of August Manns. But on 25 September Alice was unwell (not too unwell however to prevent them lunching with Mrs Roper-Curzon), so they put their furniture into store and moved down the road into furnished accommodation at No. 4. There was no piano in the house, and the obliging Mrs Roper-Curzon allowed Elgar to make use of hers. While staying here Elgar too became unwell, developing an inflamed eye which required medical attention, but eventually, twelve days later than planned, he and Alice moved into Oaklands.

Despite these domestic set-backs to the early months of marriage – ill-health and no proper, settled home – Elgar wrote to Buck from Malvern on 6 October to report how happy he was in his new life, what a dear, loving companion he had, and 'how sweet everything seems & how *understandable* existence seems to have grown'. And he adds the tantalizing sentence, 'You may forget the long discussions we used to have in your carriage when driving about but I think all the difficult problems are now solved and – well I don't worry myself about 'em now!'

What were the difficult problems that Elgar no longer worried about? Buck was a general practitioner; it is just conceivable that Elgar sought his advice on some specific physical difficulty, but problems of that kind do not usually just vanish, nor as a rule do they require prolonged discussion in a carriage while riding around visiting patients. Earlier in his letter Elgar had referred to all the talks he and Buck had had about 'the mystery of living' and it is far more likely that in Buck Elgar had found a slightly older, more experienced and already married friend with whom to philosophize and bounce off intellectual ideas and opinions for which he would have found a less receptive and stimulating audience at home.

This letter ends in a way that reminds us of the suffocating repression from which Victorians suffered. 'Give my kind regards to Mrs Buck,' Elgar wrote, '& a kiss (if he's not too big) to the Boy.' The 'Boy', the Bucks' son, was just three years old, as Elgar must well have known.

When the Elgars did eventually remove to Norwood, their stay lasted only a few months; by March 1890 they were back in West Kensington, at 51 Avonmore Road. Here Alice painted an excellent watercolour of the drawing-room and Elgar attempted to write a violin concerto, but it proved to be premature and he destroyed it. But in April the Worcester Festival Committee commissioned a short secular orchestral piece and Elgar got straight down to work on a concert overture, to be called *Froissart.*. It received its first per-

formance at Worcester on 9 September, with Elgar conducting, and although
the score is far from inspired it is of interest, for it is perhaps Elgar's first
composition to herald distinctly the possibility of things to come.

Although Elgar was still, at the age of thirty-three, learning his trade, the
music publishers Novello & Co. promised to publish the overture (they did so
as Opus 19) in spite of a less than enthusiastic welcome given to it by the
Musical Times: 'The overture is of course chivalric in style,' they wrote, 'and,
perhaps, more commendable for what it tries to say than for the manner of
its expression. There is upon it, what surprises no one – the mark of youth and
inexperience; but it shows that with further thought and study, Mr Elgar will
do good work. He must acquire greater coherence of ideas, and conciseness
of utterance – those inevitable signs of a master, only to be attained by
extended and arduous effort.' This lukewarm reception of his work came at
the end of a year Elgar had spent tramping from one London publishing house
to another trying to drum up interest in his compositions. He is said to have
sold *Salut d'Amour* outright for £5, a work that must since have been played
a million times in tea rooms up and down the land, and thus he parted with
a fortune at the start of his career. Alice sold some of her pearls, perhaps to
pay for the entertainment she felt obliged to carry out, perhaps for the gas
fittings ordered from the Army and Navy Stores, the carpets from Liberty's and
the beds from Maple's. Among the fashionable visitors to Avonmore Road was
Lady Montgomery, a widow for the past three years; her husband, Sir Robert
Montgomery, had served in India with Alice's father, distinguishing himself
during the Mutiny, when he was judicial commissioner in the Punjab, by
congratulating a deputy commissioner on his 'energy and spirit' in summarily
executing 282 sepoys without trial.[5] Eighty-five years later his grandson
Bernard was to redeem the family name in one of the decisive battles of history,
at Alamein.

On 14 August, amidst all this strange confusion of financial insecurity and
hospitality, Alice gave birth to a daughter. She and Elgar borrowed back the
name he had invented when dedicating *Salut d'Amour* to Miss Roberts, and
gave it to the baby, who in all probability became the first girl ever to be called
Carice. She was christened in London, and Elgar's parents, now aged seventy,
felt unable to make the journey again. It had naturally been a worrying time:
Alice was almost forty-two and she had left it dangerously late to give birth
to a first child, and sixteen days before Carice was born Elgar had written to
Frank Webb, 'I have been hoping to send you some good news but things go
on just as usual; it is of course a very trying anxious time but, God willing,
we hope it may pass safely by.' In the end Elgar was able to tell Webb, 'Our

5. *The Great Mutiny* by Christopher Hibbert (Allen Lane, 1978).

time of great anxiety has passed now, thank God ... All has gone well & both Mrs Elgar and the little one (Carice Irene) are very well.'

Anxiety over the impending birth of her child may have been responsible for Alice drawing up a very odd document just three weeks before the event. She made a Will, leaving everything to Elgar on trust for his children, and in the preamble she described herself as a professor of music. This strange flight of fancy was witnessed by her solicitor and 'Frances Gough, widow and cook'. Eighteen months later, even more inexplicably, she signed a codicil revoking the provisions of the trust.

In religious matters Elgar's interest in music and musicians always transcended any denominational affiliations his friends or associates may have had, and we catch a glimpse in 1890 of his connections with St Michael's College, the Anglican choir school near Tenbury in Worcestershire, founded by the wealthy Victorian musical philanthropist, baronet and canon residentiary of Hereford Cathedral, Sir Frederick Ouseley. One of the three part-songs Elgar composed that year, *My Love Dwelt in a Northern Land* (was he thinking of Miss E.E. of Inverness when he set this poem?), was dedicated to the warden of St Michael's, an Anglican clergyman. Surprisingly few of Elgar's co-religionists came to figure amongst his close friends or acquaintances.

The dedication next year, 1891, of a piece for violin and piano to Fred Ward foreshadows the close of his first attempt to succeed in London, for Ward was one of Elgar's Worcester pupils, and already a combination of London fog and the need to nurture his Worcester roots were driving him back one or two days a week to resume the chore of teaching. Among Elgar's more promising pupils at this time was Ward's younger sister. In a letter written on 8 February from Avonmore Road, Elgar told Ward, 'I am much pleased with your younger sister's progress & I think she may play *very* well: that is she has a firmness & *good tone* at present and these things mean a great deal in such early days.' The weather had given him less cause to rejoice. 'The winter has been truly awful,' he went on. 'The fogs here are terrifying & make me very ill: yesterday all day & today until two o'clock we have been in a sort of yellow darkness. I groped my way to church this morning & returned in an hour's time a weird & blackened thing with a great and giddy headache.'

Writing to Buck on 17 June 1886, before he had ever lived in London, Elgar had said, 'I suppose the London air is a tonic to those born in it; I never cd stand it long,' and when the experiment of living in London was over and he had been safely back in Worcestershire for six months, he told Buck in a Christmastide letter at the end of 1891, 'London nearly killed me.'

Whether London had nearly killed Elgar or merely failed to provide employment, by the summer of 1891 the three-year lease on the house in Avonmore

Road had been surrendered after only a few months and he and Alice were back in the West Country. He may have felt the need of an excuse for so hasty a retreat from the capital, and the fog certainly supplied one; on the other hand, groping his way to church through yellow fog was hardly likely to lead to inspiration, and until he had realized his potential as a composer he was wasting a lot of time and effort knocking on publishers' doors.

The house the Elgars now rented was 37 Alexandra Road in Malvern. They thought it had to be given a name, so they chose Forli, in honour of the Italian painter Melozzo da Forlì, who was celebrated for his paintings of angels playing musical instruments. It was a charming semi-detached house built in about 1860, covered with Virginia creeper. In Elgar's time they shared a tennis court with neighbours, and the garden extended over land on which today stands a modern house named Nimrod. There could never have been much of a view, but the house stands well away from the main road and it should have been reasonably quiet, although in a letter of 19 October 1897 to August Jaeger, his publisher at Novello, Elgar complains that the house was *very noisy* close to the station where I *can't write* at all'. There were probably five or six bedrooms, with three attic rooms to house the servants without whom the Elgars never moved far, together with two main reception rooms and a breakfast room. They were to live here in very reasonable comfort for the next eight years, furnishing the place with as many possessions as they wanted from Hazeldine, and their time at Forli coincided with Elgar's late, slow but clearly defined progress towards maturity as a musician. Late and slow though it may have been, it is doubtful whether it would have taken place at all had they stayed on in London. The move to Malvern seems to have suited Carice, too. At eighteen months she was 'a most wonderfully lovely infant!', her father told Buck. 'Everyone turns to gaze at her as she "sweeps by in her chariot" ... she is a sturdy little minx ... & never been ill a day since she came!'

It was at this time that Charles Buck aquired something called a typewriter. 'I was so very glad to see your well-known scrawl once again,' Elgar told him in response to a letter from Yorkshire, 'but was much overcome by the machine-made part: what a clever fellow you are; I have looked at those type-writing things in amazement & never could manage to make anything of them.'

The winter of 1891–2 was cold and it was snowing in March. Despite the return to the country to escape the London fog, Elgar now began to suffer prolonged bouts of ill-health. At the start of 1892 he was confined to the house for something like eight weeks, having suffered what must have been a severe attack of influenza, leaving his throat, he told Frank Webb in a letter written on 27 March, 'in a miserably treacherous state'. He said he had to be very careful and that Alice, too, 'has now an awful cold'. Only Carice was thriving: 'She is, as she always has been, *very* well.'

It was at this time that Rosa Burley, headmistress of a girls' school, The Mount, came to know Elgar, for he had been engaged, before she actually took over the school, to teach music there. Miss Burley has left us a vivid, well-written and largely believable account of Elgar's conduct and character in *Edward Elgar: The Record of a Friendship*. In testing Miss Burley's evidence, however, it needs to be borne in mind that her book was not completed until 1948, and that in recalling Elgar in his thirties, Miss Burley was casting her mind back half a century. She died in 1951 and the book was withheld from publication until after the death of Carice in 1970.

The Mount, in Albert Road, Malvern, now belongs to Malvern Girls' College. Miss Burley described it as a 'largish stucco house with that look of a Swiss chalet so much beloved by Victorian architects'. In Elgar's day it was advertised as 'being prepared to receive young ladies, the daughters of gentle-men'. As Carice was eventually admitted as a pupil, Elgar was presumably regarded as a gentleman. He was also regarded, by Miss Burley, as 'one of the most repressed people it is possible to imagine'. She has left a physical description of Elgar at thirty-four: 'A tall slight young man with a pale face and dark eyes.' His prevailing mood, she says, seems to have been one of acute unhappiness: 'It seemed evident he was suffering from some overwhelming secret trouble but what this was I had no means of knowing and he was so cold and aloof as to make it seem improbable that I ever should.' She makes no secret of the fact, however, that in her view Elgar was unhappy in his marriage, or at least that for some reason he regretted getting married. She certainly found a 'strange disparity' between Elgar and Alice. 'So incompatible did they seem,' she has written, 'that it was difficult to believe that they could be husband and wife. Mrs Elgar was wholly typical of the class to which she belonged. Like so many ladies of her time she had cultivated a number of rather indeterminate artistic pursuits in few of which she could be said to excel. She had the vagueness of manner which was then considered a mark of feminine refinement and all her utterances tended to float off into space. Even her most impressive pronouncements had to be finished by a wave of the hand rather than by anything so definite as the completion of a sentence.'

Miss Burley referred to Elgar as 'the Genius', and no doubt that was why Alice tolerated her. She tells us that 'Whatever the relationship between the Elgars may have been ... one fact was evident ... Mrs Elgar worshipped her husband with a devotion so absolute as to make her blind to his most obvious faults. It was clear from the outset that she did really believe his most trivial achievements to be works of genius and the germ was already present of an incapacity, unfortunate, because shared by her husband, to understand that hostile criticism of his music could be the result of anything but malice.' Arnold Bax recalls in his autobiography[6] being taken to meet the Elgars in 1901. 'A pleasant-looking fair-haired lady with – it struck me – rather an anxious manner, welcomed us very kindly in her gentle, slightly hesitant voice. Almost at once she began to speak enthusiastically and a little extravagantly about her wonderful husband and his work.'

Bax also gives an account of Elgar at the same period, and a fleeting glimpse of his relationship with Carice, then aged eleven. Elgar, he says, 'was not a big man, but such was the dominance of his personality that I always had the impression that he was twice as large as life'. He adds, 'There was ever a faint sense of detachment, a hint – very slight – of hauteur and reserve.' Apparently, on coming upon Carice sitting on a swing, Elgar said to her, 'Showing rather more leg than I care about, young woman!'

The Elgars recovered sufficiently from their colds in the summer of 1892 to have their first holiday in Bavaria, where they were taken by Miss Mary Baker of Hasfield Court in Gloucestershire, a childhood friend of Alice. Her family were soon to take on a number of interesting roles in Elgar's life. Elgar wrote from Germany to his sister Polly's children informing them that their aunt and uncle had 'come all this way to here music at Bayreuth'. The people, apparently, were nice, friendly and 'so polite', a quality much appreciated by Elgar in others. 'If you go by a cabstand,' the children were told, 'they do not say "Cab, please" but stand & bow & take their hats off.' The guards on the trains turned out to be equally well-bred, not shouting out 'Tickets please!' but making a bow and saying, 'Will the worshipful company be so friendly as to show their tickets!' Elgar seems to have enjoyed the holiday from every point of view, commenting in letters home on the lizards and butterflies, the pine forests, the handsome town fountains from which the poor fetched water, and the outdoor Stations of the Cross. 'In this part there are no protestants,' he noted, '& the church is open all day.' The music to be heard in church, played on a violin, hautboy, clarinet and trombone, was 'nice but very odd'. Elgar drew the Grafton children's attention to 'a very old castle' (at Nuremberg), telling them their mother would show them a poem by Longfellow, 'about the town which is one of the oldest in this country'. Remembering his mother's life-long interest in Longfellow, Elgar wrote to her from Heidelberg about a procession of students he came across, composed of three duelling guilds, 'all their faces wounded (silly fools) and many with bandages on'. He tells her it reminded him 'of Hyperion & the beer scandal etc etc'. Elgar had been reminded of Longfellow's 1839 translation of the epic poem *Hyperion* some

6. *Farewell, My Youth* (Longmans, 1943).

time before; the result was his first large-scale choral work, a cantata for chorus and orchestra called *The Black Knight*, which he began before leaving for his first Bavarian holiday and which he completed in time to be performed, under his own baton, at Worcester on 18 April 1893. Novello published it immediately, and in size and scope (it lasts about half an hour) it marked a major step forward. The year before Elgar went to Bavaria, during a sparse period of composition, Longfellow had also inspired a part-song called *Spanish Serenade*. Now, on his return to Forli, and despite having to be 'very careful *always*' with his throat, 'never going out if the weather was damp', as he told Buck in November, he was 'so horribly busy' and 'an idiot for trying to do so much'. In addition to *The Black Knight* he was at work on a number of songs, including *Like to the Damask Rose*, and the first orchestral piece to sound the authentic musical voice of Edward Elgar, the *Serenade* in E minor for string orchestra.

Many years later Elgar complained to Billy Reed that the *Serenade* had been neglected 'for years' and was only resurrected and appreciated after he had achieved fame through the *Enigma Variations*.[7] Elgar had a point as far as concert promoters were concerned: the public was given very little opportunity to hear and appreciate the work when it was first written. The Larghetto alone was played the year following composition, at a concert in Hereford in 1893, and again in 1894 at St Andrew's Hall in London. The first complete performance of the work (consisting of an Allegro, Larghetto and Allegretto) was given overseas, at Antwerp, and then not until 1896; an English audience had to wait until 16 July 1899, shortly after the first performance of the *Enigma Variations*, to hear the entire work.

At least the *Serenade* did not have to wait as long to have justice done to it as Elgar's *Chanson de Matin* and *Chanson de Nuit*, which were published as Opus 15 and first performed in 1901, and which were probably composed ten or more years before, in 1889 or 1890.[8]

On their way to Bayreuth in 1892 the Elgars had paid their respects at Beethoven's birthplace in Bonn, and during their holiday they had heard *Tristan und Isolde*, *Die Meistersinger*, and *Parsifal* twice. By 1893 Elgar's aloofness towards Rosa Burley had presumably melted, for she and a friend joined the Elgars for another holiday in Germany; before leaving for Munich, Elgar had been to Covent Garden to hear *Tristan* again, and on his first night in Munich he went to *Die Meistersinger*. He heard *Tristan* yet again and the entire *Ring* cycle, and even went to a parody of *Tannhäuser*. Not only had Elgar fallen under the spell of Wagner, he had been totally captivated by Germany, and

7. *Elgar As I Knew Him.*
8. *Portrait of Elgar.*

he and Alice were back in the Bavarian highlands for yet another holiday in 1894, when they stayed for several weeks at a pension, and to this vacation we owe the *From the Bavarian Highlands*, written in collaboration with Alice and first performed under Elgar's baton in Worcester in 1896. An orchestral version of three of the songs, dedicated to the owners of the pension at Garmisch where the Elgars had lodged, was taken up the next year at the Crystal Palace by August Manns.

At a time when no member of the working or lower middle classes ever had a real holiday, and not many members of the middle class ventured abroad, the Elgars did extremely well for holidays. Even though the Bavarian jaunt for the late summer of 1894 had already been planned, they were in Sussex in the spring of that year, paying visits to Chichester and Arundel, and it may have been on this occasion that Elgar formed an affection for the Sussex countryside which was to lead him, during the Great War, to rent a cottage near Petworth.

Among Elgar's compositions in 1895 was a song called *After*, destined to cause an uncomfortable situation some eleven years later: in his autobiography, Sir Adrian Boult recalls being present at a dinner party in 1904, during the course of which Elgar was admiring the engraved score of *The Kingdom*, just arrived from Novello. At the end of the dinner it was announced that Miss Edith Clegg would sing *After*. According to Boult, Elgar got up, shook hands and said, 'Well, you have spoiled my evening for me.'[9]

Questioned in 1980 about this incident, Sir Adrian was asked to elaborate on the impression Elgar's behaviour had made; it could, after all, have been intended as rather heavy-handed humour, or it could have been cruel ill-manners. Sir Adrian Boult had this to say: 'It was, I suppose, a kind of joke, but Miss Clegg was rather upset. I don't think it was meant to be malicious but it certainly struck me as rather a rude thing to say. I should say it was the sort of outburst that with Elgar could happen at any time.'[10] Billy Reed, a loyal and devoted friend to Elgar if ever he had one, recalls a similar incident in *Elgar As I Knew Him*. It seems that on a visit to Paris nineteen years later Elgar was accosted in his hotel by a gushing American tourist, who wanted to tell him how thrilled she had been to see him conducting, and how 'too cute' she had found the Scherzo of his Second Symphony, only to be rewarded with a cold stare from the great man before he stalked off upstairs to his bedroom. Reed was only able to persuade him to talk civilly to the woman later (she was

9. *The Kingdom* was in fact not published until 1906. In a letter to the author of 25 September 1980 Sir Adrian Boult has revised the dates given in his autobiography. He remains quite certain the score Elgar had been admiring was *The Kingdom*, and now accepts that the year of the incident with Miss Clegg was 1906, and therefore that he was about seventeen, not fifteen, when he first met Elgar.

10. In conversation with the author.

staying in the same hotel) by explaining that, if he did not, his reputation would suffer on her return to the United States. Reed is a disingenuous and honest reporter, and the anecdote rings true. A clue to Elgar's behaviour concerning the American can perhaps be found in a letter he wrote on 9 March 1904 to August Jaeger at Novello: 'I always resent any familiarity from outsiders.'

In 1895, six years after his marriage and at the age of thirty-eight, Elgar stood on the brink of success. A performance in Wolverhampton of *The Black Knight* was proclaimed from the stage as a work of genius. Another composition inspired by Longfellow, on which he had begun work the previous year, was later to be greeted, this time by the *Staffordshire Sentinel*, as the work of a composer who showed 'distinct genius'; it was the cantata for soprano, tenor, bass, chorus and orchestra entitled *Scenes from the Saga of King Olaf*. In his private life he took up golf, a game that had been played for centuries in Scotland but had made progress in England only during the eighties, and although not yet elected to anything so grand as the Athenaeum, he took to lunching, on visits to London, at the Junior Conservative Club. Another General Election victory for the Tories in July 1895 so excited him 'that he left his greatcoat and part of suits in the train', according to Alice's diary.

Despite increasing demands on his time as a composer and conductor, Elgar went again to Bavaria, in August 1895, this time stopping off at Salzburg to see the house where Mozart was born. During the early winter he was hard at work on *King Olaf* and in December he received a commission from the Worcester Festival Committee to write an oratorio, *Lux Christi*. Had Elgar died at about this time, even after completing *Lux Christi* and *King Olaf*, he would have rated barely half a column in *Grove's Dictionary*. From these years only *Salut d'Amour*, the *Serenade* for strings and *From the Bavarian Highlands* are today regularly performed. He was therefore still a man of promise rather than an established composer, although in 1895 he was on the verge of those years when we are judged to be at our most energetic and creative. Indeed, the twenty years between Elgar's forty-first and sixty-first birthdays were to be the great creative years of his life, and it is perhaps no coincidence that the beginning of this period was marked by the entry of a new influence, and one of the most important friendships of his life.

Dora Penny was the daughter of an Anglican clergyman, the Reverend Alfred Penny, rector of St Peter's, Wolverhampton. In August 1895 Mr Penny married Mary Baker of Hasfield Court, the childhood friend of Alice who had taken the Elgars to Germany in 1893, so that Mary Baker became Dora's stepmother. Mary and Alice had studied geology together as schoolgirls under the eye of another clerical gentleman, the Reverend William Symonds, rector of

Pendock in Worcestershire, and Dora tells us of a catty remark Mary stored up about her friend, relating to Alice's frequent visits to Elgar's studio, ostensibly for piano lessons, when it must have been obvious they were courting. 'Dear Alice,' Mary's step-daughter has recorded her as saying, 'how hard she worked ... she nearly wore her fingers to the bone practising and I couldn't think what for. She never would have made a fine player.'

Dora says she first met Elgar in December 1895 when the Elgars went over to Wolverhampton for the day to see her step-mother.[11] She was twenty-one and strikingly handsome. An account of their relationship is given in her book, *Edward Elgar: Memories of a Variation* (she was to become the tenth of the *Enigma Variations*), covering the period 1895–1914. It has no merits as a work of literature, and it was not written until 1936, up to forty years after some of the events it describes, but it is a fascinating document because it carries the imprimatur of Elgar's daughter and, wildly improbable though much of it sounds, it may be judged to convey precisely the image of happy home life that Carice wished to see preserved. 'You have given me the very pleasant task of bestowing my blessing on your reminiscences of what were, in spite of the difficulties and worries attendant on the life of a genius and the making of a career, such happy days,' she told Dora in a letter from Broadheath in 1936. 'And I do it most willingly because I am grateful to you for this faithful and vivid picture of my parents ... I have been reduced to a condition of helplessness over the scenes you describe ... Those who know anything of our home life will live them again with mingled tears and laughter.'

It was not long after that first meeting in 1895 that Dora had established, in her view at any rate, an intimate relationship in which both Elgar and Alice were dependent upon her, in which she would be summoned to their home whenever Elgar was down in the dumps and needed cheering up, in which his well-meaning but frankly incompetent 'dear' little wife had to be nudged along in her elementary domestic duties and tucked up in bed at night as early as possible in order to leave the coast clear for the creative genius and his perceptive, tactful helper to get down to work together on a few more pages of heart-rending music. 'When I came to know them very well,' she explains, 'it was the usual thing, almost directly after I arrived, for me to slide into a seat by the piano ready to turn over.' There is in a great deal of her book an element of the absurd of which neither she nor Carice was remotely aware.

Elgar's letters indicate very clearly his affection for Dora, and her brain cannot have been half as scattered as her book would suggest, for she also enjoyed the confidence and shared the musical experiences of August Jaeger,

11. She gives the date as 6 December 1895, which contradicts Percy Young's assertion, in *Elgar: OM*, that she accompanied the Elgars to Munich in August 1893.

Elgar's publisher at Novello, a widely respected musical figure of his day who was destined to achieve immortality as 'Nimrod' in the *Enigma Variations*. (Not everyone admired Jaeger, however; Rosa Burley described him as 'a true friend but an almost commonplace little German'.) Among the many invaluable letters Jaeger wrote to Dora was one describing the vital 1902 Düsseldorf performance of *The Dream of Gerontius*, in which the part of the Angel was sung by Muriel Foster; Dora destroyed it one day when 'clearing out', and correspondence from Alice was among other valuable source material relating to the life of Elgar which she threw away.

When his oratorio *Lux Christi* (for soprano, contralto, tenor, bass, chorus and orchestra) received its first performance at Worcester on 10 September 1896, with Elgar conducting, he and his new work were in select company: also in the programme were Beethoven's *Pastoral* Symphony, Schumann's *Rhenish* Symphony and Verdi's *Requiem*. The Elgar work moved one critic to write, 'His masterful orchestration and originality of thought and idiom convinced all who heard Mr Elgar's music that a great musician was arising of whom much would be heard later on.' *Lux Christi* was an important milestone, and it must have been an exciting time for Elgar and his friends; they had only seven weeks to wait for another first night, this time at the North Staffordshire Music Festival in Hanley when Elgar conducted his *Scenes from the Saga of King Olaf*. Among the audience was Dora Penny. Instead of resting in the artists' room, Elgar joined her in the interval and, not content with *King Olaf*, in the evening the pair of them went off to another concert to hear Beethoven's *Choral* Symphony. 'Mr E. sat with me most of the time,' Dora recorded in her diary. It was as a result of the performance of *King Olaf* that the *Staffordshire Sentinel* had written, 'While we have now in this country plenty of composers of great merit, Mr Elgar is the first among them who has shown distinct genius.' The *Athenaeum* said the orchestration was worthy of Wagner. Prior to the first performance of *King Olaf* Elgar received generous good wishes from one of those 'composers of great merit' to whom the *Sentinel* had referred, Charles Stanford. After the concert Alice recorded, 'Glorius King Olaf a magnificent triumph,' adding, somewhat piously, 'D.G.'. Sometimes when things were going well she wrote out her thanks to God in full, as she did after the first London performance of *King Olaf* the following spring, at the Crystal Palace under the faithful Manns. 'Most magnificent. Deo gratias,' she noted.

Alice's judgement of the first performance of *King Olaf* differs somewhat from Rosa Burley's third-hand account (she gives the date of the performance as 13 October when it was in fact 30 October), the gist of which is that Elgar, 'already nervous and fidgety', lost his grip on the performance because the tenor, Edward Lloyd, made some minor error, the situation only being saved by the leader leaping to his feet 'and straightening the thing out by his presence and his bow'. Lloyd's lapse was the result of missing the final rehearsal 'through a train error', and Elgar is said to have vented his spleen on Charles Swinnerton Heap, founder of the North Staffordshire Festival, to whom he had dedicated *Lux Christi*. Miss Burley says that Heap was deeply injured and the breach was never healed, though this seems most unlikely as four years later Heap undertook to rehearse *The Dream of Gerontius*.

Promising though Elgar's progress at this time may seem in retrospect, a friendly letter he wrote to one of his pupils in March 1896, enclosed with an account, helps to place his prospects in perspective. For a whole term's tuition he had charged three guineas, but he told the young lady she was to let him know if that was too much. He had other irons in the fire besides teaching; it had not escaped his notice that 1897 was the year of the queen's Diamond Jubilee, and as a contribution to the jingoism the occasion was bound to engender he had composed an *Imperial March*. On 9 January 1897 he wrote to his publisher apologizing for even mentioning terms, 'but,' he explained '... the Term [at The Mount] will shortly recommence & it will depend entirely upon this matter whether I return to teaching or continue to compose – or try to.' Another thought struck him. 'Would it be of any material good,' he asked, somewhat disingenuously, 'to get permission to dedicate it [the March] to the Queen? If so I should be greatly obliged if you cd advise me how to set about it. I know Sir W. Parratt & wd ask him unless there is a recognised way unknown to me.' Sir Walter Parratt had been Master of the Queen's Music since 1893. In the event, nothing came of this attempt to cash in on Queen Victoria's sixtieth year on the throne, and Elgar had to wait another twelve months before his sovereign was to grant him her favours. In the meantime he got in some practice with a foreign potentate, having Novello send a presentation copy of *King Olaf* to the King of Norway and Sweden.

Even without a royal dedication the *Imperial March* caught the popular mood and boomed across London during the summer of 1897. Its first performance was given by massed bands at the Crystal Palace in April, and there were encores at a royal garden party on 28 June, the actual anniversary of the queen's coronation, at a state concert in July and at the Albert Hall in October. For a time it became almost a second national anthem: in 1899 it was played at St Paul's Cathedral, Westminster Abbey and St George's Chapel, Windsor. And approval of an earlier work, *From the Bavarian Highlands*, came at this time from Sir Charles Grove, founder, among so many other things, of the musical dictionary; Alice had sent him a copy of the score and he told her it was 'lively, heartfelt music'.

Still in patriotic mood, Elgar received a spur to his inspiration in the spring of 1898 from his mother, now in her seventy-sixth year. She had remembered from her youth tales of a British chieftain called Caractacus, who was said to have roamed the Malvern Hills. One day, so she told her daughter Polly in a letter written in December, she and Elgar had stood looking at the Beacon and she had said to him, 'Oh! Ed, look at the lovely old hill. Can't we write some tale about it? I quite long to have something worked up about it; so full of interest and so much historical interest.' Elgar told her to write the tale herself; and this part of the narrative she related to Polly in almost Biblical language: 'He held my hand with a firm grip. "Do," he said. "No, I can't, my day is gone by if I ever could," and so we parted.'

Elgar must have got down to research immediately, for in less than a month he told his mother that *Caractacus*, a frankly operatic cantata for soprano, tenor, baritone, bass, chorus and orchestra, was 'all cut and dried'. Obviously proud and delighted, Anne told Polly she felt a sort of godmother to the work, and shortly before Christmas she and Elgar 'had a jolly time, all to ourselves' while he 'played and sang a lot of choice bits from *Caractacus* oh lovely, for ever so long'. Elgar had managed to negotiate a fee of £100 but he had to provide the choral and orchestral parts, and Alice lent a hand copying them out. The queen consented to have the work dedicated to her, and on the eve of the first performance, in Leeds on 5 October, William Elgar wrote to his son and daughter-in-law a simple, rather moving note: 'Dear Ted and Alice, I hope you are well and enjoying yourselves and getting the steam up for tomorrow. I have not the least doubt your works will go well and give great satisfaction and also astonish the good people. I have looked through it well and am much pleased. I only wish I was there to hear it. I shall think of you and shall look in the papers wishing you every success, From your old warnout Dad.'

The critic of the *Musical Standard* wrote a piece which tells us as much about the confused state of his mind as it does about *Caractacus*. 'The difficulty in criticising Mr Elgar's music is that the score is such a good example of clever modern work, in which mere cleverness is never allowed to obtrude itself, that to praise it as it deserves from that aspect would be to give a totally wrong impression of the manner in which it affected me. But having enlarged sufficiently on the failures of the cantata, it is a pleasure to turn to the excellent workmanship of *Caractacus*. After having heard the work at the London band rehearsals I wrote last week that it is one of the most considerable of British modern compositions, and Wednesday night's performance has not made me alter that opinion. The elaborate and appropriate use of representative themes has never been approached by any living, native composer; the symphonic accompaniment is varied and elastic; the harmony if out of the way according to the purist has always the merit of sounding natural and unforced; the part-writing is well carried out; and the whole texture of the music flows on from note to note with an easy mastery which proclaims Elgar a composer of decided gifts. You may say of him with truth that he writes *music*; that his mastery of technique comes not from a laborious effort but from his real talent as a composer.'

Elgar, not unnaturally, was pleased with this somewhat garbled notice. The day it appeared he wrote to Troyte Griffith, a Malvern architect seven years younger than himself whom he had first met in about 1896 and who was to become one of his greatest friends and the seventh of the *Enigma Variations*, to say he would send him a copy of the *Musical Standard* 'which is the first to give me the place I've fought for'. And on 9 December he posted the score of *Caractacus* to Sir Arthur Bigge, private secretary to Queen Victoria, with the following note: 'Sir, I beg leave to forward with this letter a copy of my Cantata Caractacus produced at the Leeds Musical Festival, the dedication of which Her Majesty the Queen was graciously pleased to accept. If Her Majesty would deign to receive this copy of a work which is founded on a passage of our ancient British history, it would be a further honour for which I should be most humbly grateful. I have the honour to be, Sir, Your faithful servant, Edward Elgar.'

He received from Windsor Castle a brief and rather oddly worded reply from Sir Arthur, dated 12 December. 'Dear Sir, I am commanded to express to you the thanks of The Queen for the specially bound copy of your cantata Caractacus which you have been good enough to offer for this acceptance.'

In October the previous year, in a letter to Jaeger marked 'very private', Elgar maintained that in two years he had received £86 15s. after writing half a dozen works (including *Lux Christi* and *King Olaf*), that after paying his own expenses at two festivals he felt a damn fool for thinking of music at all, and that no amount of kind encouragement could blot out 'these simple figures'. (On 28 May 1899 he was to return to the subject of royalties, at the same time taking the opportunity of expressing his views on choral society conductors. He wrote to Jaeger: 'Another "Enigma" – the Black Knight you say is un-successful commercially – and its the only thing I ever recd. any royalty on yet – I see how it is. I think it is too artistic for the ordinary conductor of Choral Societies – I find they are an inordinately ignorant lot of cheesemongering idiots. The chorus & orchestra *go* for my things but the *conductors* always, or nearly always, find them too difficult – to conduct.') In spite of being hard up, and not content with the comfort and relative seclusion of Forli, in the summer of 1898 he and Alice took a step typical of people anxious to proclaim their upper-middle-class status: they rented, as a country retreat, an isolated cottage called Birchwood Lodge at Storridge, just off what is now the A4103 Hereford to Worcester road, a few miles north of Malvern. The Lodge is approached through heavily wooded lanes full of yellowhammers and jackdaws, and stands on high ground with superb views across the rolling West Country; in Elgar's day the cottage was well protected by tall, mature trees. It would have been impossible to live and work there unless one was inspired by absolute solitude and rural sounds ('One line to say we arrived here & are in the intense quiet & solitude which I love,' Elgar wrote to Jaeger from Birchwood on 11 July 1901), and the evidence that in Elgar's case he was inspired in such surroundings lies not just in the letters in which he writes with real joy of the trees and animals at Birchwood (also, alas, of otter-hunting) but in the glorious music he was soon to write in this simple, sturdy little house miles from anywhere.

During the late summer the Elgars were staying at Hasfield Court, the sixteenth-century childhood home of Dora Penny's step-mother, the former Mary Baker. Dora was not there and Elgar inquired of Mary Penny, 'How is my sweet Dorabella?' Mrs Penny expressed some slight, amused surprise at the way the question was worded and Elgar hastily explained he was quoting from *Così Fan Tutte*. From that moment Dora became Dorabella, and it was as Dorabella that she gave her name to the tenth of the *Enigma Variations*. On 24 September Elgar wrote to her to say, 'We missed you at Hasfield very much and I could have made you useful as well as – ah! I didn't write the other word.' What was the other word Elgar did not write? Whatever Dorabella was meant to think it was, he had written a teasing, mildly flirtatious letter, even if it was signed 'Edward Elgar'. Signatures in those days betrayed very little. The most overtly affectionate letters to close and intimate friends were frequently signed in full, even when the salutation had been by use of a Christian name; General Gordon, for example, signed letters to his sister using his surname.

For reasons best known to herself, Dorabella now decided to refer to Elgar as 'His Excellency', and Alice she christened 'the Lady'. From 1898, the year of *Caractacus*, the renting of Birchwood and of an event later in the autumn that marked the most significant turning point yet in Elgar's fortunes, Dorabella has left us a picture of Carice, then eight years old and shortly to be packed off to Rosa Burley's school as a weekly boarder. 'She was a dear little girl,' says Dorabella, 'very properly behaved and rather prim.' At meal-times, 'Carice used to stand behind her chair with an expression of patient disapproval on her face, waiting for silence till she could say grace.' Elgar called her 'Fishface'. On introducing Miss Burley to a visiting professor from Yale, Elgar explained he could not have written *Gerontius* without Miss Burley. 'You see,' Elgar said, 'she took Carice off our hands while I was writing it.'

One evening after returning from the stay at Hasfield Court, Elgar got home from what he later described as a 'long and tiresome day's teaching'. He sat at the piano, lit a cigar and began to play. Alice asked what it was. 'Nothing,' he replied. 'But something might be made of it.' It was the theme for the *Enigma Variations*. He had begun to compose his first great work and was about to enter the short, twenty-year period of his musical maturity. The fame for which he longed, but which would never bring him happiness, was just around the corner.

CHAPTER THREE

'A Triumph Everywhere'

1898–1902

Elgar's *Variations on an Original Theme (Enigma)* for orchestra, published as Opus 36, were written at Forli and Birchwood during 1898 and 1899 and were first performed at St James's Hall, London, on 19 June 1899. The conductor was the great German maestro Hans Richter, who had become famous in England after conducting at a three-day Wagner Festival in London in 1877.

Dedicated to Elgar's friends 'pictured within', the work consists of an original theme and fourteen variations, the first variation depicting Alice, the eleventh a bulldog called Dan, and the last Elgar himself. The other eleven are miniature portraits of seven men and four women. Originally the variations were headed by initials or nicknames though little difficulty was experienced unmasking the recipients of these flattering and faultless gifts. The 'enigma', if indeed it really exists, has always referred to the theme and not to the identity of the friends pictured within, for the theme, or tune, is said to mask yet another theme over-riding the whole work. Whether this supposed second theme is a musical one or an abstract idea Elgar would never say, for he enjoyed far too much the game of keeping everyone guessing.[1]

Dorabella asked Elgar to explain what he meant by 'the tune that "goes and is not played"'.

'Oh, I shan't tell you that, you must find out for yourself,' he told her.

'But I've thought and racked my brains over and over again,' Dorabella replied.

'Well,' said her tormentor, 'I'm surprised. I thought that you, of all people, would guess it.'

'Why me, of all people?'

'That's asking questions!'

Dorabella never did guess, Elgar never told her (always assuming there was anything to tell), and she came to believe that the only two people who knew the secret were Alice and August Jaeger. If either of these two did know

1. For a detailed and interesting analysis of the 'enigmatic' content of the *Enigma Variations* see Michael Kennedy's *Portrait of Elgar*.

anything that musicologists have since failed to discover, they took their secret to the grave. Alice was later to speak freely enough (although she was almost certainly misinformed) to Dorabella about the other great Elgarian mystery, the secret identity of 'the Soul' enshrined in the Violin Concerto, and Jaeger was so enthusiastic a champion of Elgar's music and such a pleasantly garrulous sort of person that he was unlikely to have denied posterity a secret in itself so harmless. There is therefore no reason to believe that Alice or Jaeger discovered for themselves or were told by Elgar anything of consequence about the supposed 'enigma'.

The *Enigma Variations* are among Elgar's most endearing compositions. As Sir Frederick Ashton fully realized in his ballet of 1968, they are an evocation of the Victorian concept of friendship, a concept almost entirely lost in our day. We know quite a lot about the people whose idiosyncrasies Elgar reveals and we can judge from the music the depth of feeling he entertained for each one, ranging from benign affection to overwhelming love and admiration. Some of the friends were acquainted with each other, some were related, others hardly knew one another at all. Together they represent a cross-section of the provincial society in which Elgar had moved and developed since his marriage nine years before.

A gentle, rather wistful Andante for Alice opens the set of variations, and this is followed by Hew Steuart-Powell's Allegro; Powell himself was a pianist who played in a trio with Elgar and Basil Nevinson, the subject of Variation XII. Richard Townsend, commemorated by a movement marked Allegretto (Variation III), was apparently completely unmusical, had a 'brick-red, weather-beaten face, bright blue eyes and a shock of grey hair'. He rode a tricycle round Oxford with an alarm bell constantly ringing so that people could hear him coming; he explained that as he was deaf he was unable to hear them. Typical of many such moneyed Victorian eccentrics, he was also a classical scholar, and had once tried his hand as a cattle rancher and a gold prospector. During one of those amateur theatrical entertainments Victorian house parties went in for – on this occasion at Hasfield Court – Townsend had been recruited to play the part of an old man, but the bass voice with which he tried to impersonate the character kept breaking down, for his natural voice was a rather embarrassing high falsetto; this set the other guests off into fits of laughter, and the comedy of the episode stuck with him. His friends claimed to be able to detect in his variation both the tricycle and his funny manner of speech.

William Baker (Variation IV), the Old Etonian owner of Hasfield Court, was the brother of Dorabella's step-mother and had come into Elgar's life through Alice's friendship with the family; he and Richard Townsend (Variation III) were brothers-in-law. Nicknamed 'the Squire' by the Elgars, Baker ran the kind of establishment that housed in the stables a brougham, a brake and a dog cart, and he thought nothing of dressing for dinner in hunting pink and kneebreeches. Dorabella described him as a small, wiry man (he was forty-one when the *Variations* were written), very quick and energetic, with a decisive way of speaking. He was an alpine climber, and the music, an Allegro di molto, certainly depicts a man of energy used to giving quick, decisive orders as he bustles about organizing the day's activities for his guests. At the end of the variation there is said to be a door slamming as he dashes out of the room to get some new plan under way.

Richard Arnold (Variation V) was the son of Matthew Arnold, the poet; he is depicted in a variation marked Moderato and his 'funny little nervous laugh' is said to be taken off in the woodwind. Dorabella thought him 'charming, interesting, amusing and a delightful talker, a gentleman of the old school if ever there was one'.

The principal instrument in Variation VI, an Andantino, is the viola, and the movement is dedicated to Isabel Fitton to whom Elgar had given viola lessons in order that she should be able to play in one of the orchestras at The Mount. Isabel's mother, who lived to be nearly a hundred, was a great friend of Dorabella's step-mother and thus Isabel, too, was a member of the Hasfield Court set. All Isabel's family were musical; her mother, in particular, played the piano well and was regarded as a brilliant sight-reader.

Dorabella has quoted Ivor Atkins, organist at Worcester Cathedral from 1897 to 1950, describing Troyte Griffith, whose character provides the subject for Variation VII, marked Presto, as highly argumentative, and certainly a cascade of rushing scales suggests this side to his nature. But Dorabella herself, who knew him fairly well, says he used to sit and grin but seldom speak. Elgar first met him at his next-door neighbour's house shortly after moving into Forli, and Rosa Burley says, 'There was something doglike in his quiet admiration of Edward and also in the readiness with which, dressed in Harris tweeds with a mustard-coloured tie, he followed him on long tramps round the Malvern countryside.' Griffith's background was very different from Elgar's (he was an Old Harrovian), and it was certainly not a shared interest in music that drew them together; Griffith was an amateur painter in watercolours but no musician. Of all those who appeared in the *Variations* he was the last survivor but one; Dorabella, the youngest, outlived them all.

Winifred Norbury, a granddaughter of Lord Guillamore, lived at Storridge and had therefore become a neighbour when the Elgars rented Birchwood Lodge; she was very much a country woman of her time, devoted to church work, tennis, hockey and the new craze of cycling. For some years she was joint secretary of the Worcester Philharmonic Society. The subject of Variation VIII, an Allegretto, she has been given a charming little country tune. A good pianist, she tried out much of Elgar's music with him (Elgar on the violin), and she also helped copy the orchestral parts for *Caractacus*.

Variation IX, nicknamed by Elgar 'Nimrod' ('the Great Hunter'), depicts one of the best friends Elgar ever had, August Jaeger of Novello & Co. (*Jäger* is the German for hunter, as Alice, who spoke German, would have known.) Born in Düsseldorf in 1860, he had settled in England when he was eighteen, and was married in the year the *Variations* were written. Until his tragically early death in 1909, when he was only forty-nine, he fought tooth and nail with his employers on Elgar's behalf, for he believed passionately in Elgar's music and in his creative genius. In 1907, with only two years to live and already dying, he wrote to Dorabella to say he had worked terribly hard for Elgar and ruined his health over it very likely. Jaeger's enthusiasm for Elgar was warmly reciprocated: Dorabella recalls Elgar telling her – on a 'lovely, fine afternoon' after the two of them had set out for a bicycle ride, leaving their cycles under some trees to sit on the banks of the River Wye – that he thought Jaeger had 'a grand and noble mind', and that the tune for the ninth variation had been written in tribute to Jaeger for the trouble he had taken in writing to him and going to see him to encourage him to go on composing. That Elgar believed Jaeger to have 'a grand and noble mind' can hardly be in doubt if the music of 'Nimrod' is anything to go by, though it was only later that Elgar became indebted to Jaeger for this kind of encouragement. It is true that on 17 December 1898, while still at work on the *Variations*, Elgar wrote to Jaeger to complain that the previous year he had 'subsisted on £200' but that as this was 'the end of all things' it did not matter, and that in reply Jaeger had written, 'A day's attack of the blues, due to a touch of indigestion or a blast of east wind will not drive away your desire, your necessity which is to exercise those creative faculties which a kind providence has given you. Your time of universal recognition will come. You have virtually achieved more towards that in one year than others of the English composers in a decade.' Jaeger's major morale-boosting efforts did not in fact have to come into play until after the disastrous first performance of *The Dream of Gerontius* in 1900, by which time the *Variations* had been written and performed.

The fact that Elgar did write his tribute to Jaeger so early in their relationship makes his appreciation of the man all the more interesting, for it would surely be impossible to write music so full of love and tenderness for anyone you did not wholeheartedly admire, and it is hard to imagine how Jaeger himself ever sat through performances of the work knowing that 'Nimrod' had been written for him.

Dorabella's variation (X) follows; it is a playful, teasing little tune, and in *Edward Elgar: Memories of a Variation* Dorabella has recorded the first occasion on which she heard it, when played on the piano by Elgar. Dorabella seems to have been in her usual place, seated beside the composer, turning over the music for him. When she arrived at a sheet headed 'No. X, Dorabella,' she was 'overcome by many emotions' and sat silent until Elgar had finished playing. Then he turned to her and asked, 'Well, how do you like that – hey?'

Dorabella murmured something about it being charming and rather like a butterfly but, she confesses, she could think of nothing sensible to say. Her mind was in a 'whirl of pleasure, pride, and almost shame that he should have written anything so lovely about *me*'. She was 'rescued' by a voice from the fireplace: 'Isn't it beautiful, dear Dora,' said Alice, 'I do *hope* you like it.'

There follows a scene reminiscent of a novel by Charlotte M. Yonge, for suddenly, it seems, Elgar took her 'by her two hands' and half lifted her up.

' "And how did you like *yourself*, my Dorabella?" he inquired.

'I tried to tell him how wonderful I thought it, and how it was far too delicate and lovely for the likes of me.

' "Well," Elgar responds, "of course it is, we all know that."

'But I wouldn't be put off and I said how marvellous it was to feel oneself part of the music which had been acclaimed by half the world as being his greatest work.

' "You dear child," he said, "and kissed me on the forehead." '

If Elgar had been playing through the score on the piano with Dorabella turning over, and she had never previously heard the work, this incident must have taken place prior to the first performance, and yet she tells Elgar how marvellous it was to feel oneself part of the music 'which had been acclaimed by half the world as being his greatest work'.

Elgar has left us his own opinion of the tenth variation. In a letter to Dorabella dated 22 February 1899 he says, 'The Variations are finished [they were in fact finished on 19 February] & yours is the most cheerful; everybody says it is the "prettiest" – of course intending to compliment the music not the *Variationee* – that's you. I hope it may be done soon and then we shall have some curious opinions. I *have* orchestrated you well.' Dorabella took the last remark to refer to the entire set, not just to her own variation.

The initials 'G. R. S.' at the head of Variation XI denote George Sinclair, organist of Hereford Cathedral, though the actual subject of the variation is his bulldog, Dan, who used to lie under the conductor's desk during Hereford Festival choral rehearsals and did not seem to mind if sometimes he got kicked by mistake. Sinclair told Dorabella that the one thing Dan could not stand was people singing out of tune – he growled if they did. After evensong it became something of a ritual for Dr Sinclair to throw a chunk of wood into the river for Dan, and in 1944 Dr Percy Hull, who had succeeded Sinclair as organist and no doubt had inherited the folklore concerning Dan and his doings, explained that the first bar of the Allegro di molto represented Dan rushing about the bank, bars three and four depict Dan plunging in and paddling after the stick, and that this paddling passage led to a 'fierce growl of joy' in bar five as he seized hold of it.[2] Hull claimed to be the first person ever to play the *Variations* in duet form with Elgar, from rough proof sheets. 'My hat! how we both sweated with sheer excitement!' he told Dorabella forty-five years later.

It was sad that Elgar had to commemorate someone else's dog in the *Enigma Variations*; he was never without dogs after Alice died, and it is reasonable to assume it was she who would not have one in the house. Like Richard Townsend, Dan's owner also seems to have been a bit of an eccentric. He once called on Elgar to suggest they go for a bicycle ride together (this must have been after the *Variations* had been written, as Elgar did not take up cycling until 1900). Elgar liked to ride alongside his companion, talking about the scenery, whereas it transpires that Sinclair would speed ahead, wait at the top of a hill for Elgar to catch up, and before the two of them could exchange more than a couple of words he would shoot off again, leaving Elgar to ride some ten miles or so to all intents and purposes alone. At the end of the afternoon he annoyed Elgar by saying, 'Well, cheerio, it *has* been nice sharing your company.'

The domination of Variation XII by a cello is because this movement, an Andante, was written for Basil Nevinson, the cellist in the Elgar–Nevinson–Powell trio. He had a house in Tedworth Square, Chelsea, where Elgar frequently used to stay when in London on business.

Variation XIII was originally headed by three asterisks because Lady Mary Lygon, 'the most angelic person' for whom it was intended (that was how Elgar described her in a letter to Jaeger in March 1899), had just sailed for Australia to act as hostess for her bachelor brother, Earl Beauchamp, who had been appointed governor of New South Wales at the age of twenty-seven. Elgar wrote asking permission to dedicate the variation to her but she missed his letter and permission had to wait until after the first performance. No doubt Elgar was anxious to act with such perfect formality because Lady Mary was a lady-in-waiting to the Duchess of York (later Queen Mary). Lord Beauchamp and his sister had entertained the Elgars at Madresfield Court, near Malvern, one of the grand county houses where in less prosperous days Elgar's father had earned his living tuning the piano. Lady Mary was a discerning patron of music festivals; Lord Beauchamp carried on the family's tradition of public

---

2. This analysis of Variation XI was given to Dorabella by Percy Hull in a letter dated 13 June 1944, which she quotes in *Edward Elgar: Memories of a Variation*.

service and involvement in local and national political life. (In 1931, after serving as Lord Steward of His Majesty's Household, twice as Lord President of the Council, receiving the Garter in 1914 and holding the post of leader of the Liberals in the House of Lords for six years, Lord Beauchamp's distinguished career was ruined and his domestic life shattered when he was compelled to resign most of his offices and flee abroad in order to avoid prosecution for homosexual offences. It was of him that George V – at whose coronation Beauchamp had borne the Sword of State – is reputed to have said, after being informed by Beauchamp's obnoxious brother-in-law, the Duke of Westminster, that for twenty-seven years a homosexual had worn the Garter, 'I thought men like that shot themselves'. Beauchamp did indeed contemplate suicide, but was dissuaded by one of his sons, and eventually he died, in 1938, in New York.)

Elgar's view of Lady Mary's angelic characteristics was not shared by all who knew her. Writing to her husband from Osborne in 1898, Marie Mallet, a maid of honour to Queen Victoria, reported that the Duchess of York ('a thorough Puritan at heart', who could not bear 'the prancings and millinery of the High Church party') had confessed to her that she could not bear to discuss religious topics 'with the medieval Mary Lygon' – an unexpectedly forthright comment from a princess normally regarded as very shy and reticent.[3]

Lady Mary's variation has a strong tune that leads to the finale, another Allegro, which represents Elgar's estimation of himself at the time, a piece of grandiose writing by turns bombastic and serene. At first there was some puzzlement over the initials 'E. D. U.' at the head of this last variation; they were in fact a diminutive of Eduard, the German form of Edward by which, after four holidays in Germany four years running, Alice sometimes addressed him.

Completion of the *Enigma Variations* in 1899 coincided with a change of home, to what is now 86 Wells Road, Malvern, 'a better house than Forli, larger and far more comfortable', according to Dorabella. By jumbling up his own surname with Alice's married initials (C. A. E.) Elgar arrived (not entirely successfully) at an anagram for the new home, Craig Lea. It was staffed by a cook and a maid called Mary, and it may have been bigger and more comfortable than Forli but it was a far less attractive house, being constructed of brick and pebbledash in the least inventive style of respectable Victorian domestic architecture. Tucked into the damp, tree-clad hillside, it did have spectacular views across the Severn Valley, and it was this that especially appealed to Elgar. For Alice it was probably sufficient that the property was bigger. Elgar

3. See Marie Mallet, *Life with Queen Victoria: Letters from Court, 1887–1901*, ed. Victor Mallet (John Murray, 1968).

wrote to Jaeger on 10 March from a club in Malvern to explain that because of the move his letter-writing was in an awful muddle – he was, in fact, 'awfully worried with this move & [would] do anything to escape'. But only five days after he had settled in he took the opportunity, while Alice was at church and he was stopping at home to 'try and mend an untidy eye', to write to Dorabella to report, 'This *is* a nice house & a gorjus view.'

While escaping on one occasion, Elgar had an amusing encounter which he recounted to Jaeger. Having '*fled* out yesterday straight across country to think out my thoughts & to avoid everyone', he had walked nine miles when apparently a man rode up behind him on a bicycle and began to inquire whether Novello had performing rights in various works. 'I was speechless,' says Elgar.

Elgar's was not the only letter-writing to get into a muddle at times; it took Jaeger six months to become accustomed to Elgar's new address, and on 17 September Elgar was reminding him that he had addressed no fewer than three letters to Forli since they had left. But Jaeger was already over-stretched, writing for the *Musical Times* after he had done a day's work at Novello, where he was preparing scores by Parry and Coleridge-Taylor with the same conscientiousness he was devoting to Elgar's career, and already in June 1899 Elgar was expressing concern about his health. 'I want you to get a further opinion about your nasal business,' he told Jaeger on 2 June. 'I have asked a doctor friend in town who recommends Greville MacDonald. I will remind you of this when I'm up again next week & we'll talk it over.' MacDonald was an ear, nose and throat specialist at King's College Hospital. On 5 November Elgar was again writing to Jaeger about his health: 'I'm sorry to hear about your own worry – do see a Specialist if you haven't already done so.'

Elgar had no doubt that his *Variations* were a major achievement and required an impressive launching for he was also under no illusions that despite the relative success of *King Olaf, Caractacus* and *From the Bavarian Highlands* he was still virtually unknown in the musical world outside the Midlands. So, without Novello's knowledge (although he let Jaeger in on the secret), he contacted Hans Richter's agent, and even sent a copy of the score to Richter in Austria. 'For mercy's sake don't tell *anyone* I pray you about Richter becos' he may refuse,' Elgar wrote to Jaeger early in February. He went on to explain his reason for approaching the conductor who had first performed Wagner's *Ring* cycle at Bayreuth: 'It wd be just too lovely for anything if R. did an English piece by a man who hasn't appeared yet ... I have begged for a very early reply from Vienna.'

The reply was favourable and Richter was engaged to conduct the first performance, at St James's Hall on 19 June. The preparations for such a major première illustrate well the state of orchestral playing at the time, of which they were entirely typical, resulting again and again in under-rehearsed performances. Coleridge-Taylor's *Death of Minnehaha*, for instance, was given at Hanley in 1899 without any choral or orchestral rehearsal at all. At the turn of the century there were in fact relatively few symphony concerts, and orchestral players earned the greater part of their living by playing in theatres and music halls. A symphony orchestra was nothing more than a collection of reasonably competent players who came together for one or two particular occasions and were then disbanded. This state of affairs led to what became known as the deputy system, whereby any musician hired to fill a particular post in an orchestra was responsible for supplying a deputy if on some occasion he was unable to perform because he was engaged to play elsewhere. The player who had been hired would pay part of his fee to his deputy, keeping back part as commission. The difficulty in bringing together a permanent collection of musicians to form a stable orchestra made the holding of rehearsals some-what pointless, as half the players at the rehearsal might not be in the orchestra for the performance. The deputy system extended even to con-ductors, and a rehearsal in the morning under one conductor followed by a performance at night under another was a common occurrence. It was held that one benefit of the system was that British orchestral players had perforce to become expert sight-readers, and their reputation for giving competent per-formances after less preparation than their continental counterparts en-couraged visits to this country by such great European conductors as Richter, Nikisch and Weingartner. It was Henry Wood who eventually decreed that his Queen's Hall Orchestra must abolish the deputy system and sign proper contracts, and many of his leading players objected so strongly that they left to form their own cooperative, the London Symphony Orchestra, ruled by a committee of its own members and without a permanent conductor. But in 1899, two rehearsals to read through the programme and correct any obvious errors were all any new work was likely to be allotted, and any question of a conductor impressing his own interpretation upon a work under those conditions was seldom likely to arise.

In the case of the *Enigma Variations*, the work was first rehearsed by Henry Wood on 3 June, and then there was a gap of thirteen days before Elgar went through the score with Richter, formerly conductor of the Vienna State Opera and the Hallé's conductor from 1897 to 1911. Richter himself then rehearsed the work on 17 June, and again on the morning of 19 June. In the event, the piece elicited 'a nice rapturous letter' from Parry – 'most kind of him,' Elgar wrote to Jaeger on 27 June – and a nice, rapturous notice in the *Musical Times*, contributed by none other than Nimrod. The *Athenaeum* was a bit stuffy about the dedication. 'We regret that the composer has dedicated his work "To my friends pictured within",' they wrote. 'There was no harm in his working, like Beethoven, to pictures in his mind, but it would have been better not to call attention to the fact . . . If the friends recognise their portraits it will, no doubt, please them; but this is altogether a personal matter.' The writer was on safer musical ground when he made the point that the variations stood in no need of a programme, for as abstract music they were fully satisfying; and after noting that under the direction of Dr Richter the performance was perfect and the composer loudly applauded, he concluded the evening was no mere *succès d'estime* but that the variations would be often heard and as often admired.

In first sending news to Jaeger, in a letter of 24 October 1898, that he was at work on a set of variations, Elgar had given his own explanation of what was in his mind and he made it clear that he was writing a piece of music quite independent of any programme: 'Since I've been back [from a stay at Hasfield Court] I have sketched a set of Variations (orkestra) on an original theme: the Variations have amused me because I've labelled 'em with the nicknames of my particular friends – *you* are Nimrod. That is to say I've written the variations each one to represent the mood of the "party" – I've liked to imagine the "party" writing the var: him (or her) self and have written what I think they wd have written – if they were asses enough to compose – its a quaint idea & the result is amusing to those behind the scenes & won't affect the hearer who "nose nuffin".'

In his review for the *Musical Times*, Jaeger drew attention to the work's 'effortless originality – the only true originality – combined with thorough *savoir faire*, and, most important of all, beauty of theme, warmth, and feeling are his credentials, and they should open to him the hearts of all who have faith in the future of our English art and appreciate beautiful music wherever it is met.' Alice wrote to Jaeger on 4 July to tell him of the intense pleasure his notice had given her. 'It seemed exactly to realise my idea of what I wanted said regarding the music,' Jaeger was no doubt relieved to read.

A month before the *Variations* received their first performance Elgar had a part-song, *To Her Beneath Whose Steadfast Star*, dedicated to the queen and sung at Windsor Castle, and he was back at Windsor in October for another Royal Command performance of his music, arranged under the patronage of Sir Walter Parratt. On 5 October Clara Butt, dressed, said Elgar in a letter to Troyte Griffith, like a mermaid, gave the first performance of his song-cycle *Sea Pictures*, with Elgar conducting, at the Norwich Festival for which it had been commissioned, and Queen Victoria had invited Clara Butt up to Balmoral to sing this new work to her as well. The cycle, for contralto or mezzo-soprano and orchestra, was written at Birchwood and has become one of Elgar's most popular works; it is certainly one of his more successful settings of poems, the second of the five, *In Haven*, having been written by Alice.

Elgar's most successful setting of any poem could be said to have had its origins in the crisis over the Liberal government's dilatory efforts in 1884 to rescue General Charles Gordon at Khartoum, which had led to the Conservative victory in which Elgar and Scap had played their part. Gordon, a half-mad Christian fundamentalist who was said always to have a Bible by his bedside, also rather surprisingly possessed a copy of a poem called *The Dream of Gerontius*, written in 1865 by another remarkable individualist, Cardinal Newman. Shortly before his death, Gordon had given his copy, with annotations, to Frank Power, a correspondent for *The Times*, and this copy seems to have been borrowed or acquired by Father Knight, one of the parish priests at St George's Church in Worcester. Father Knight must have known of Elgar's sympathy for Gordon, for he transcribed Gordon's annotations into another copy of the poem and gave it to Elgar as a wedding present. Elgar, we know, began to absorb the poem almost immediately,[4] though the first sketches for *The Dream of Gerontius* date from 1898. The peacefulness of Birchwood and the new confidence he had found through writing the *Variations* now encouraged him to work in earnest in the summer of 1899 on the composition many people regard as his masterpiece. He may well have been at work on the score in his study at Birchwood – the room to the right at the top of the stairs – on the last day of July 1899, the day that Dorabella tells us she cycled forty miles from Wolverhampton to Storridge (no mean feat for a man in training, and for a young woman of twenty-five it showed commendable stamina). In the afternoon 'the Lady' was busy so Dorabella and Elgar went off into the woods together, where eventually he lay down and apparently went to sleep. The idyll was only disturbed by the sound of Alice ringing a bell to summon the pair of them back for tea.

The year ended with a false alarm. In a letter written to Charles Buck on 29 December Elgar said his 'poor old father', whom he had seen the day before, was just hovering ' 'twixt this world & the next'. 'He knew me,' he told Buck, 'but the end cannot be far away.' The end was in fact seven years away, and old and feeble though he became, William lived long enough to watch his son walk past the High Street shop to collect the Freedom of the City of Worcester; long enough, too, to be photographed with him the day after the news had come that he was to be knighted. These were gratifications still in store, but in October 1899 Elgar already had good cause to tell Troyte Griffith, in a letter

4. In a letter dated 7 May 1900, Elgar invited August Jaeger to suggest cuts to the libretto of *The Dream of Gerontius* because, he said, he knew the poem too well himself to be able to do it.

written from Basil Nevinson's Chelsea home just before setting out for Windsor, 'I am longing to get home although the whole thing has been a triumph everywhere.'

The first news that Elgar was engaged on what was to prove another triumph, though only after one of the most disastrous first performances in musical history, did not reach Jaeger until February 1900. 'I am setting Newman's "Dream of Gerontius" awfully solemn & mystic,' he wrote on 5 February. Elgar seemed to think the matter deserved an air of mystery, too: 'There's no harm in your knowing,' he very decently informed his most ardent advocate, 'only *don't* tell anybody else.' Jaeger responded with a note of warm encouragement. He wrote on 25 March, 'The poem is wonderful & must appeal to you most forcefully. But by Jove! what a task for you. Yet I feel sure you will be equal to it, for like most first-class composers, you seem to grow with your task, & the greater the difficulty the more surely you will rise to it. So I don't think you will disappoint us over your present great task.'

In musical terms, *The Dream of Gerontius* remains unique and impossible to label. 'I say, *need* you call it a *Sacred Cantata*,' Elgar wrote to Jaeger on 4 July 1901, after Jaeger had produced an analysis of the work. 'That is of course the *trade* description but it occurs nowhere on the title I think, so don't perpetuate that dreadful term unless we're obliged.' And three years later, when Jaeger was preparing a catalogue for Novello, Elgar wrote to say, 'By all means, put Gerontius in the Oratorio list – there's no word invented yet to describe it.' Whatever precisely it was, *Gerontius* was due to be performed at Birmingham Festival on 3 October 1900, and the 'great task' was to take up most of Elgar's time during the summer. The first part was sent to Novello on 2 March. A second set of manuscripts was posted on 20 March, but between these two dates Elgar found time to go through the *Sea Pictures* with Charles Stanford, who was due to conduct them at the Royal College. Stanford was at that time professor of music at Cambridge and was generally regarded as England's leading composer. There was something of a mutual benefit society in existence between the two men: in May Elgar got Stanford elected to honorary membership of the Worcester Philharmonic Society and he also used his influence to have Stanford's *Last Post* performed; in the same month Stanford was trying to use his own influence to get Elgar an honorary doctorate of music at Cambridge, but the lists seem to have been filled at that time, and conferment of his first academic honour had to wait until the end of the year. When it did come it was not, as might be thought, in recognition of *The Dream of Gerontius*, for it would have been virtually impossible for the Cambridge convocation to have met and voted on the matter between the first performance on 3 October and receipt of the offer by Elgar on 17 October. The degree can be directly attributed to Stanford's admiration for the *Enigma Variations*.

On 3 April proofs of the first part of *Gerontius* had been returned to Elgar for checking, a task he had to carry out while sketching and scoring other portions of the work. Progress cannot have been assisted by Elgar being unwell (with a chill and a bad throat), and Alice, too, felt so under the weather that 'dear Dorabella' had to be sent for. She and Elgar, his chill and bad throat notwithstanding, enjoyed 'an uproarious time' correcting the proofs: his efforts to try out various parts of the score on the trombone apparently gave her such hysterics she had to go out of the room, where she sat on the stairs and clung to the banisters to ease the pain.

Next day she had 'little difficulty in keeping the Lady in bed'. Alice is reputed to have said to her, 'I *do* like hearing you both laugh. Then I know that His Excellency is happy and that makes me feel better.' She asked Dorabella to find out if there was anything 'dear Edward' wanted in Malvern. Dorabella tapped at the study door, and the following dialogue ensued:

'Come in.'

'I'm going into Malvern on some errands for the Lady; is there anything you want?'

'Yes, you. Come in and shut the door.'

'I really can't stop now; I've put the flag out [the Elgars had taken to hanging out a Union Jack, not just any old flag, when they wanted the public brake to stop at Craig Lea] and the brake is almost due – I simply must go.'

'I can't see what is the good of you coming all the way from Wolverhampton if you go and spend half the day in Malvern directly you arrive.'

'You unreasonable thing – Mercy! there's the brake,' and Dorabella dashed downstairs and out of the door.

The theatricality of the incident owes a lot to a sense of the importance of little things, and those who care to follow drama on this scale will be relieved to know that Dorabella caught the brake, was lucky in Malvern, did all Alice's errands and 'got back to Craig Lea in time for luncheon'. That afternoon Alice had a good sleep and Dorabella went out for a short walk with 'E. E.'.

According to Dorabella it was during this visit that Elgar took time off from correcting proofs of *Gerontius* to go on a short visit to Leeds. Dorabella was commissioned to pack his portmanteau. It is true that Alice was unwell, but they did have a maid (who even accompanied them to Birchwood). Nevertheless, on the morning of Elgar's departure he summoned Dorabella to bring his luggage into the room where he was playing, saying he would change for the journey in front of the fire. She went out of the room, but she could hear him continuing to play the piano. So, getting anxious about the time, she went back in. Elgar said to her, 'You can just do some work and dress me. I'm not going to stop playing.'

'How I got him dressed I don't know,' Dorabella confessed, thirty-six years later. 'I laughed so much I could hardly fasten anything ... I went and told the Lady how naughty he had been and I was really afraid she would laugh more than was good for her.'

The picture that begins to emerge from these platonic frolics is of a *ménage à trois* consisting of two women, one young (twenty-six) and attractive, the other middle-aged (fifty-one) and complacent, treating Elgar like a little boy, and sharing the experience in the way that two good friends might confide to one another about their boyfriends, except that in the case of Alice and Dorabella there was only one boyfriend, and he was not exactly a boy but a pampered, moody genius of forty-three.

From this same period Dorabella has left us another vivid impression of the humorous antics of the Elgar household, as well as a rare glimpse of the two self-indulgent parents with their only child, now ten years old. One Sunday Carice came home from The Mount. Jaeger and Troyte Griffith were there for luncheon and it was 'all most amusing'. When the adults came into the dining-room Elgar saw Carice, standing behind her chair, waiting.

' "Hallo, Fishface! Quite well?" ' seems to have been the greeting he gave his daughter.

' "Yes, thank you, Father," ' Carice replied.

' "Yes, thank you, Father," imitated E. E. in a high sort of squeak.'

As an only child with a mother forty years older than herself, Carice's position cannot have been easy at the best of times; it seems that if she was present Alice would try to stop Elgar's 'running fire of absurd remarks, comments, chaff and repartee', and this must have made her feel all the more conspicuous, out of place and possibly not even wanted.

Meanwhile, Jaeger was coming to enthuse more and more over *Gerontius* as batches of score arrived in his office. He recognized its originality and genius from the start and he championed it until the day he died. To Dorabella he wrote on 25 May, 'Gerontius grows more and more masterly as it proceeds. It is quite wonderful in parts: mystic, sublime, superb. I have to write a preliminary review of the work in The Musical Times for October, so I am already studying it hard, in Buses, Trains, everywhere. Have it always in my pocket, in fact & go to Bed with it.' He was writing to her again, eight days later, to say, 'In Gerontius we have a great, deep thinker and dreamer allying wonderful music to wonderful words, a powerful intellect doing its greatest for a great poem'. And to Elgar himself, Jaeger had written on 22 May, 'I have just spent an hour over your last batch of proofs ... and Oh! I am half undone, and I tremble after the tremendous exaltation I have gone through. I don't pretend to know everything that has been written since Wagner breathed his last in Venice 17 years ago, but I have not seen or heard anything since Parsifal that has stirred me, and spoken to me with the trumpet tongue of genius as has this part of your latest, and by far greatest work. I except, perhaps, the Pathetic Symphony, although that is but worldly, pessimistic, depressing, whereas your wonderful music is inexpressibly and most wonderfully elevating, "aloof", mystic, and heart-moving, as by the force of a great compassion. I cannot describe it! ... That solo of the "Angel of the Agony" is overpowering and I feel as if I wanted to kiss the hand that penned these marvellous pages.'

'I can't tell you how much good your letter has done me,' Elgar replied. 'I *do* dearly like to be *understood.*'

Elgar and his Great Hunter understood one another very well by now. In July 1899 Elgar was sending a message about business via Jaeger to someone he refers to as 'that nice woolly-lamb young man'. To Jaeger himself he writes as 'Dear sea-serpent', 'All Hail, great Faun!', 'My dear Jay', 'Dear Jagerissimus' and 'My deary Jaeger'. 'Yours ever & ever' and 'Yours ever with undying affection' were ways in which he was taking to signing off. On 20 May 1900, in a letter promising more manuscript the next day, Elgar ends, 'Bless you my Angel. Send your long letter about nothing,' signs himself 'E.' and adds a postscript, 'I wish you were here.' In the letter to Dorabella written in 1907, telling her he had worked terribly hard for Elgar and ruined his health over it very likely, Jaeger was to temper his complaint by adding, 'I have never loved and admired a man more, made myself more a slave for any man out of sheer enthusiasm.'

On 7 May Elgar told Jaeger he had gone through the libretto of *The Dream of Gerontius* with a priest from the Birmingham Oratory, cutting out 'all we thought possible', but on 14 June Jaeger was sounding a warning note about possible theological objections to the work: there was 'a lot of Joseph and Mary' about it, likely 'to frighten some d—d fools of Protestants'. He advised removing Mary and Joseph to 'a more distant background' if this could be done without bowdlerizing a superb poem. Elgar replied on the day he received Jaeger's comments, 'As to the Catholic side, of course it will frighten the low Church party but the poem must on no account be touched! Sacrilege and not to be thought of: them as don't like it can be damned in their own way – not ours.'[5]

5. The Worcester Festival Committee was to express doubts, on 12 April 1902, about the propriety of performing *The Dream of Gerontius* in Worcester Cathedral, doubts which were upheld by the bishop (although total responsibility remained, as always, with the dean and chapter). It was agreed that they should omit the Litany of the Saints, to substitute the word 'prayers' for 'masses' and to expurgate the word 'purgatory'. The bishop then wrote 'a very kind letter' to Elgar thanking him. (Letter from Elgar to Jaeger of 9 May 1902.)

On 21, 22 and 23 May Alice recorded in her diary that Elgar was 'writing hard'. On 25 May he had been 'very engrossed last chorus' and on 29 May he had again worked 'very hard at last chorus'. The next day he had 'nearly finished great chorus'. Six days later Alice wrote perhaps the funniest contribution to our documented knowledge of the progress made by Elgar on one of his greatest works: 'E. finished the Dream of Gerontius. Deo gratias. Rather poorly.'

On 5 June Elgar had in fact only finished work on the vocal score. He still had a vast amount of work on the orchestration to complete in time for the first performance in October. And in June his brother, Frank, was ill enough to warrant Elgar mentioning in a letter to Jaeger how worried he was. It should not be imagined that Jaeger saw his task merely in terms of boosting Elgar's ego and offering nothing but unstinted praise; he offered constructive advice and criticism, and although Elgar sometimes pretended furious indignation, he demonstrated again and again his dependence on him and his faith in his judgement. After asking him to look very carefully at Part II, and discussing various details of the work, he ended a letter on 7 May, 'Anyway keep an eye on it, there's a dear.' On 20 June he wrote, 'Now I've had time, I've been through all your suggestions for which a heap of thanks; I'm truly glad you like the thing cos I've written it out of my insidest inside.'

This remark should almost certainly not be taken to imply that he had written *Gerontius* as an overt religious testament: for Elgar, music came before anything else, and he was never a particularly religious person. Most great artists who happen to have been Christians have usually found expression for their religious feelings in their art rather than in formal worship, and many also have a private 'religious' vision quite apart from a Christian one. On the other hand, Elgar had certainly chosen, quite deliberately, a deeply religious and indeed deeply Catholic poem to set; he had, moreover, dedicated it to God, and the marvellous way in which his music complements Cardinal Newman's sentiments could never have been achieved by a man who did not himself believe. Bernard Shaw made an attempt to explain Elgar's religious position, when asked by his biographer, Hesketh Pearson, whether Elgar was a devout Roman Catholic. Shaw, whose own religious affiliations were always somewhat ambiguous, told Pearson that Elgar avoided the subject with a deliberate reticence; he was convinced he was 'a nineteenth-century unbeliever, though he wouldn't have admitted it and wouldn't have liked to be told so.' He added that all Elgar's emotion went into his music.[6]

So far as it is possible for us to judge, it seems likely that as a young man Elgar believed in God and participated regularly in the life of the Church as a communicant member, and that he remained broadly in sympathy with

6. *Bernard Shaw: His Life and Personality* by Hesketh Pearson (Macdonald, 1975).

religious belief during the period he wrote his three religious works – *The Dream of Gerontius* (set to the words of a convert, incidentally, and both Elgar's parents had been converts), *The Apostles* and *The Kingdom*, which was completed in 1906. Up to the outbreak of war, by which time he had written the Violin Concerto and both symphonies, there is no clue from his compositions that he had lost his faith. If eventually he did so, the war and the death of his wife were the two events most likely to have undermined an intellectual belief never very firmly supported by emotional involvement, although it seems unlikely that the composer of *The Dream of Gerontius* should not have retained at least the essentials of belief on his own death-bed.

As far as the musical content of the work was concerned, Jaeger warned Elgar in his long letter of 22 May against expecting it to be appreciated 'by the ordinary amateur (or critic) after once hearing'. He would have to rest content, as other great men had had to do before him, if a few friends and enthusiasts hailed it as a work of genius. And on 9 June Jaeger returned to the same theme in a letter to Dorabella with an ominous and prophetic warning: 'The majority of the B'ham audience,' he told her, 'will not be able to appreciate Gerontius first time; too subtle and original & too mystic & beautiful, but a few like yourself & others will wax "Wild" with enthusiasm.' Jaeger was to be proved right, though for the wrong reasons, as it was not to be the Birmingham audience so much as the performers who were to fail to appreciate *Gerontius* first time.

The training of the choir due to sing the first performance was to be in the hands of Charles Swinnerton Heap, who had now been a friend of Elgar for the past half-dozen years. Trained in Leipzig, Swinnerton Heap was considered the leading choral conductor in the Midlands (he had trained the chorus for the first performance of *King Olaf*), he understood Elgar's style of music and he was sympathetic to him as a composer. Elgar in turn appreciated his support, dedicating to him *Lux Christi* and his Organ Sonata of 1895. In June, however, at the age of fifty-three, Swinnerton Heap died, and a replacement for him was urgently needed. W. C. Stockley, in whose Birmingham orchestra Elgar had once played among the first violins, was now seventy and was living in retirement in the city. Inexplicably, and disastrously, he was called out of retirement to train the choir in Swinnerton Heap's place.

Unaware of impending problems, on 11 July Elgar was 'well into Part II', he told Jaeger, referring to work on the orchestration. His letters throughout the time he was writing *Gerontius* are among his most relaxed, and one can imagine him at this time almost happy. He must have known he was writing great music. He told Jaeger the trees were singing his music. 'Or have I sung theirs?' he asked. 'I suppose I have? It's too lovely here.' He was writing from the solitude of Birchwood, where he was learning to progress from a tricycle to a bicycle, and where on 19 July he was again visited by Dorabella. This time she was prudent enough to catch the train from Wolverhampton to Worcester, parking her bicycle in the guard's van and only cycling the last nine or ten miles from Worcester to Storridge. The Elgars had been out shopping, and Dorabella got to the cottage before they had returned. She made herself at home, and after supper, 'E. E. and I went out of doors. I wanted to stay and help the Lady but she wouldn't hear of it. "I can manage quite well, thank you, dear Dora," ' the obliging Lady told her. ' "Do go out with Edward, it will be lovely and cool out there." Nothing loath, of course I went.'

Off they trotted into the woods, where they watched the glow-worms, encountered an owl and admired the moonlight. Elgar was finding in middle age not only the musical expression for which he had been searching all his life, but the pleasure of a mild and innocent flirtation and a courtship ritual he had never experienced with his wife. Alice, in her turn, was being relieved by Dorabella of any necessity to play a romantic role.

Elgar finished orchestrating *Gerontius* on 3 August, and just as he was signing his name at the foot of the score a friend from Ledbury, William Eller, a governor of the Royal College of Music, who had been invited to lunch, cycled up to the front door of Birchwood Lodge. He found Elgar upstairs in his study, at a table 'absolutely covered with musical manuscripts'. Realizing the historical significance of the occasion he dashed downstairs to his bicycle, came back with a camera, and photographed Elgar at the table (Plate 8). This unfortunately allowed Elgar time to pose himself, in pensive mood, his left hand resting on his cheek, looking dreamily away through the window. The result represents Elgar's image of himself, and the picture lacks the sense of occasion and spontaneity that a modern news photographer might have captured, but it still says much for the initiative of Mr Eller.

Up to this date there can be no doubt that Elgar had worked as fast and as hard as any man could have done, correcting, revising, scoring, orchestrating, badgering his publishers to get a move on, fretting when he was kept waiting for material from the printers, anxious to consult with 'the Birmingham people early'. Recalling these events more than half a century later in an article in the *Musical Times* in 1959, Dorabella, then eighty-five (she lived to be ninety), criticized Elgar for being 'dilatory in getting the chorus parts corrected and returned to the printers'. Her memory had suffered with age, for had she accused him of holding up final corrections to the orchestral parts she might have been nearer the truth. Copies of the vocal score were ready by the third week of July, and originally the orchestral parts and the full score were corrected in August, but as late as 18 September Jaeger was almost screaming at Elgar, 'For God's sake return all *proofs* at once or we shall get landed in a fine quandary.' Just thirteen days before the first performance, Elgar was still tinkering about with final corrections to the orchestral parts. It was small wonder that after attending an orchestral rehearsal in London on 21 September he wrote to Jaeger, 'Somehow, after thinking of the rehearsal, I feel very much ashamed of myself as author of Gerontius – a sort of criminal – and wonder if I shall ever get up sufficient courage to go to Birmingham at all.' By this he meant to the first performance – Richter had agreed to conduct – for he had already been to Birmingham to attend a rehearsal on 12 September.

Earlier in the summer a hopelessly optimistic rumour had reached the Elgars, most probably via Dorabella, concerning reception of the choral writing. Dorabella had an aunt who sang as a soprano in the choir and who, unlike many of her colleagues, was a good sight-reader. Telling her niece how lovely she thought the music, she added (and this part of her comment clearly did not get passed on to Malvern), 'But shall we ever learn it in time?' In Alice's diary this report at first got abbreviated and then exaggerated, and came to read, 'Heard chorus were delighted with Dream of Gerontius.' They were nothing of the kind. One of the tenors told Dorabella that the choir had only been supplied with single-voice parts, so that one section had no idea what the other section was doing.[7] Some of the basses did not know their parts at all and seemed not to care.

At the joint choral and orchestral rehearsal on 29 September, four days prior to the first performance of what was a major new work, Elgar sat next to Hans Richter and tried desperately to explain what he wanted. It was too late. There was to be a long delay between the final rehearsal and the first performance, possibly because the Birmingham Festival was crammed with other major works – Parry's *De Profundis*, Byrd's Five-Part Mass, Coleridge-Taylor's new *Hiawatha's Departure*, not to mention Bach's *St Matthew Passion* – all of which were being rehearsed by old Stockley, and the sheer weight and diversity of the programme may have accounted for much of the trouble. On 29 September things were said to have become chaotic, with everyone worked up to a high pitch, 'and unfortunately E. E. more than anyone'. Elgar was invited by Richter to address the choir, but by this time he was feeling desperate, and instead of encouraging the singers to do better he told them they had turned his work into a drawing-room ballad. That night Alice's diary entry read, 'Rehearsal not so good as London & chorus dull and wretched.'

The festival was due to open on the Tuesday, *Gerontius* being performed on the Wednesday. By Saturday evening it was beginning to dawn on Richter that he had grossly underestimated the scope of the score, and sensing a real

7. *Edward Elgar: His Life and Music* by Diana McVeagh.

emergency, he did something almost unprecedented at the time: he called an extra rehearsal for the Monday.[8] He spent what was left of Saturday and the whole of Sunday pacing up and down his hotel bedroom with the score propped on the mantelpiece, a cigarette holder preventing his straggly beard from catching alight as his chubby hands lit cigarette after cigarette, thumbing the pages in a frantic and hopeless fight against the clock. It could not have mattered by this time how well he knew the score, as it was going to be impossible in the course of one last rehearsal to drill the choir and blend the choral and orchestral writing in time to prevent a shambles. Arnold Bax records Elgar telling him in 1901 that neither the choir nor Richter knew the score,[9] but in spite of this condemnation of the man ultimately responsible, Elgar, to his credit, never blamed Richter for the disaster, and went out of his way in 1908 not only to dedicate to him his First Symphony but to entrust him with its performance. It is also worth noting that Elgar could have taken over from Richter and did not – perhaps wisely, for a switch of conductors would have been necessary well before the final rehearsal to have had much effect on the outcome. In future, however, he did take the precaution of conducting the first performances of *The Apostles*, *The Kingdom*, *Cockaigne*, *In the South*, the *Introduction and Allegro*, the Violin and Cello Concertos and the Second Symphony. He continued to admire Richter, and writing to him in 1910 he assured him he would never forget his kindness, nobility '& the grandeur of your life & personality'.

While ultimate responsibility for any performance must lie with the conductor, almost everyone connected with the first performance of *Gerontius* had a share in the nerve-racking proceedings. Even the extra rehearsal on the Monday, which lasted six hours, was probably a well-intentioned mistake, for over-rehearsal can leave a choir tired just as under-rehearsal can leave them hesitant. During Parry's *De Profundis*, the *Sunday Times*'s critic came to the conclusion 'that something was wrong', and the performance of the *St Matthew Passion* seems to have been given a performance 'worthy of a fourth-rate provincial choral society'. Having got off on that sort of footing with a great religious work in the standard repertoire it must have seemed unlikely that the choir would suddenly cover themselves in glory for Mr Elgar's benefit. Losing his nerve completely, Richter stupidly harangued the choir in their dressing room just before the performance was due to commence,

8. One of Hans Richter's successors at the Hallé, Sir John Barbirolli, writing in 1965 about his own experience in preparing to conduct *The Dream of Gerontius*, recalled in the EMI record notes, 'I began to realise for the first time the great delicacy, imagination and subtlety of much of the scoring. Alas, this is often obscured by lack of sufficient preparation. It is a work that has that dreaded reputation "Everybody knows it", so that one rehearsal, or at the most two, is deemed sufficient.'

9. *Farewell, My Youth.*

beseeching them 'with unforgettable voice and gesture' to do their very best.

No doubt the general air of nervousness had infected the soloists, account-ing to some extent for their poor showing. The tenor, Edward Lloyd, who had sung in the first performance of *Lux Christi*, *King Olaf* and *Caractacus*, was fifty-five and about to retire. Dorabella's verdict on him, that he was a fine singer of drawing-room ballads, seems to have been borne out by Vaughan Williams's unkind and amusing comment: 'He sang *Gerontius* like a Stainer anthem, in the correct tenor attitude with one foot slightly withdrawn.'[10] Rosa Burley was even more unkind and forthright in her attack on Lloyd, whom she described as a lyric tenor well able to sustain a straightforward part such as Olaf, 'but with no understanding whatever of anything more profound than *I'll Sing Thee Songs of Araby* into which one almost expected him to burst at any moment'.

Miss Burley has left us an account of the performance which leaves little to the imagination. 'Before the end of the Kyrie,' she says, 'it was evident that the chorus did not know the parts they were trying to sing and as the music became more chromatic, they slipped hideously out of tune. It was appalling – far far worse than one had thought possible. Those of us who knew the score and the lofty aims Edward had had in writing it suffered agonies as we thought of the misery it must be causing him and did not dare to look at him.'

Elgar had been teaching at The Mount while writing *The Dream of Gerontius* (he was still having to give lessons there at the end of 1901), and Miss Burley knew the score because he had played it over to her on the school piano. She considered that Richter took the whole thing too slowly, and that the bass, Hugh Plunket Greene, failed no less than the tenor to realize Elgar's intentions. 'Suddenly,' she wrote, 'there was the dramatic pause which follows Gerontius's death and I waited for the ringing cry of the Priest whose "Proficiscere" should, as I knew, sound like a trumpet call. But here again there was a ridiculous anticlimax for Plunket Greene, despite the immense reputation he was later to earn – and deserve – for interpretation, had anything but a strong voice and was always uncertain in intonation.'

Part I concludes with the great and beautiful chorus, 'Go forth upon thy journey, Christian soul!' This the choir sang out of tune, and Richter spent the interval pacing up and down the artists' room as he had paced up and down his hotel bedroom, with as much effect. Plunket Greene began the Angel of the Agony's solo in Part II a semitone flat – 'or was it sharp?' Dorabella inquired of herself afterwards. At any rate she recorded that he 'stuck to it (bless his heart!) and was so upset about it afterwards'. Miss Burley says the Demons' Chorus 'sounded like something out of a pantomime', but she gave credit to the soprano, Marie Brema, 'a goddess from Valhalla if ever there was

10. *The Works of Ralph Vaughan Williams* by Michael Kennedy (Oxford University Press, 1964).

one', for being the only person who 'appeared to have any grasp of the emotions the music was supposed to express'. On the other hand, Miss Brema came in for another of Vaughan Williams's barbed remarks: whilst it may have been true, he said, that Plunket Greene had lost his voice, Marie Brema had none to lose. Miss Burley summed up the dreadful morning by saying that had the soprano made the most brilliant success of her part, 'she could not have saved a performance which had been hopelessly wrecked by the choir, whose pitiful stumblings indeed remained the outstanding impression. There were times when they seemed to be a whole semitone out and when the orchestra, disregarding the directions on the score, would play fortissimo in order to drag them back to the true pitch. The whole thing was a nightmare.' She ends her account with the unlikely statement that the only person who was not in the least disturbed was Richter; having 'on the same day given a performance of Hiawatha which had distressed its composer only a little less than Gerontius had distressed Edward, the great conductor went home and finished the day with a rousing performance of the Tannhäuser overture on the pianola'.

Dorabella's summing-up in her diary read, 'Too wonderful and clever to describe here, but performance not good.' Later, she noted, 'It was all rather dreadful and I felt afterwards that I wanted to get home quickly and meet nobody. The poor Elgars had escaped back to their hotel.' Writing to Dorabella eleven days after the performance, Jaeger was a good deal more forthright. Stockley, he said, ought to have been boiled and served on toast for having had the audience in purgatory for two hours. His faith in the work itself had in no way been diminished, and at the end of December he was again writing to Dorabella to tell her, 'I'm still trying hard to get Gerontius performed in London, but it is almost hopeless. I still hope Wood will do it.' On 18 February the next year his hopes were to be partially realized, when Henry Wood did, somewhat cautiously, conduct the Prelude and the Angel's Farewell. 'Oh, Dorabella,' Jaeger wrote afterwards in ecstasy, 'the stuff sounded most beautiful, most moving, most elevating. It is the highest thing in English art (musical art) & honestly I can say it seems to me the noblest, aloofest thing since Parsifal. Wood conducted it with loving care ... the result was a performance which completely put Richter's in the shade. I was deeply affected & I felt more than I could express to dear E. E.'

At the end of the score Elgar had copied out a quotation from Ruskin's Sesame and Lilies: 'This is the best of me; for the rest I ate, and drank, and slept, loved and hated, like another; my life was as the vapour, and is not; but *this* I saw and knew; this, if anything of mine, is worth your memory.' It was an apt quotation, and its memory and meaning must have stabbed him as he 'escaped back to his hotel'. The exhilaration of those months at Birchwood had turned to ash. After twenty years of struggle, after teaching in a lunatic asylum and a girls' school to earn a living, he had written out of his 'insidest inside' a work far superior to the commonplace run of Victorian oratorio, motivated by religious feelings, inspired by a fine poem and dedicated to God. He brooded on his terrible fate, and all the paranoia and despair that all his life lay just beneath the surface of his often painfully forced humour took control. Six days after experiencing perhaps the most miserable day of his life, he took up his pen and wrote to the one man he knew in his heart would minister to him, to a man who loved and admired him, believed in his music and shared his own romantic, emotional outlook on life. Jaeger could take the full blast of his anguish.

'I have not seen the papers yet,' he wrote, 'except one or two bits which exuberant friends insisted on my reading and I don't know or care what they say or do. As far as I'm concerned music in England is dead – I shall always write what I have in me of course.

'I have worked hard for forty years & at the last, Providence denies me a decent hearing of my work: so I submit – I always said God was against art and I still believe it. Anything obscene or trivial is blessed in this world and has a reward – I ask for no reward – only to live & to hear my work. I still hear it in my heart and in my head so I must be content. Still it is curious to be treated by the old fashioned people as a criminal because my thoughts and ways are beyond them.

'I am very well and what is called "fit"! I had my golf in good style yesterday and am not ill or pessimistic – don't think it, but I have allowed my heart to open once – it is now shut against every religious feeling and every soft, gentle impulse *for ever*.'

In some ways this letter need not be taken too seriously, for it is an easily disentangled mass of contradictions. 'Music in England is dead', but of course Elgar will go on writing it. 'I have worked hard for forty years' suggests that he began composing at the age of three. The general rage against God is typical of the bruised believer: no one can truly hate God unless he believes in his existence. Rather than blame Richter, by general consent a great conductor, or even old Stockley, who after all had employed and to some extent encouraged him when he was young and penniless, why not lash out at Providence, someone or something less likely to answer back? 'I ask for no reward': all his life Elgar was complaining that he was not properly rewarded, financially or by artistic recognition. The idea that he had been treated like a criminal was ludicrous; his work had been mauled by people who were themselves the victims of a system of musical presentation in serious need of reform. 'I am not pessimistic' hardly needs comment. As to his heart being shut for ever, one can only be grateful for the fact that it was not.

No letter written by Elgar better demonstrates the dichotomy of his personality: he was now a mature musician and still a desperately immature man. But the purpose of the *cri de cœur* was achieved, for Jaeger came galloping to the rescue, telling him it was weak and wicked to write the way he had.

The following week, on 17 October, Elgar was offered a doctorate of music from Cambridge, Stanford having continued to exert his influence, and we may be forgiven if we allow considerable scepticism to settle on the story that Elgar ever entertained a serious inclination to refuse. He is said to have hesitated on two grounds: that he could not afford the robes and that he did not wish to be associated with academic distinctions because he despised 'academic' musicians, those who earned their living on the fringes of the establishment. He had already, however, used his own friendship with the Master of the Queen's Music to get two works dedicated to Queen Victoria, he had shown no objection to having his music played at Windsor and Balmoral, and the whole course of his career was to involve a headlong dash into the arms of royal patronage, the honours system and academic recognition from half a dozen countries. He may genuinely have disliked the music the academic musicians wrote but that was no reason not to become Dr Edward Elgar. A handle to one's name always has commercial benefits and Elgar was far more commercially astute than he pretended – had he not already inquired of Novello in the year of the Diamond Jubilee whether it would be 'of any material good' to get his *Imperial March* dedicated to the queen?

As to the problem of finding £45 for a set of robes, it is typical of Elgar that he should have pretended poverty over such a relatively small sum connected with such a milestone in his career. Even allowing for a recent loss on the stock exchange and the expense of a minor throat operation, Alice could easily have dipped into her private resources to cover the expense, but in the end a collection was organized by Granville Bantock, with the majority of people contributing a guinea each. Those who sent money included the owner of the German pension, Henry Bethell, to whom (with his wife) Elgar had dedicated *From the Bavarian Highlands*, Hew Stueart-Powell and Basil Nevinson of the *Enigma Variations*, Stanford himself, whose kindness to Elgar at this time was prodigious, Jaeger (who never had any money), Parry, Henry Wood (who sent three guineas), and poor Hugh Plunket Greene, obviously anxious to make amends for singing out of tune at Birmingham. Parry said he would send a further guinea if one proved insufficient, but in the end the money was raised; considering that by this time Elgar had a number of wealthy friends to whom an outright gift of the robes would have cost roughly what they spent on cigars in a week, the impressive subscription list should perhaps be regarded as a joint tribute by a wide circle of friends to the musical hero of the hour.

Elgar was overwhelmed when he heard about it: 'I say I'm knocked over,' he exclaimed to Jaeger on 9 November; 'I don't know what to make of you all & am in a fit of the *blues* thinking of the kindness of you all for which I have done nothing to deserve – it's very odd & dreamlike & I don't know who I am; or where we are, or who's who, or anything – perhaps in a week I shall realise the thing.'

As far as *Gerontius* was concerned, Elgar had underestimated the ability of his fellow musicians to distinguish between a poor performance and a great work. The *Enigma Variations* of the previous year were becoming increasingly popular and his friends were in no doubt that he was poised to write more great music. He received his doctorate at Cambridge on 22 November, St Cecilia's Day, and the year ended with another first performance, on 27 November, at St James's Hall, of a piece for small orchestra, the *Sérénade lyrique*.

One of the famous rows in which Elgar engaged – always with men – was with Stanford, and the seeds of this childish tiff are said to have been sown at the birth of *Gerontius*. 'It stinks of incense' was the offending quip made by Stanford and tactlessly passed on to Elgar. It was a liturgical point of view, one perhaps shared by Stockley, who was a Nonconformist, but as a serious musical critique it was on a par with describing Verdi's *Requiem* as good opera. Stanford's sincere championship of Elgar and his music at this time can be in no doubt. He invited Elgar to conduct the *Variations* at the 1901 Leeds Festival, he conducted the *Variations* himself in December 1901, and he took the trouble to write to Elgar congratulating him on his concert overture *Cockaigne*, the brilliant work in which Elgar brushed aside his depression over the initial failure of *Gerontius*.

First news of this new piece had reached Jaeger in a letter from Elgar dated 4 November 1900. As so often, it had to be cloaked in an air of secrecy: 'Don't say anything about the prospective overture yet – I call it "Cockayne" & it's cheerful and Londony – "stout and steaky".' Few people of Elgar's background and education would have known of the connection between Cockaigne – an imaginary land of idleness and luxury – and cockney. 'Ye gods! what a capital title,' Jaeger enthused to Alice on 7 November. 'I can smell the Steak and Stout already. I'm glad that E. has done something *jolly* after the serious and awesome Gerontius. Let him finish with a "*Bang*" though, and give us a really *rousing* piece. We can all do with it.'

Elgar subtitled his concert overture 'In London Town' and dedicated it to his friends the members of British orchestras. It received its first performance – in London – at a Philharmonic Society concert at the Queen's Hall on 20

June 1901, with Elgar conducting. It was only his second work to receive its première at the Queen's Hall, opened in 1894 – the first had been his song *Pipes of Pan*, on 12 May 1900. According to Dorabella, Alice 'literally sobbed with laughter' on hearing Elgar play *Cockaigne* for the first time, presumably on the piano, but most audiences since have tended to find it enjoyable rather than funny. In a letter to Hans Richter written six weeks after the first performance, accompanying a copy of the score, Elgar said the overture was 'intended to be honest, healthy, humorous and strong but not vulgar'. He added, 'I hope I have not quite missed my aim and trust I may one day hear the overture under your conductorship – I need not tell you what a joy that would be.' Within two months Richter had taken up the new work, and Elgar wrote to Richter on 25 October to thank him. 'My own overture was most exhilarating and I was glad indeed to hear it under your sympathetic and most masterly direction – but, it has taught me that I am not satisfied with my music and must do, or rather try to do, something better and nobler.'

The idea of dedicating *Cockaigne* to his orchestral friends may have occurred to Elgar in April, when he attended a rehearsal of the *Enigma Variations* under Henry Wood and received the rare distinction, at a rehearsal, of an ovation from the orchestra. Jaeger reported on Wood's treatment of the *Variations* to Dorabella: 'I have never heard anything more daringly, devilishly brilliant & boisterous than Troyte or G. R. S., more gorgeous in colour than Nimrod, more dainty and graceful than the lovely Dorabella.' He added that Wood played 'that stunning coda' superbly.

On 10 May Dorabella was present to record a fragment of history. She tells us that Elgar called out to her, 'Child, come up here. I've got a tune that will knock 'em – knock 'em flat', and he played through the Military March No. 1 in D – the first of the *Pomp and Circumstance Marches*. 'I was thrilled,' she recalled years later. Poor man, he had just written one of the great tunes of the world, and it has been knocking 'em flat ever since. Interestingly, Dorabella recalled Elgar playing it that evening in almost strict quick-march time, making very little of the 'largamente'. Over a period of thirty years Elgar was to write another four marches (the second was contemporary with the first, and the others followed in 1904, 1907 and 1930), that complete the set of five later grouped together under the title *Pomp and Circumstance*. Their popular appeal has been used to disparage their author, for no great composer is supposed to write popular music, and the more popular it becomes the worse it is generally assumed to be. In the case of the infamous *Pomp and Circumstance March* No. 1, the truly offending portion is the trio section, the tune Elgar thought would knock 'em flat. The *Manchester Guardian* critic, Arthur Johnstone, suggested in 1902 that it was as broad a melody as *God Save the*

King, Rule Britannia and *See the Conquering Hero Come*, and perhaps the broadest open-air tune since Beethoven's *Freude, schöner Götterfunken*. Elgar certainly had a gift for writing big, some people believe great, tunes. According to Adrian Boult, 'Elgar enjoyed his own tunes and was not in the least ashamed of them.'[11] Indeed, there was no reason why he should have been, and it needs to be remembered that even before any words had been set to the piece we now know as *Land of Hope and Glory* it was instantly recognized as a stirring and memorable piece of music. At its first London performance, at the Queen's Hall on 21 October 1901, Henry Wood had to conduct it three times before the audience would let him get on with the rest of the concert.

Reporting on the event to Elgar two days later, Jaeger told him, 'Your splendid marches [No. 2 received its London première the same day] were the greatest success I have ever witnessed over a novelty at any concert.' Modern aversion to the *Pomp and Circumstance Marches*, when it exists, usually owes as much to social and political attitudes as it does to any serious consideration of their musical merit.

The Military March No. 2 in A minor was dedicated to Granville Bantock, perhaps in gratitude for organizing the subscription list for Elgar's convocation robes. The March No. 1 was dedicated to Alfred Rodewald and the members of the Liverpool Orchestral Society, and it was Rodewald and the Liverpool Orchestral Society who were in fact entrusted with the very first performance of both marches two days before the London performances under Henry Wood. Elgar had probably first met Rodewald, whom he usually addressed as Rody, during the summer of 1899, so that their relationship must have got off to a flying start; it was destined to last a tragically short time. Rodewald was one of a circle of wealthy, gifted, generous and amusing friends who were gathering around Elgar at this time. Many were Jews and many were German or, like Rodewald, of recent German descent. Rodewald had been born and brought up in Liverpool, where he made his money out of the textile industry, played the double bass and championed the music of Richard Strauss and Wagner. He was an excellent amateur conductor and a patron of Granville Bantock. He entertained Elgar at his Liverpool home and his Welsh cottage, and it was he who had been entrusted to tell Elgar that his friends were to rally round and buy his Cambridge robes. The key to his friendship with Elgar lies in one sentence in a letter he wrote to Elgar after hearing *Cockaigne*: 'Ah my dear boy, you write from the heart, and not from the brain, there's the secret.'

Shortly before embarking on the *Enigma Variations* (in 1898), and still almost inevitably caught up in the national cult of hero-worship that had surrounded General Gordon since his untimely death in 1884, Elgar had toyed

---

11. In conversation with the author.

with the idea of writing a programmatic symphony based on Gordon's life, a life now held up, as a result of the nation's guilt, as the epitome of Christian service. In the end the original project came to nothing, but between 1898 and 1901 Elgar produced some sketches and a theme, sketches which whetted Alice's appetite to the point where on 20 January 1901 she was writing to Jaeger to tell him, 'There could be no *nobler* music than the symphony. I *long* for it to be finished & have to exist on scraps – Do write & hurry him.' It may have been Alice who then enlisted Rodewald's aid; at all events, Rodewald, a wealthy man, offered to commission the work. Elgar declined, perhaps because at the time he did not wish to feel under the kind of pressure to complete a work by a certain date that a commission inevitably imposes, a pressure made all the more embarrassing if the obligation is to a personal friend, but a few months later he accepted a commission from another quarter for precisely the same project.

Once Alice had got Jaeger excited over the prospect of a symphony, Jaeger was alerting Henry Wood to the good news and on 26 October he told Elgar that Wood was hoping to conduct the symphony at the next Leeds Festival if it was ready. Only the day before, Elgar had mentioned in a letter to Richter that he was at work on a symphony, so possibly Richter, too, had spoken to Wood or Jaeger, or both. Elgar was never averse to fanning rumours about impending works (the most notorious example was to be in relation to the unfinished Third Symphony), and instead of explaining in a straightforward way that the work was by no means written, and there was no saying when it would be, on 9 November Elgar returned the misleading and ambiguous message, 'As to the Symphony – we did talk of it & *if ready* the festival shall have it, of course, but there's not the slightest chance of my doing it I fear.' There was 'a real paying commission' for Norwich to be completed '& 100 other things to come first'. This promise – to let the Leeds Festival have a symphony there was no chance of him completing in time – led, in December 1902, to a firm fifty-guinea commission from Leeds for a symphonic work to be performed at their 1904 Festival. Elgar was not satisfied with the fee and told them they could have a choral work instead. Early the next year Elgar then told Leeds they could not have a choral work after all, so they raised their original offer of fifty guineas to £100 – for the original symphony. Elgar accepted. Seven months later, by this time having got himself into a hopeless tangle, Elgar returned the commission for the symphony on the extraordinary grounds that it would mean he could never write a large choral work for Leeds in the future. He tried to justify his prevarication in a letter to Troyte Griffith by saying he had promised the dedication of the symphony to Richter and the first performance to Leeds, then learnt that Richter was counting on conducting the first performance at Birmingham, and so withdrew it from Leeds; it was now promised to Richter and hence to Birmingham. Eventually Richter did get his symphony, though he had to wait until 1908 since Elgar did not even begin to compose it in earnest until June 1907; the early sketches to which Alice had referred in her letter to Jaeger on 20 January 1901 may have been used up eventually in the Second Symphony, completed in 1910. The immediate upshot of Elgar's behaviour was a refusal by the Leeds Festival to play any work of his in 1904. Some of their indignation may have been exacerbated by the publication of an erroneous story in the *Daily News* to the effect that a new orchestral work shortly to be heard at Covent Garden was 'the symphony announced for Leeds'. Had the reporter checked his facts he would have discovered that the new orchestral work was in fact to be a new concert overture – *In the South*. Despite the degree of responsibility for the muddle that could fairly be laid at Elgar's door, Stanford, who had been the conductor of the Leeds Philharmonic Society since 1898, took up Elgar's case with the chairman of the committee, asking what earthly harm it could do to play *Cockaigne* 'at the end of the Wednesday evening performance'. He went on to outline an extremely sound principle: 'A man's artistic work,' he wrote, 'ought to rank independently of his personality. If it had not been that Hans von Bülow had taken this view of Wagner, the Bayreuth theatre would not be standing now.' The committee took Stanford's point, *Cockaigne* was performed and once again Elgar found himself in Stanford's debt.

Another friend whom Elgar met for the first time two years before the *Enigma Variations* made him famous was Alice Stuart-Wortley. Third daughter of the painter Millais (and hence the daughter of a baronet), she was five years younger than Elgar, very beautiful (Elgar called her 'Windflower'), and she is now generally assumed to have been 'the Soul' enshrined in the Violin Concerto. Safely married, she was typical of the assured, aristocratic and handsome type of woman Elgar was content to place on a pedestal and worship from afar. Elgar and his Alice were on perfectly proper terms of friendship with Mr Stuart-Wortley and his Alice, so that there was no social or emotional impediment to a dedication of the Violin Concerto to Alice Stuart-Wortley by name; had she been a man, like Hans Richter, Ernest Newman, Billy Reed or Edward VII, she might well have gone down to posterity with her own name unashamedly at the top of an Elgar score, but Elgar never dedicated a major composition to a woman, not even to his wife or daughter. The women Elgar professed to admire may have been archetypes of the elegant, upper-class mother he would have chosen given the chance, but as they also represented a class, and in some instances a narrow provincial mentality, that disdained his parents for being tradespeople, they were presumably as much despised as admired; never a reticent man where the outpourings of his emotions were concerned, Elgar nevertheless reserved his most overt expressions of emotional involvement for men, his often petty rows for men, the most precious gift in his possession, his dedications, for men and, with the single exception of his wife, his deepest sorrow in bereavement for men.

One of Elgar's most important friends, whom he first met in 1899, the same year as his first meeting with Rodewald, was Leo Schuster, always known as Frank. (His father, a banker, was also Leo.) Schuster was five years older than Elgar (forty-seven when they met), an old Etonian bachelor of German Jewish extraction, and a wealthy patron of the arts who regarded himself privileged to be able to keep the company of people more clever than himself. Crippled by a childhood injury, 'he spent his life making other people happy', Sir Adrian Boult tells us in his autobiography, and 'never seemed to mind what his guests said or did provided they were enjoying themselves'.[12] (Siegfried Sassoon commented in his diary that Schuster was content to be exploited by his friends provided he was sure he was getting good value in return.) Schuster had no doubt that Elgar was a genius. He was a friend and patron of Fauré, and he claimed to have been the first person to recognize that Adrian Boult would make a good conductor. The guests whose company Schuster so much enjoyed were entertained by himself and his elder sister, Adela, in London at 22 Old Queen Street, Westminster, and in the country at The Hut, a large house near Monkey Island, outside Bray; the name of the house was changed to The Long White Cloud some time between August 1924 and April 1925.[13] The Hut had gardens that ran down to the Thames, and Billy Reed recalled the place as 'a sweet riverside house, raised several feet above the level of the lawn, with wooden steps leading up to the verandah from the gravel path ... Across the lawn, and almost screened by trees, was the studio, away from the house and approached by stones placed in the grass about a pace apart.'[14] Elgar was to work in this garden studio on the slow movement of his Violin Concerto.

In *Alice Elgar: Enigma of a Victorian Lady* Percy Young dismisses Frank Schuster as 'one of Edward's wealthy friends, a homosexual dilettante whom Alice did not like'. Her alleged dislike of Schuster did not however prevent her appointing him a guardian to her daughter nor accepting his hospitality at The Hut. It was through Schuster that Elgar now met fashionable artists like Sickert, Sargent and Tree, and other wealthy patrons – the Marquess of

---

12. In conversation with the author.

13. In a codicil to his Will, dated 28 August 1924, Frank Schuster's home is referred to as The Hut; in another codicil, dated 14 April 1925, it is referred to as The Long White Cloud. As Schuster did not die until 1927 it would appear that it was he who changed the name, not Leslie Wylde (who inherited the house) as stated in a Parkin Gallery catalogue for 1–18 October 1980 on the authority of Wylde's widow, the painter Wendela Boreel.

14. *Elgar As I Knew Him.*

Northampton, for example, and Lady Maud Warrender, who, like Alice Stuart-Wortley, was a handsome, talented and aristocratic woman who was admirably placed to help with his career. She was a sister-in-law of the Hon. George Allsopp, for whom Elgar and Scap had canvassed in 1885. She was also a close friend of Queen Alexandra. From 1901 to 1922 her brother, the Earl of Shaftesbury, was comptroller of Queen Mary's household. In 1932 her elder son was appointed vice-chamberlain to George V, and at the end of Elgar's life Lady Maud was actually to make use of her relationship with the royal family by addressing a letter personally to King George V on Elgar's behalf. He was frequently to stay at Leasam House, her beautiful home near Rye.

Perhaps the most surprising of Elgar's newly acquired friends at this time was Lord Charles Beresford, who had served in the entourage of the Prince of Wales on his tour of India in 1875, had later carried to Lord Randolph Churchill the prince's absurd challenge to a duel (occasioned by Lord Randolph's disgraceful disclosure to the Princess of Wales of the existence of indiscreet letters written by the prince to Lady Aylesford, mistress of the Marquess of Blandford, Lord Randolph's elder brother) and had ultimately written a libellous letter to his wife accusing the prince of behaving like a blackguard and a coward. By the time that Elgar met Lord Charles, he and the prince had been reconciled (in 1897), but for a time he had been intended by the prince for a social outcast, and Elgar's attachment to him seems all the stranger in view of his common reputation as a notorious adulterer. It was said he enjoyed making women cry because it was 'such fun to hear their stays creak'. Lord Charles became an admiral and between 1874 and 1910 he was several times returned to parliament as a Conservative. In 1916 he was raised to the peerage as Baron Beresford by George V on the advice of Herbert Asquith, and in 1917 Elgar dedicated to him his setting of four poems by Kipling, *The Fringes of the Fleet*.

One of the pleasing and interesting facets of Elgar's friendships is their diversity. His later affection and respect for Bernard Shaw might at first glance seem surprising, but as fellow self-made men, artists and egoists they enjoyed each other's company because they knew they did not have to take one another – in particular one another's politics – too seriously. They also had in common a totally non-academic musical training. Elgar's pose as a country gentleman was a good performance in a role that epitomized all that Shaw secretly cherished in the English character, and Shaw's warm-hearted brand of Fabianism no doubt stirred a liberal conscience in Elgar, whose own conservatism, in any case, owed more to an emotional set of values than to any political creed. Elgar's politics did not get in the way of other valuable friendships: Troyte Griffith and the Marquess of Northampton, for example, were active supporters of the Liberal Party, while Earl Beauchamp, Lady Mary Lygon's brother, was to become leader of the Liberals in the House of Lords. However, Lord Northampton did once feel it necessary to caution Elgar when inviting him to stay: 'As long as we keep off politics we are not likely to fight,' he wrote.

Other men and women from the worlds of literature, the theatre, music and politics who congregated at The Hut, many of whom Elgar came to know well (though not all, for Schuster may have tended to compartmentalize his friends – Enid Bagnold, for instance, was a frequent visitor to The Hut yet she retained no recollection of ever meeting Elgar[15]), included Siegfried Sassoon, Claude Phillips, W. B. Yeats, Lady Randolph Churchill, Lauritz Melchoir, Nellie Melba, Roger Fry and Constance Collier (who went on tour with Elgar and the London Symphony Orchestra in 1915). Had Elgar met Schuster four years earlier he might also have met Oscar Wilde, but by 1899 Wilde was living in exile in Paris. Adela Schuster had known Wilde well, and after learning of his bankruptcy following his arrest in 1895 she had sent him £1,000 with the assurance that it was 'a wholly inadequate recognition of the pleasure his conversation had given her' (she told Wilde's biographer, Hesketh Pearson, that in order to get a faint idea of what Wilde's conversation was like one could take the duologues from *Intentions* and stir them up with *The Importance of Being Earnest*).[16] No doubt Frank Schuster, too, had taken pleasure in Wilde's conversation, but the two men had in common another pleasure besides. Sickert (admittedly an aggressive heterosexual, who once, at the age of fifty-four, proposed marriage to a girl of eighteen who was already his mistress) is reported to have remarked apropos of Schuster, 'A pansy in my day was just a flower'[17]; and among Schuster's many friends who visited The Hut were a number of well-known homoerotic artists, like the poet Robert Nichols and the painter Glyn Philpot; it was Nichols who introduced Elgar to Siegfried Sassoon, a regular visitor to The Hut after the war.

Schuster was a banker, and bankers were peculiarly respectable at the turn of the century, possibly because of Edward VII's friendship with bankers and businessmen generally. Another wealthy banker, whom Elgar met in 1901, was Edward Speyer. Born in Frankfurt, he had become a naturalized British subject. In 1915, when he was accused of being a German spy, Elgar came

---

15. Letter of 28 October 1980 to the author written on behalf of Enid Bagnold.

16. *The Life of Oscar Wilde* by Hesketh Pearson (Methuen, 1966). Wilde described Adela Schuster in *De Profundis* as 'one of the most beautiful personalities I have ever known'. On his release from prison she contributed to a fund to enable him to survive in Paris, and it was to her that Robert Ross wrote his vivid and detailed account of Wilde's last illness. She was among those who sent wreaths to his funeral.

17. Wendela Boreel, quoted in the Parkin Gallery catalogue for 1–18 October 1980, and referring to parties given in Tite Street by Frank and Adela Schuster, to which Sickert was sometimes invited.

to his defence, but in 1921 Speyer had his naturalization revoked, and so lost
the baronetcy conferred on him in 1906. He had taken with panache to the
life of an English country gentleman, entertaining the Elgars at his house at
Shenley in Hertfordshire. He also retained valuable connections with his
fatherland, and was influential in encouraging German orchestras to take up
Elgar's works. Indeed, the German critics present at the first performance of
The Dream of Gerontius had been among the first to appreciate its worth, and
while Jaeger was still receiving criticism for showing so much enthusiasm for
the work and was still having difficulty persuading anyone to put it on again
in England, it was to Germany, the home of Elgar's hero Wagner and of
Richard Strauss, soon to become another influential friend, that Elgar sailed
on 16 December 1901 for a performance of *Gerontius* at Düsseldorf.

Things seem to have gone much more satisfactorily on this occasion than
they had done in Birmingham, as we can glean from an affectionate but
wickedly funny account of Alice's reactions, sent home by Jaeger in a letter
to Dorabella: 'As for dear Mrs E.,' he wrote on 29 December, 'you can imagine
her style of seventh-heaven-beatitude, with eyebrow lifting, neck twisting,
forget-me-not glances towards the invisible Heavens! Don't think I am making
fun of her! I am not; but you know her signs of deep emotion over the Dr's
music don't you?' Jaeger had sat with the Elgars and Arthur Johnstone, the
perceptive music critic of the *Manchester Guardian*, in the third row of the
balcony. He went on to report that the chorus was perfect and that the tenor
had brains, although in Part I he did not seem in very good voice and made
one serious blunder. However, in Part II he was '*great*, especially in the "Take
me away" '. Unfortunately the performance nearly came adrift because of an
inadequate Angel, whom Jaeger described as 'anything but angelically perfect',
and Elgar suffered 'sundry twitches and pangs' when she threatened to fall.
Julius Buths (to whom the Elgars had lent Craig Lea for a holiday that summer)
was conducting, and Jaeger says that thanks to his alertness the audience
could not have realized how dangerously near collapse the performance came,
'through this d— Angel's shortcomings'. After the performance Jaeger had the
initiative to dash to the telephone and wire 400 words to *The Times*, earning
himself twenty marks in the process. Hence he arrived late for a supper
party, where he sat next to the Angel, who was very depressed because Buths
had ticked her off during the performance after she had missed an important
entry; Buths used the expression '*es war scheusslich*' which, according to
Jaeger, was 'pretty strong stuff' (it was indeed – it meant her performance was
atrocious). During the course of this German visit Elgar was much fêted,
greatly to Jaeger's delight, for he regarded his German compatriots as much
more civilized in musical matters than the English.

Elgar returned to London on New Year's Day, 1902, and by 3 January he had forgotten to feel refreshed by the appreciation shown him by his German hosts, for he was complaining to Jaeger about 'the horrible musical atmosphere' of England, into which he had plunged at once and which had 'nearly suffocated' him. 'I *wish* it had completely,' he moaned. And on 9 January he was asking his publisher if any money was due to him, as it was 'an awkward time of year financially'. He refused to be cheered by a letter from Jaeger with the good news that a second Düsseldorf performance of *Gerontius* had been arranged for May, again under Buths, whom Elgar had described in a letter to Novello only a month before as 'unsurpassable' as a conductor, a man who had taken 'infinite pains' to make everything 'go'. He told Jaeger his music had no commercial value as it did not arrange well for the piano, and all he wanted to do was write chamber music and a symphony. The previous year, hoping perhaps for financial success, he had written the *Concert Allegro* for the piano, performed in December by Fanny Davies and dedicated to her, but it was not published at that time and the manuscript in fact disappeared for many years. (The score of what was to prove to be Elgar's only major piano work was rediscovered in 1968 and was published by Novello in 1982 as Elgar's Opus 46.)

Elgar's own troubles did not entirely blind him to other people's: he and Alice had lent Craig Lea to Jaeger and his wife at the same time as Professor Buths was staying there, for otherwise Jaeger could not have afforded a holiday, and on 13 January Elgar was again writing to Jaeger, having paid Dr MacDonald's bill himself, to say, 'I'm awfully distressed to hear you are again ill & terribly disappointed that our operation was not finally successful. I wish you all the good things & only wish I could put this right for you; do tell me what can be done & how & when? I think hourly about you & worry about it till I'm sick – which is human but not poetic.' Elgar had also lent a generous helping hand to Herbert Brewer, the thirty-six-year-old organist and choirmaster at Gloucester Cathedral, whose cantata *Emmaus* was still unscored three months before it was due to receive its first performance. On the point of withdrawing it, Brewer (who was knighted in 1926 and died two years later at the age of fifty-two) received a letter from Elgar saying he had heard from Jaeger that he was worried about getting his work ready and offering to help with the orchestration. 'I know it's a cheek to offer,' Elgar wrote, 'but if I can save you a little worry let me do so.' In the end Elgar scored a substantial amount of the work, returning it to Brewer with the accompanying note: 'I have taken great pleasure in trying to interpret your thoughts and feelings and only hope I have not grossly misrepresented them. Now: please accept my work on your score and never think I want any return whatever: keep a kind thought for a fellow sometimes – that's all.'

The Elgars were back in Düsseldorf for the May performance of *Gerontius*; on this occasion the part of the Angel was beautifully sung by an English soprano, Muriel Foster, and the whole performance was a triumphant success. According to Henry Wood, who was there, Elgar took no less than twenty calls at the end of Part I, and the faithful Arthur Johnstone, who had again travelled to Germany for the *Manchester Guardian*, informed his readers that full justice was done to the instrumental part, that Miss Foster sang with 'considerably greater and more expressive eloquence than any previous experience might have led one to expect from her', and that the semi-chorus 'acquitted themselves almost to perfection'. An even more enthusiastic account might have survived had Dorabella not thrown away Jaeger's letter telling her all about it. At a luncheon in Elgar's honour the next day, 20 May, Richard Strauss, with *Don Juan, Macbeth, Till Eulenspiegel, Don Quixote, Ein Heldenleben* and his First Horn Concerto already to his credit by the age of thirty-seven, proposed a toast to Elgar, describing him as 'the first English progressivist'. Strauss's speech became famous because his endorsement of Elgar, in Germany, was felt by many people to have been largely responsible for Elgar's success on the continent in advance of his true recognition at home. Three weeks after the luncheon, his head not in the least turned, Elgar expressed his own comment on the toast when he wrote to Jaeger to say, 'What a fuss about Strauss's speech! too ridiculous & nobody seems in the least to know what he said or meant.' Strauss had in fact meandered on about Arne being somewhat less than Handel, Sterndale Bennett less than Mendelssohn and some Englishmen 'of later day' not quite so great as Brahms, so it is small wonder that Elgar had no idea what Strauss was talking about, and it seems odd that it occurred to nobody to suggest at the time that he may quite simply have been drunk.

If the Rhenish wine did flow freely at that luncheon it served to seal a friendship between the two composers. Four months previously, on 2 January, when writing to Strauss to send him tempo markings for *Cockaigne* which was due to be conducted by Strauss in Berlin at its first performance in Germany, Elgar had addressed him as 'My dear Sir'. At the end of the year, on 10 December, Elgar heard a performance of *Ein Heldenleben* at the Queen's Hall, at which Strauss was present, and he wrote immediately afterwards to tell him – 'which in the hurry & crowd after the concert I could not do' – how tremendously he felt his music and how he rejoiced to see and hear how the audience appreciated his 'gigantic work & genius', and on this occasion he began his letter 'Dear Friend', signing it 'Your sincere friend'. The note was headed 'Richard Coeur de Lion! Ein Held!' In *Elgar: OM*, Percy Young says that Elgar found Strauss's music perplexing, and he appears to support this comment by referring to a footnote in his *Letters of Edward Elgar*, the footnote reading, 'The

Diary notes – "Very astonishing" '. Elgar himself kept no diary between the years 1889 and 1920, and the comment – which referred to *Ein Heldenleben* – would have been Alice's. It is perfectly true that no comment made by Alice would have been likely to differ from the views of her husband, but 'very astonishing' could surely be interpreted to mean 'very good; very original; very clever'.

In *Elgar As I Knew Him*, Billy Reed tells us that Elgar had 'great admiration for Strauss', although Sir Compton Mackenzie in his autobiography[18] has recalled attending a concert with Elgar in 1924 which opened with Strauss's *Don Juan*, 'by which Elgar seemed bored'. Other aspects of Elgar's musical taste seem to have led to conflicts of opinion. Dr Young has said, 'Elgar disliked *L'Oiseau de Feu* and *Petrushka* of Stravinsky as much as he adored the Rossini of *La Boutique Fantasque*'; but Reed, who knew Elgar well for nearly thirty years, informs us, 'Elgar's boyish pleasure in Suppé did not in the least interfere with his relish for Stravinsky, and the fun he got out of *L'Oiseau de Feu* or *Petrushka* never put Mendelssohn, Gounod, Grieg or Schumann out of court.' For the record, Reed has recalled that Elgar liked 'all Beethoven, Mozart and Haydn', reading the scores of the Haydn quartets for relaxation, and that he liked the tone poems of Liszt and thought Handel a genius, speaking of him with tears in his eyes. Reed tells us that in 1933, the year before he died, Elgar was still studying the score of Mendelssohn's *Elijah*, but spoke very little of the works of contemporary composers, 'especially of the younger school', although 'he liked some of them in a mild sort of way'.

Reed confirms what is undeniable, that Elgar was 'a Wagner enthusiast', and that he admired most of Berlioz, although Elgar apparently told Compton Mackenzie that much of the *Symphonie Fantastique* was rubbish. He was particularly fond of *Tosca* (Puccini was just one year younger than Elgar) and used to play the score on the piano. Other operatic works that found favour, according to Reed, were the 'older' (he must have meant earlier) operas of Rossini and Meyerbeer. If Elgar did not care for 'the younger school' of 'serious' composers, at least 'some of the later jazz records fascinated him so much he would play them again and again on his gramophone'. Most of Elgar's strictures, so far as the great masters were concerned, seem to have been reserved for what he felt to be weaknesses in orchestration. He loved Schumann and would discuss his symphonies at great length, but although the music entranced him 'he felt the weakness of the orchestration'. The same seems to have been true regarding his attitude to Brahms: the concluding F major chord at the end of the first movement of Brahms's Third Symphony was one of his favourite examples of weak scoring. Fred Gaisberg of the

18. *My Record of Music* (Hutchinson, 1955).

Gramophone Company was even to record that Elgar found the *Alto Rhapsody* and the *Requiem* 'dull and uninspiring'.

Elgar once played the whole of Gounod's *Faust* as a piano duet with the Ranee of Sarawak (according to Reed, Her Highness was an excellent pianist and a discerning musician), and it is also slightly surprising to learn from Reed that he loved 'some of Bach's music but by no means all', and that he liked Purcell but found Byrd insipid, 'except for a few works'. Of his contemporaries he regarded Fauré, who died in 1924, as dreadfully neglected, and in this he was surely right: Fauré's original and beautiful *Requiem* had to wait until 1935 for a performance at the Three Choirs Festival. Many of Reed's observations are borne out by Dorabella, who confirms that Elgar admired the orchestration of Strauss and Berlioz, and recalls him playing on the piano the works of Wagner, Mozart, Beethoven, Bach, Brahms and – perhaps not so unexpectedly – the operas of Gilbert and Sullivan.

CHAPTER FOUR

'Remember Poor Nim'

1902–8

The birth of the twentieth century brought about, somewhat belatedly, the end of the Victorian age; with it came a new king, a carefree and often bilious enjoyment of their money by the rich, and a rapid acceleration of technical achievement. The second half of the nineteenth century had been a progressive, expanding time in which to be born, provided one was blessed with reasonable health and was not living in grinding poverty. Advances in hygiene and medicine and the increasing use of electricity, the telephone and the motor-car were now to furnish for the Edwardians, and their vulgar, lavish, insular era that bridged two irreconcilable worlds divided by the Great War, a veritable paradise of modern conveniences. Those who benefited most, among them the Elgars, were of course the middle and upper middle classes, who took their station in life, and their enjoyment of cheap food, cheap labour and unspoilt countryside, entirely for granted.

Elgar suffered a certain amount of ill-health, mostly after his marriage and a lot of it arguably psychosomatic, but he never suffered from unrelievable pain and he only had to undergo one operation, for the removal of his tonsils in 1918 (plus a small exploratory operation in 1925), before he developed at the end of his life the cancer from which he died. Alice seldom suffered more than a headache or a cold. The Elgars had maids and cooks, gardeners and handymen, and by 1909 Elgar even had a valet. They furnished, with beautiful possessions, progressively more and more luxurious houses. They maintained country cottages and flats in London as an adjunct to their main home. They frequently went on holiday abroad. They entertained and they stayed for weekends in country houses. They did not need a large income to live well, because money went so far, and on a modest income the Elgars lived in a style that few upper-middle-class families and no middle-class families have since been able to emulate.[1] Alice never lifted a finger in the house nor,

1. To get some idea of the cost of living in Elgar's day, it is interesting to note that in 1917 Lytton Strachey was renting a house in Berkshire with an orchard, six bedrooms and three reception rooms for as little as £1 a week; and even in 1934, the year of Elgar's death, *The Times* was carrying an advertisement for a house on the border of Bedfordshire and Hertfordshire with four reception rooms, nine bedrooms, three bathrooms, a tennis court and three acres of land at an asking price of £1,600.

apart from playing around with a hosepipe in the evenings, did she or Elgar ever personally cultivate a garden. They sent their only child to school as a weekly boarder, and one cannot help gaining the impression that sometimes when Alice complained of feeling tired it was a tiredness brought on, as in the case of so many women like her, by the worry of wondering what on earth to do to pass the time.

At Court, the suffocating constraints of Queen Victoria's reign gave way to the flamboyance and extravagance of Edward's dyspeptic decade. In the arts, with Wilde in disgrace and his plays virtually banned, the theatre was far from exciting. There was not an English composer, not at that time even Delius, with whom the composer of *The Dream of Gerontius* could be compared (all Elgar's musical peers – Strauss, Puccini, Dvořák, Mahler, Debussy – were to be found on the continent). In literature Tennyson's successor as Poet Laureate was Alfred Austin. Painting was just about alive thanks to Sargent, Sickert and a few now neglected artists like Henry Lamb and Brake Baldwin. Increasingly the public's appreciation of beauty was to be shaped not by artists so much as by pure designers, the men who manufactured ocean liners and motor-cars.

Like so many of their contemporaries, the Elgars looked ten years older than they were; Elgar was seventy before his age caught up with him. Ivor Atkins, who first saw Elgar in 1890 at the Worcester Festival, described the thirty-three-year-old first violinist as having a fine intellectual face, with nervous eyes and beautiful hands. In 1907, while in Italy, Elgar was to have a cast made of his right hand (now in Elgar's Birthplace at Broadheath) and it is indeed a beautiful, small and very feminine hand. But in 1900, when he was forty-three, Elgar bore the care-worn looks of an over-worked clerk of at least ten years older. It is hard to say what he must have looked like off-stage, for in front of the camera he always struck a pose, but a good image of him was given by Billy Reed when he described going to see him on one occasion at Brinkwells, a cottage in Sussex rented by the Elgars in 1917. The cottage was surrounded by acres of chestnut trees, and here Elgar played the role of a country gentleman by cutting some of them down. Reed describes how, on arriving, he saw Elgar 'standing like a tall woodman leaning a little forward upon an axe'. The picture, says Reed, was perfect, and the pose magnificent; he had 'placed himself there leaning on his axe and fitting in exactly with his surroundings'. Reed suggests, perhaps rather naïvely, that Elgar did these things without knowing it, 'by pure instinct'.[2]

Elgar's musical output and the jingoistic side of his nature came perilously close together during the reign of Edward VII, and however his music of this

2. *Elgar As I Knew Him.*

period is judged it does seem an inescapable fact that the composer's personal aspirations, his identification with the old order and his admiration for the person of the monarch as well as the institution of monarchy had a bearing, even if it was not a major one, on the uses to which he put his artistic gifts. He had already savoured royal patronage, and he had not hesitated to cash in on the Diamond Jubilee. Now he saw in the first coronation for sixty-five years another golden opportunity to turn out occasional music. His contributions to Edward VII's coronation in 1902 consisted of a setting of the national anthem for soprano, chorus and orchestra, a hymn to be sung in Westminster Abbey, *O Mightiest of the Mighty*, dedicated to the Duke of York (later that year created Prince of Wales), and the largest work of all (dedicated, of course, to the king), a *Coronation Ode*. Originally intended for performance on 30 June at Covent Garden in the presence of the king and queen, during a programme that would also have included excerpts from *Carmen*, *Rigoletto* and *Tannhäuser*, the first performance of the *Coronation Ode* had to be postponed, along with the coronation itself, when the king suddenly underwent an operation for appendicitis. It was eventually heard for the first time at Sheffield on 2 October.

In a volume of reminiscences published in 1933, *My First Sixty Years*, Lady Maud Warrender recounts an anecdote she attributes to 'the first performance' of the *Coronation Ode*, at a concert she organized at the Albert Hall in 1903 in aid of the Union Jack Club, at which the king and queen were present and the audience had been given Union Jacks to wave. Elgar conducted, and Alice was in a box with Lady Maud next to the royal box. Anxious lest Alice should notice that the king had fallen asleep, Lady Maud managed to distract her attention by getting her to change her seat. Apparently the king woke up 'when Land of Hope & Glory blazed forth'. Although incorrect in laying claim to having sponsored the première of the *Ode* (it was not even the first London performance, which took place at the Queen's Hall on 26 October 1902), Lady Maud is most unlikely to have invented the story; a rabid royalist, she was a frequent guest at Queen Alexandra's birthday parties at Sandringham, and Queen Victoria had stood as godmother to her elder son.

The *Ode* consists of seven settings for soprano, contralto, tenor, bass, orchestra and chorus of pieces with such titles as 'Britain, Ask of Thyself' and 'Only Let the Heart be Pure'; the Finale which awoke the king, an adaptation of the trio section of the *Pomp and Circumstance March* No. 1 to words by Arthur Benson, is the *Ode*'s chief claim to fame. It was apparently King Edward, not best remembered for his interest in music, who spotted the possibility of singing words to such a splendid tune, but Jaeger warned Elgar against the project: 'I say,' he wrote on 6 December 1901, 'you will have to write another tune for the Ode in place of the March in D tune. I have been trying much to fit words to it. That drop to E & bigger drop afterwards are quite impossible in singing *any* words to them, they sound downright vulgar. Just try it. The effect is fatal. No, you must write a new tune to the words & not fit the words to this tune. Consider this carefully & give no Choir a chance of scooping down. It will sound horrible.'

Elgar was never one to let a good tune go to waste; he took the view that if a tune was good enough the words could look after themselves, and Jaeger's advice fell on deaf ears. Elgar had been in correspondence over the words since 21 March 1901 and the choice of the man to supply them, Arthur Benson, may well have been the king's. Benson's father had become Archbishop of Canterbury in 1882 and Arthur had assumed an unofficial role as private poet to the royal family. A wedding hymn he originally wrote for the marriage of a fellow Old Etonian was eventually sung at the wedding in July 1896 of Edward's daughter Princess Maud to Prince Christian of Denmark (later elected King of Norway); he had contributed to a Diamond Jubilee hymn, and another hymn he wrote for a service at the Royal Mausoleum was set to music by Victoria herself. Princess Beatrice, too, seems to have collaborated with Benson, who turned out hymns for royal confirmations, hymns for royal christenings, an ode to celebrate Queen Victoria's surprise visit in 1900 to Ireland, a hymn to keep up British spirits during the Boer War and another to celebrate the proclamation of peace. In February 1902 he even found something suitable to write on the occasion of the signing of the alliance with Japan, and with the coronation planned for the summer, King Edward had in fact asked Benson to provide words for Wagner's *Kaisermarsch* as well as suggesting he should collaborate with Elgar on the *Coronation Ode*. The king was also to invite Benson to work with Lord Esher on an edition of Queen Victoria's letters, for which he was made Commander of the Royal Victorian Order. In 1924 he co-edited the *Book of the Queen's Doll's House*.

Elgar had already, in 1901, set to music a song by Benson entitled *Speak Music*, but they do not seem to have met until a performance of the *Ode* in London towards the end of 1902. Elgar, who conducted, was described by Benson in his diary as 'taller and shapelier than I have imagined ... a long nose – red hands – large cuffs. He conducted with a smiling aplomb – has a funny fumbling movement of the hands after *end* of piece.' Benson added that the *Ode* ('wizard-like music') impressed him very much. After the performance he went to the 'premier artists' room where he 'just had three pleasurable words with E., who was very genial and pleasant'. Referring presumably to Elgar's accent, Benson added, 'Once or twice I detected a twang, I thought.'[3]

Benson was certainly a snob. He became very wealthy through an unexpected legacy and was a lavish benefactor, as Master, of Magdalene College, Cambridge. He had a lot in common with Elgar, for while both had jingoistic tendencies they were also men of liberal inclination and tender conscience. When the Great War caused its obscene outbreak of anti-German feeling at home, Elgar stood against the general trend by supporting his friends with German origins, while Benson, too, bravely attacked the more hysterical anti-German propaganda and helped young conscientious objectors to prepare their cases for tribunal. Benson's personal life was, like Elgar's, a ceaseless and painful search for fulfilment although he was surrounded by many who admired and loved him, and they were both plagued by depression. In 1907, when the two met in Cambridge, Benson recalled Elgar greeting him after a performance of *The Kingdom* at King's College as 'an old friend and collaborator', and apparently Elgar went back with Benson to Magdalene, where 'Elgar was interesting. He told me his eyes were overstrained and he could do no work – then he said simply that it was no sort of pleasure to him to hear The Kingdom, because it was so far behind what he had dreamed of. It only caused him shame and sorrow ... He seemed all strung on wires, and confessed that he had petitioned for a seat close to the door so that he might rush out if overcome – by shame and sorrow, I suppose.'

It was on a visit to Rome later that year (1907) that Benson, in the midst of a severe breakdown, again ran into Elgar, and in his diary he recorded his impressions of both Alice and Carice, for the family were on holiday together. 'Lady E. *very* kind,' he wrote, 'but without charm and wholly conventional, though pathetically anxious to be *au courant* with a situation. Elgar's daughter, about sixteen, a quiet, obediently silent, contented sort of girl.' As for Elgar himself, Benson said, 'The worst thing about him is the limp shake of the thin hand, which gives a feeling of a great want of stamina.' On the strength of a fairly brief acquaintance with Elgar, Benson had no hesitation in linking his name with Margot Asquith's, Hubert Parry's and others who, he said, 'had to carry this cross' and tread 'the same sad path as myself', by which he meant they were prone to nervous breakdowns.

Shortly after preparing the words for the *Coronation Ode*, Benson is reputed

3. *On the Edge of Paradise* by David Newsome (John Murray, 1980), a splendid life of Benson in which a full account of Elgar's collaboration with Benson can be found, and from which the ensuing quotations have been drawn.
  Rosa Burley confirmed in her book *Edward Elgar: The Record of a Friendship* that Elgar had a marked Worcestershire accent which he never wholly lost, although neither Sir Adrian Boult nor Mr Edgar Day, when questioned recently by the author, could recall any particular accent.

to have written the song (to Elgar's music) *My Heart* in ten minutes. In 1904 there was talk (as intermittently there was to be for thirty years) of Elgar writing an opera, and Benson was invited by Boosey & Hawkes, one of Elgar's publishers, to discuss the possibility of collaborating with Elgar on an opera based on 'the theme of Cleopatra'. Benson was assured by the firm that 'it would be highly lucrative' and that he was 'the only man in England etc'. Benson neither accepted nor refused the commission in principle, but he seems to have had doubts about his own ability to carry it out, and in the end nothing came of the suggestion. It was in fact the end of Benson's working relationship with Elgar, and his meeting with the family in Rome in 1907 seems to have marked the conclusion of what might have developed into a fruitful and interesting friendship.

Other relationships continued to prosper, however. Elgar had taken to addressing Jaeger as 'My dear Augustus darling'. On 21 December 1902 he ended a letter to him by sending 'much love to you all' and added, in brackets, 'I must read up Love in the Ency' (Elgar had acquired the *Encyclopaedia Britannica* the day before). Percy Young is surely right when he comments in his preface to his edition of Elgar's letters to Jaeger, *Letters to Nimrod from Edward Elgar*, that Elgar was writing 'without care for his posthumous literary reputation, or for aesthetic theories, and only for the eyes of an intimate'.

Amidst all the excitement in June of the forthcoming coronation, Dorabella had been summoned to Malvern by telegram. She found 'the poor little Lady' in bed, and Alice told her that having someone there to keep Elgar cheerful 'made her comparatively happy and carefree'. Alice was not so ill that she could not be left alone from time to time, however, so Elgar and his guest were able to go for bicycle rides and to sit by the Severn. The day after Dorabella left, Elgar wrote her one of his teasing, flirtatious notes: 'I rode 50 miles (who with?) yesterday ... lovely but lonely (I was solus).'

Dorabella was for ever receiving letters asking her to come and cheer up Elgar, and she attributes their getting on so well to her sensitivity to atmosphere and her ability to attune herself quickly to the mood of the moment, the implication being that all this was beyond the capabilities of Alice. Dorabella says there were times when Elgar was quiet and disinclined to talk. Then there were days when 'he longed for the open air, and we spent hours out on bicycles or walking on the hills or sitting in the woods or by the river'. Then he would tell her 'all sorts of interesting and amusing thing's and she kicks herself for being so silly as not to be able to remember any of it. 'I ought to have written down everything I could remember every evening,' she admits. 'I can only remember that the walks and rambles were a sheer delight. His witty and unexpected comments on things were a never-ending source of amusement, and, when he was feeling like it, he was funny beyond words.' But there were rarer occasions, she warns us, 'when he was frankly miserable and dispirited and bored'. These were when people had been 'provoking' and things had been 'tiresome'.

Rosa Burley was another of Elgar's constant cycling companions. 'Our cycling trips began in earnest after the production of Gerontius at Birmingham and there is no doubt that they did Edward an immense amount of good,' she tells us. Apparently there cannot have been 'a lane within twenty miles of Malvern that we did not ultimately find'. Alice's one attempt to learn to cycle had in fact been confined to mounting a tricycle, and she had even managed to fall off that. She seems to have been perfectly content to stay at home while Elgar sallied forth with unchaperoned young ladies; the behaviour of Dorabella and Rosa Burley in rambling around the West Country on their own with a married man was radical even by standards of liberation still to be set by the Bloomsbury group.

On one occasion, when the Elgars were still living at Craig Lea ('I *fear* they are going to build in front of us. If so, we're nomads once more,' Elgar had told Jaeger in June 1902), Dorabella was greeted by Alice with the words, 'Oh, *dear* Dora, what a *blessing* you've come! Now you will be ready to amuse dear Edward for a bit and I shall be able to get on with some work. I simply *must* go into Great Malvern and do some business.'

'It is terribly difficult to have to begin "amusing" anybody – like turning on a tap,' Dorabella wrote. 'But I usually managed to think of something that pleased him.' In fact, on returning from the inevitable cycling excursion, 'we generally came home happier than when we went out'.

Witty and amusing though Elgar may have been, Alice is made by Dorabella to sound like a pathetic wound-up little doll. Into the room she comes with a letter in her hand, and she says to Elgar, 'Dear darling, do you think you could write a letter to that *nice* Mr Smith?' When Elgar protests that he is too busy to write letters (he wrote hundreds during the course of his life), even to somebody whom Alice then describes as a 'nice *kind* little man,' she tries again, coaxing him this time with the truly unbelievable words, 'Yes, but sweet darling, I'm just going into Malvern and I could catch the early post and then he'd have it tomorrow morning.' Perhaps the most astonishing thing about this sickly dialogue so faithfully ascribed to Alice is that it should have received the positive and enthusiastic recognition of Carice; taking Dorabella's account of life in the Elgar household as a whole, one has to consider the possibility that in adult life Carice secretly, or at least subconsciously, enjoyed the posthumous portrait of her mother as a simpering, incompetent ninny incapable of ministering to the most elementary needs of a famous husband. Yet her endorsement of Dorabella's portrait compares strangely with her desire that a record should exist – a record she toyed with the idea of writing herself and then left to Percy Young to produce in *Alice Elgar: Enigma of a Victorian Lady* – 'of the great devotion and self-sacrifice of [Alice's] life ... which may have been equalled but can hardly have been surpassed in human history'.

After the May 1902 performance of *The Dream of Gerontius* at Düsseldorf, Strauss had made another speech, the Elgars had got to bed at 3 a.m. and Alice had written to her mother-in-law to tell her all about the visit. Replying on 23 June from the shop in the High Street where she had lived since 1863, watching the world go by and her son go up in it, Anne Elgar wrote, 'What can I say to him the dear one. I feel that he is some great historic person – I cannot claim a little bit of him now he belongs to the big world.' As far as her own family news was concerned, she told Alice, 'Dad is only poorly,' and gamely added, 'I am very well now.' Two months later she was dead.

Elgar's parents seem to have been content in their relatively humble home, and they retained, while all their children did reasonably well for themselves, an unaffected simplicity and a quiet pride in Edward's outstanding gifts. In the normal course of events parents do not expect to witness the ultimate achievements of their children, and Anne was fortunate, especially in view of Elgar's late development, to have survived long enough to have heard *The Dream of Gerontius* even if she was never to hear his concertos and symphonies. She undoubtedly inspired at least one of his formative works, *Caractacus*, and it is no dishonour to her that the cantata was dedicated to Queen Victoria rather than to herself.

It was a part of Elgar's destiny that he should all his life be ingratiating himself with the royal family. In a letter to Lady Mary Lygon in 1901, asking her to thank Elgar for the *Coronation Ode*, Queen Alexandra referred to him as 'the great master', and shortly afterwards her widowed sister-in-law, Princess Henry of Battenburg, Queen Victoria's youngest daughter (formerly Princess Beatrice), received him at Kensington Palace. He was presented to the princess by Sir Walter Parratt, and in view of all that the Master of the King's Music had done to further his career it is not surprising to find Elgar dedicating to him that year a set of five part-songs.

During the nineteenth century the oratorio had tended to take pride of place for composers instead of settings of the Mass; Dvořák had considered setting *The Dream of Gerontius* before Elgar did so, and for many Victorian composers the writing of oratorio had become almost a ritual genuflection to the stability of Victorian life symbolized by the dull, virtuous Anglican services packed out every Sunday by the gentry and their servants. It was therefore inevitable that Elgar should contemplate the writing of oratorio, and it was now that the concept of tackling a trilogy of oratorios took definite shape in his mind. He was to complete two great works in this field, *The Apostles* and *The Kingdom*; the third part of the trilogy, sometimes provisionally referred to as *The Last Judgement*, was begun but never finished. As always with Elgar, when he came to settle down to a definite project he would go back to his sketchbooks, and some of the themes that came to be used in *The Apostles* date from the 1880s. Elgar began concentrated work in 1902 on *The Apostles*, an act of some courage in view of the fact that *Gerontius* had still not been performed in London. But despite the disaster at Birmingham in 1900, he knew at least that he could be assured of a performance there for any major new work, and *The Apostles* came to be scheduled for the Birmingham Festival of October 1903. On 3 August 1902, in telling Jaeger he was engaged on the work, Elgar could not resist a sly dig at his friend's profession: 'My eyes are better, I think,' he told Jaeger, '& I'm working on the Apostles – which you will not like – it's too philosophical for your *cheap publisher's side* of your mind, but just the thing for the *real* A. J. J.'

Elgar prepared his own libretto from the Bible, and despite his professional background as an organist and choirmaster, the hours he had spent as a young man in Worcester Cathedral, his own practising Christianity and a sufficient personal religious interest and faith to want of his own free will to write so soon a second religious work, Dorabella asks us to believe that he was now realizing for the first time, in his forties, the marvels of the gospels and the historical and literary possibilities of the Bible:[4]

'I say, do you know that the Bible is the most wonderfully interesting book?' Elgar inquires of Dorabella.

'Yes,' Dorabella responds, 'I know it is.'

'What do you know about it?' Elgar asks. 'Oh, I forgot, perhaps you *do* know something about it. Anyway, I've been reading a lot of it lately and have been quite absorbed.'

Dorabella, brought up in a rectory, was soon recruited in the hunt for suitable texts, and turning up Psalm 85 found it was just what Elgar wanted. 'I think it is very astonishing,' she wrote, 'when one looks at the words which are set in *The Apostles* and sees the immense skill with which they have been selected and put together, that the work was mainly done by one who was finding out the beauties of the Bible for the first time.' More discerning scholars have been less enthusiastic about the outcome. In his *Portrait of Elgar*, Michael Kennedy goes so far as to suggest that some measure of respon-

---

4. Billy Reed, on the other hand, writes in his book *Elgar*, 'As is well known . . . [Elgar's] knowledge of the Bible and the Apocrypha was profound.'

sibility for the failure of *The Apostles* to grip the public is attributable to the fact that compilation of the libretto was a 'scissors-and-paste job'. In fact both *The Apostles* and *The Kingdom* have tended to find greater favour with musicians than with the public.

By 5 May 1903 Jaeger was writing to Elgar to tell him, 'Your work grows on me tremendously & by leaps and bounds. It's great stuff & quite wonderfully original & beautiful. Bless you, this is your finest work so far & your greatest.' On 21 June Alice wrote in her diary, 'Finished – all but the very end', and on 1 July Elgar was inquiring of Jaeger, 'Do you know any *clean* wholesome young man who wd like a couple of months in the country to copy my score as fast as I do it: he wd have to be in a lodging near & be able to write clearly & decipher my blind work – any *musician* can do that with prayer & fasting. I could not pay *much*. The Johnny might also – under my direction – make out the band parts with proper cues etc.' Within a couple of days Jaeger had found a young man, presumably clean and wholesome, but on 6 July he was told by Elgar that an amanuensis was no longer needed: 'It's too late to be of any use ... my fault, I ought to have asked sooner.' So what had happened in the space of five days to make two months work vanish into thin air? Elgar had earlier written to Jaeger, on 1 July, telling him (which could hardly be true) that he lived on £1 a week, so perhaps he had had second thoughts about paying 'the Johnny' anything at all.

On the day on which he was explaining it was 'too late to be of any use', he was in fact writing from Rodewald's cottage in Wales, where he had decided to stay in order to work on the orchestration himself. Within a few days he was writing to Jaeger again, to say he *must* come up and join them; 'it shall *cost you nothing*'. As further inducement, Elgar added, 'It is quite free & easy here – you dress as you like & do exactly what you please – no formality or any nonsense.' At first Jaeger protested that he could not afford the journey (perhaps because Elgar had failed to explain exactly why it would cost him nothing) but eventually he did join the party towards the end of the month.

Elgar was back at Craig Lea at the beginning of August, and the task of orchestration was completed on 17 August. The next day Jaeger wrote to Elgar confirming his original views, and by implication saying that he regarded *The Apostles* as a greater achievement than *The Dream of Gerontius*: 'The beauty of the music moves me to tears & the longer I study the work the more & the greater beauties I find,' he wrote. 'The Apostles are certainly your maturest & greatest work; the certainty of touch & style displayed throughout is wonderful, & the feeling of the most touching, heart-searching kind. But it is all so original, so individual & subjective that it will take the British Public 10 years to let it soak into its pachydermal mind ... As for the poor critics (the dullest among them I mean) they will be bewildered I fear.' Jaeger's letter goes on to provide firm evidence that by this time a trilogy had already been planned, which makes Dorabella's suggestion that Elgar had only just come to discover the Bible even less plausible. 'I believe that by the time you have completed Part III,' he went on, 'you will have given to the world the greatest oratorio since the Messiah, though this seems a rash statement to make, & time alone can prove the accuracy or futility of such a guess.'

A few days later Elgar was playing 'heaps of it' to Ivor Atkins and to Bantock. Stanford heard a choral rehearsal in September, and according to Elgar's report (of 17 September) to Jaeger, he was *enthusiastic ... telling people all round (Albani etc. etc.) of its and their glory!* Proofs were still being corrected at this time, and with the first performance due on 14 October, Elgar was complaining to Jaeger in September that Novello's men 'must be jolly slow'. Elgar began rehearsing the orchestra on 5 October and he conducted the first performance himself of what was, as far as the *Daily Telegraph* was concerned, 'perhaps the most remarkable work of the present century'. The century was in fact scarcely three years old, but perhaps they meant for the past hundred years. Arthur Johnstone of the *Manchester Guardian* still preferred *The Dream of Gerontius*, writing that *The Apostles* 'was of greater depth and significance but less perfectly finished'. Elgar was warmly applauded, but while the performance was no doubt a vast improvement on the première of *Gerontius*, English audiences came to reserve their real enthusiasm for that work and their polite respect for *The Apostles*. One technical detail that tends to militate against frequent performances of *The Apostles* is Elgar's decision to set the solo parts not only for the normal complement of soprano, contralto and tenor but for no less than three basses.

Towards the end of 1902 Elgar had begun to master a typewriter. With proofs of *The Apostles* arriving, Alice too thought that a typing machine, although she was rather slow on it, might prove a useful aid in the work she did on manuscripts to help her husband. Unable to resist patronizing her sixteen years after her death, Dorabella recorded a most unpleasant story. Alice's typing, she says, was 'not only slow at that time, dear thing! but rather inaccurate as well', so that passages from St John's gospel which should have contained exclamation marks turned out with pound sterling signs instead, and Elgar and Dorabella thought this so risible they actually reduced Alice to tears.

It was not long after this incident that Dorabella made one of her most successful attempts to usurp Alice's position as assistant to Elgar. She found Alice 'struggling' with a pile of press notices and offered to take over, and for the next fifteen years Dorabella was known as 'Keeper of the Archives' and found the work of pasting in Elgar's press cuttings 'tremendously interesting'. Having once again illustrated Alice's utter incompetence and her own managerial abilities, Dorabella completes her caricature of the composer's wife: 'The Lady, dear little person, was so delighted and so interested and would turn over the pages with almost childish pleasure, admiring the arrangement of the programmes and pictures with their gay spots of colour brightening the dull newspaper columns.'

Writing *The Apostles* had been a major undertaking, leaving Elgar, in September 1903, 'dead with fatigue'. Sketches had also been accumulating at the same time for a symphonic work, over which Elgar, notwithstanding the muddle he had already been in with Richter and the Leeds Festival, again got himself into an embarrassing situation. At some point he must have intimated that progress towards a symphony was a good deal further forward than composition of *The Apostles* could have allowed it to be, even had there been no other factor inhibiting the project, for in 1905 the Russian conductor at St Petersburg, Alexander Ziloti, was writing to Elgar to inquire 'if the symphony you speak of is in print, or if not how soon it will be'. He said he would not need the parts until early autumn but the score as soon as possible. Having fallen 'quite in love' with the *Enigma Variations* Ziloti even went so far as to assure Elgar he would take anything of his without seeing it. There was, however, nothing to see, at least nothing performable, and yet the tone of Ziloti's letter makes it quite clear he had been led to believe a symphony was all but written. It is hard to believe that on occasions like these Elgar deliberately set out to mislead or deceive, and if he did not, then pressure to produce a symphony (in 1903 he was forty-six) must have been growing to intolerable limits, to the point perhaps where in order to convince himself that he really was capable of writing a symphony he almost came to believe that he had virtually done so.

An explanation for Elgar's failure to produce a symphony before the age of fifty has been offered by Jerrold Northrop Moore. Discussing the matter at a meeting of the Royal Society of Arts on 13 December 1978 he said, 'The reason can be clearly seen in his earlier orchestral works. One and all, they lack a proper development section. Elgar was self-taught as a composer, and his natural expression was to extemporize variations on a single idea rather than to develop a combination of several ideas at great length. But the linchpin of the traditional symphony is its first movement sonata-allegro, and the centre of the sonata-allegro is its development.'[5]

The year that saw *The Apostles* come to fruition was an uncomfortable one in a number of ways. At the beginning of March, Elgar had had 'such awful

5. *Journal of the Royal Society of Arts*, March 1979.

sciatica' that he could hardly move, and his cycling had hit a rough patch: in April he reported to Schuster that a new bicycle had collapsed 'with ME ON IT', and in May Winifred Norbury's sister Florence had received perhaps slightly exaggerated news to the effect that Elgar had been knocked off his bicycle on to the pavement by a man in Upton-on-Avon and nearly killed. His fortunes revived when on 25 June, during the interval of a concert at the Albert Hall, he was presented to the king and the Prince of Wales, but it may have been a combination of physical pain and over-work that had caused him, in April, to make what was surely a strange error of judgement. In a genuine and perfectly sensible attempt to ease his mind over financial worries, firm proposals were drawn up by Adolf Brodsky, the Russian violinist, who was also principal of the Royal Manchester College of Music, for the creation of a new post specially for Elgar, that of professor of instrumentation and compo-sition. It was made clear to Elgar that it was his name they wanted to secure, for a fee of £400 a year, and that there would be no question of his having to undertake any formal teaching. 'It is your personality we want to attract,' Brodsky wrote to Elgar. 'Your name would give glory to the Institution & attract, I am sure, all the talent of the country.' Elgar was simply to criticize the students' compositions 'and develop their taste by which to be guided when composing'. It was an honourable offer, £400 a year was well worth having, and the post would have carried the title and prestige of a pro-fessorship. His decision to turn down the offer is hard to understand, though perhaps the explanation is that in spite of Brodsky's assurance that Elgar would not be tied to any formal teaching he may have developed over twenty years at The Mount an ingrained loathing of pupils in any shape or form.

The turn of the century coincided with the beginnings of the heyday of popular journalism (the *Daily Mail* had been launched in 1896). Newsprint was cheap, the style of the day was loquacious, and newspaper readers were assumed to have an insatiable interest in the comings and goings of every traveller on board every ocean liner, and every actor staying at every pro-vincial hotel. A week before the first performance of *The Apostles*, the *Sketch* ran a two-page feature on Elgar, complete with a dozen photographs, all of them carefully posed and all designed to show that, when at home, great men behave just like anyone else, doing perfectly ordinary things like smoking a pipe, riding a bicycle, playing a round of golf and composing an oratorio.

Referring to Elgar's boyhood, the *Sketch* writer recalled his brief apprentice-ship to a solicitor: 'Law, however, could not claim the soul which the Muses had marked for their own,' the readers were told, and there was much else in similar vein. The interview is interesting because it records Elgar's 'immovable opinion that his first real introduction to the large musical public was through the kindness of Mr W. C. Stockley, the pioneer of orchestral music in the Midlands, to whom Dr Elgar expresses sincere and lasting gratitude'. Stockley, it will be recalled, was the choirmaster Jaeger considered ought to have been boiled and served on toast for his efforts over the first performance of *The Dream of Gerontius*, and Elgar's tribute to Stockley's earlier patronage, like his refusal ever to blame Richter for the Birmingham disaster, is a side of Elgar's nature worthy of the greatest respect.

The *Sketch* reporter gives us a contemporary picture of Elgar's physical appearance: 'With his slight physique, his brown hair, cut short, and his heavy moustache, his quick, nervous movements and quick speech, Dr Elgar gives no hint of the popular notion of a musician, and might rather pass for an Army officer in mufti than anything else.'

Nine days after the première of *The Apostles*, Alice recorded in her diary Elgar's worry and disappointment over the 'finance side of new work', despite the fact that he had negotiated with the secretary of the Birmingham Choral Society the enormous fee of £1,000. Even so, Elgar may have begun to regret turning down £400 a year from the Royal Manchester College of Music. A month later, he had an even more dramatic cause for regret. Early in November he received what he was later to describe to Jaeger as a cheerful postcard from Rodewald, saying he thought he had influenza but was over the fever and hoped to be all right soon – and that he was looking forward to seeing Elgar on 14 November. Shortly after receiving his postcard Elgar heard that Rodewald was unconscious – this was on 7 November – and that four doctors had pronounced his recovery impossible. 'It came as the most awful shock to me,' he wrote to Jaeger. 'It is too awful & my heart is quite broken.' It was indeed a shock, particularly as Rodewald was only forty-three. Elgar hesitated in Malvern for forty-eight hours, and on the morning of 9 November he travelled to Liverpool where he wrote to Jaeger from the North Western Hotel shortly after Rodewald had 'passed away quietly' at 12.30 p.m. 'I am heart-broken & cannot believe it. God bless him. He was the dearest, kindest, *best* friend I ever had. I don't know how I write or what I've written – forgive me. I am utterly broken up.'

It has to be remembered that Elgar had known Rodewald for only about four years. No doubt he had been a good and kind friend, but the idea that he was the 'dearest, kindest and *best*' friend he had ever had was somewhat tendentious, and in view of all the encouragement and constructive criticism he had received from Jaeger it was perhaps tactless to start constructing a friendship league. Schuster, whose emotional reaction to the death of a male friend Elgar may have guessed he could count upon, was the next to be informed of the details of the drama. Elgar wrote to him on 10 November on his return to

1. Buckler's watercolour of the cottage at Lower Broadheath where Edward Elgar was born. His parents, William and Anne, are shown strolling in the garden with their eldest daughter, Lucy, and in the porch with her nurse is their second daughter, Polly.

2. Elgar (on the right) at the age of seven, with his younger brother, Joe.

3. A studio photograph of Elgar at the age of eleven.

4. The music shop at No. 10 High Street, Worcester.

5. Elgar's mother at the age of about sev

6. Edward and Alice Elgar, three or four years after their marriage in 1889.

7. Polly Grafton, Elgar's second sister

William Eller's snapshot of Elgar just as he finished orchestrating *The Dream of Gerontius* 3 August 1900.

Elgar with his father in 1904, after he had cycled the twenty miles from Malvern to ·msgrove to bring the news of his knighthood.

The German conductor, Hans Richter, who gave the successful first performance of the *gma Variations* in 1899.

The *Enigma Variations*:
the 'friends pictured within'

11. II (H.D.S-P.) *Hew Steuart-Powell*

12. III (R.B.T.) *Richard Townsend*

13. IV (W.M.B.) *William Baker*

14. V (R.P.A.) *Richard Arnold*

15. VI (Ysobel) *Isabel Fitton*

16. VII (Troyte) *Troyte Griffith*

17. VIII (W.N.) *Winifred Norbury*

18. IX (Nimrod) *August Jaeger*

19. X (Dorabella) *Dora Penny*

20. XI (G.R.S.) *George Sinclair with Dan*

21. XII (B.G.N.) *Basil Nevinson*

22. XIII (* * *) *Lady Mary Lygon*

23. Severn House in Netherhall Gardens, Hampstead.

24. Carice at the age of about sixteen, with her pet rabbit.

25. Alice, photographed at Severn House, at the age of about sixty-five.

26. A tea party in the garden studio at The Hut, Frank Schuster's house near Bray. Schuster is standing on the right, next to Alice and Elgar; on the left is Claude Phillips, Keeper of the Wallace Collection (the couple in the centre have not been identified).

27. An unusually informal snapshot of Elgar, enjoying a cigarette at The Hut.

28. With Billy Reed in the late twenties.

29. With Bernard Shaw at Malvern in 1929.

30. At the Three Choirs Festival in 1933 with Percy Hull, organist of Hereford cathedral. Elgar is in court dress, wearing the Broad Ribbon, Star and Badge of the GCVO, and round his neck the Order of Merit, his baronetcy badge and the Belgian Ordre de la Couronne.

31. Enjoying a glass of wine with Carice and Fred Gaisberg at a garden party and looking, as Osbert Sitwell said, 'every inch a personification of Colonel Bogey'.

Malvern. 'O my God,' Schuster was told, 'it is too awful ... I could not rest &
fled to Liverpool yesterday only to be told all was over ... this is all too
cruel and horrible ... I can only weep over the awfulness of it.' But that letter
was to prove a mere dress rehearsal for the letter Elgar sent to Jaeger the
next day, 11 November, in which he relayed the truly traumatic details of the
night he spent in Liverpool after hearing that Rodewald had died.

First of all he did not go to Rodewald's house but to the home of a friend
in the same street. There he was told the news, and 'broke down and went out
– *and it was night* to me. What I did, God knows. I know I walked for miles
in strange ways – I know I had some coffee somewhere – where I cannot tell.
I know I went & looked at the Exchange where he had taken me – but it was
all dark, dark to me although light enough to the busy folk around. I thought
I wd go home – but could not – so I stayed at the hotel.' Having booked in
for the night, Elgar ordered dinner and wine, 'and I believe ate all thro' the
menu', excusing such banal behaviour by explaining that had he been less
stricken he would not have eaten – and he did order the meal 'in a dazed way'.
Fortunately, having dinner 'probably saved my life I think – but I lived on as
an automaton – & did everything without thought – then I went to my room
and wept for hours – yesterday I came home without seeing anyone & am
now a wreck & a broken-hearted man'. Elgar then told Jaeger not to send
him 'any more score yet', for the reason that he used to pass every sheet to
Rodewald as he finished it and heard his criticisms, and altered passages to
please him. Michael Kennedy believes the score referred to was *The Apostles*
and if so it was presumably the proofs being prepared for publication. 'I can't
tell you what I feel,' Elgar concluded, 'but I have lost my best & dearest – I
thank heaven we all had that bit of time together in Wales; you know a little
of what he was.'

Throughout this painful episode Elgar portrayed himself with studious self-
dramatization as one suffering a degree of grief more normally reserved for
the death of a spouse, a lover or a child, and one cannot help feeling that just
as it is possible for an immature person to fall in love with the idea of love,
Elgar was mourning more over the concept of death than over the death of an
individual. One might also ask where Alice was while all this was going on; not
by his side, at any rate. It may or may not be significant that the friend being
so extravagantly wept over died at exactly the age that little Joe, Elgar's
second brother, would then have been had he lived, and Elgar's grief was
perhaps a drama played out in the face of death itself, the final catastrophe
with which as a boy he had never come to terms. He had certainly not come to
terms with the concept of death when he heard of Rodewald's fatal illness.
'I could not rest & fled to Liverpool,' he told Schuster. This is simply not true,

for he had waited two whole days before travelling to Liverpool, arriving, as perhaps he half hoped he would, when all was over and when he would not be obliged to visit the death-bed.

At the end of November the Elgars left England for what was intended to be a three-month working holiday. This time they gave their beloved Germany a miss and decided to see what effect a quite new environment might have on Elgar's spirits, downcast as they were by the death of Rodewald and by his inability to make any real progress with a symphonic work. The unprecedented honour of a three-day festival at Covent Garden devoted entirely to Elgar's music had been arranged for the following March, the king and queen had agreed to attend, and a new work for the occasion was called for; this was another excuse for a change of scene, and they went first to Bordighera in Italy, where Alice had first been taken by her mother in 1882 when the two of them went abroad following the death of Alice's brother Frederick. Although Elgar admitted the place was lovely – he wrote to Schuster on 8 December, shortly after their arrival, to tell him so – he complained that it was 'too cockney'; he wanted something either more Italian or more civilized, Bordighera being too 'betwixt & between', full, as he told Troyte Griffith in a later letter, of English nursery-maids and with the feel about it of Malvern. Nevertheless he had already found 'a lovely little place' a mile up a mule track that he had set his heart – probably not too seriously – on buying. He had acquired a donkey called Grisia, and he and Alice were taking their meals out of doors in the sun. They were both, he told Schuster, riotously well, and in the first flush of holiday enthusiasm he announced they would never be coming home.

Before long they moved on to Alassio, where they had taken a villa; this was a town, Elgar told Troyte Griffith, that was 'really Italian'. The weather unfortunately was bad, but they had the house warm, and were enjoying the amenities of two servants and splendid cooking. Elgar had a study 'looking out over the old town with the sea beyond', with 'citrons, lemons & all sorts of flowers in the garden'. Like many a casual English traveller before and since, he did not trouble to sleep under a mosquito net and got badly bitten. Otherwise, all was well: 'we are really "having a life" here & everything is lovely except the rain,' he assured Troyte, and in a postscript he noted that the cook was a 'clinker', and he himself was 'delirious!'.

The bad weather persisted. On Boxing Day Elgar was writing home on business matters and noted, 'We have a nice house here & Italian servants & want nothing for the moment except fine weather; at present it is beneath notice.' Elgar informed Schuster early in January 1904 that he had written to Novello to say 'the symphony is impossible', but that he had 'partly promised' a concert overture for the Covent Garden festival – 'In the South ... or some better title if you can suggest one'.

By 18 January Elgar was concerning himself over details for the festival programme, suggesting all sorts of items to Schuster for inclusion, noting the length of time each took to play and pressing for Clara Butt to sing a song called *The Wind at Dawn*, as it 'would be novel and give her something more to do'. On 20 January Elgar reported to Troyte that he had a cold but was 'working away'; as to future plans, they had the villa until the middle of February and he had to be back in London on 1 March. He had met the Dean of Westminster on the top of a mountain and had taken (shades of his previous conduct towards other people's dogs in Worcester) to hitting cats with shoes fired from a catapult; no doubt Elgar had devised this amusing pastime to ease the frustration brought on by 'eleven days in the house with bitter east winds'. There had also been visits by the doctor to attend to 'crippling rheumatism and colds'. These details were related to Schuster on 28 January, six days after an event had occurred to make a premature retreat respectable. On 21 January Elgar had received a letter from the comptroller of the Prince of Wales's household inviting him to dine at Marlborough House on 3 February. It was just the excuse he needed to get away from a holiday home that had lost its charms. Elgar had written to Jaeger on 3 January, marking part of his letter *'Private'*: 'Now,' he said, 'there's nobody in my precious confidence more than you: this visit has been, is, artistically a complete *failure* & I can do nothing: we have been *perished* with cold, rain & gales five fine days have we had & three of those were perforce spent in the train. The symphony will not be written in this sunny land ... I have never regretted anything more than this horribly disappointing journey: wasting time, money & temper.' Alice lost no time in explaining to the local people that they were leaving not because Elgar had been invited to dinner by the Prince of Wales but because her husband 'had command to meet the King'. But in case Schuster should think he was returning early merely to rub shoulders with royalty Elgar assured him, 'You see I *only* want to go home to finish my work. I cannot work anywhere else.'

Soon after his return home he would need to give serious consideration to finding a new house, as the lease on Craig Lea was due to expire in September. At the end of October 1903 he had already given up Birchwood, a piece of news he conveyed to Jaeger in reply to a letter in which Jaeger had enclosed an insect, with the comment, 'I found this BUG, with letter attached, in my letter. Surely it is meant for *another* boy?' 'You are right the Bug was not for you,' Elgar replied, '& his pretty body is about done for in the post. Never mind, I'll catch another – altho' this year has not been good for flies & stinging beasts. We gave up Birchwood last week for ever! The weather has been too bad really for it to be of use & my regrets, which were bitter, are assuaging themselves.' These sound like brave words. On 27 August he had written to Jaeger, 'You saw my dear place & I hate having to give it up. My life is one continual giving up of little things which I love ... I do like my *little* toys.' Two days later he had reverted to the subject: 'As to Birchwood: we give it up on occ. of the difficulty of keeping it aired etc ... I would like to end my days there – only it's too remote for my wife & Carice is now growing up! & must be in the loathed world. Alas! alas!' Sir Arnold Bax tells us in his autobiography that it seemed that Elgar's days at Birchwood 'counted as the happiest in his tormented life' and that he 'kept a special regard for anyone who had seen him in those surroundings'.

Jaeger seems to have been frequently in Elgar's thoughts, for on 6 February 1903 Elgar had written offering to give him his old 'Bike' as he was changing it for 'a free-wheel'. It was apparently a three-year-old Royal Sunbeam and the only scratches on it had been made by railway porters. 'Gosh! Augustus darling! you might write some music on it!!' Elgar gushed on his new typewriter. Ten days later he wrote, 'The machine – known affectionately in the family since its birth as "Mr Phoebus" goes to-day – packed by experts,' but the bike's train journey was not to be a smooth one. On 26 February Elgar explained it had been 'removed from here *last Monday week*, ordered to be packed in crate & forwarded at once. I learn to-day that it was sent on *Saturday* last & now you say it wasn't packed. Oh! Malvern tradesmen.' Elgar took the opportunity, in that letter, of telling Jaeger not to expect too much at first, and above all not to give up 'under a month's hard work at it'. Such was the craze for cycling at that time that Elgar reverted to the subject on 11 March, even offering to pay for Jaeger to take half a dozen lessons, and eleven days later he was back on the subject again. 'The best way to learn to Bike,' he said, 'is to have a good strong strap round your waist & let your coacher grab that: that's how I learnt.'

On his return from Italy Elgar was soon caught up in a social whirl. At Marlborough House he sat between Lord Howe and Lord Suffield (the one talked to him about music, the other, a Lord-in-Waiting-in-Ordinary, about horses) and there he was presented to Prince Christian of Denmark (King Edward's son-in-law) and to Prince Louis of Battenberg. After dinner the royal party went on to a smoking concert where Elgar conducted the *Pomp and Circumstance March* No. 1, which the king, who had been dining with the Prince of Wales too, asked him to repeat. The next day Elgar signed the visitors' books at Buckingham Palace and Marlborough House. He had obviously made such a favourable impression on the royal family that on 14

March, the first day of the three-day Covent Garden festival in his honour, he was invited to a levée at Buckingham Palace. The king and queen sat through *Gerontius* the first night and *The Apostles* the second, and on the third night the queen went alone to hear a programme consisting of the early overture *Froissart*, selections from *Caractacus* and, to end the first half, the *Enigma Variations*. Elgar then conducted the first performance of the work he had written in Italy, the new concert overture *In the South* (which was dedicated to Schuster), and was sent for by the queen to be congratulated. The programme continued with Clara Butt singing not *The Wind at Dawn* but *Sea Pictures* (she would have had even more to do had she not priced herself out of *Gerontius*), the overture *Cockaigne* and the *Pomp and Circumstance Marches* Nos 1 and 2. The Hallé Orchestra played, the Manchester Chorus sang and, except for *In the South*, Hans Richter conducted. The programme note remarked that 'Dr Hans Richter having, with his Manchester orchestra and chorus, devoted special attention to Dr Elgar's works, a perfect ensemble may be anticipated.'

When Elgar got around to writing to Richter eleven days after the festival 'to thank you from my heart for your conducting of my music at Covent Garden', he singled out the *Enigma Variations* as having been '*marvellously*' played. 'I have never heard them better,' he wrote, 'and "Cockaigne" also.' He ended, 'Without you the thing could not have been done at all, and with you it was a great artistic success and your presence gave it a *dignity* which would otherwise have been wanting.'

Jaeger was so hard up that he had written to Elgar to ask him to 'remember poor Nim' should he find he had any tickets he did not need. 'I really can't afford to pay,' he wrote, '& I *should* at least like to hear the overture [*In the South*]. You have no poorer friend than yours ever.' He had been asked to write a book on Elgar, and on 27 February he had written to Dorabella to ask if she would help him; nothing seems to have come of the project, but at least he did get to hear his hero's new work, and he reported to Dorabella that *In the South* was '*beautiful* and new, & shows a surer touch than almost anything else I know of E. E.'s'. He had been given tickets for *The Apostles* too, which impressed him tremendously, 'though nothing "came off" as the composer meant it'. He thought the acoustic defects of the 'theatre' were too great. But on the social side Jaeger realized that all was perfection: 'Elgar had a rare time,' he told Dorabella, 'and everything was splendid. Ask dear little Mrs E. She must have been in the 7th Heaven of Happiness. *Such* swells they met, from the Queen downwards. A great time for E. E., & some of us who have believed in him & fought for him (I had to fight hard for him at Novello's) are happy.'

The piano-tuner's son who had been born in a country cottage and brought up over a shop was now being swept into the arms of the establishment. Thanks to Stanford's nomination Elgar had been elected the previous year to the Athenaeum, and now he was to meet the prime minister, Arthur Balfour, at the home of his friend Lord Northampton. In June, Durham University decided to confer on him an honorary doctorate of music, and while Elgar was in the north receiving the degree a letter arrived in Malvern from Mr Balfour containing the offer of yet another honour. Alice, who had stayed at home, must have recognized by the envelope where the letter had come from, and could have been in little doubt of its contents; she placed it in the safe. When Elgar got home Alice told him the letter was there, and recorded in her diary that Elgar said, 'with such a light in his face, "has it come?" but then thought it wd only be about copyright'. Prime Ministers are not much given to communicating with composers on the subject of copyright, and after all the fêting of the past year Elgar was probably less than surprised to find that the letter from Downing Street contained the offer of a knighthood. 'Both very pleased,' Alice's diary tells us. 'D. G.'

Elgar was eventually to be festooned with honours (the Order of Merit, three knighthoods and a baronetcy from his own king and country alone) and some unlikely views have been put forward concerning his reaction to the honours system in general and to his own receipt of recognition in particular. In his book *Portrait of Elgar*, Michael Kennedy says 'his natural inclination was to refuse honours', although it is hard to see where the evidence exists to support such a statement. Much has been made of the idea that Elgar only accepted honours to please Alice, a theory launched in 1920 by the theoretically anonymous author of Alice's obituary in *The Times*, who was in fact A. H. Fox Strangways, editor of *Music and Letters* (according to Carice he wrote the obituary notice at Elgar's 'special request'[6]). It stated that Elgar 'broke his resolve to remain "Mr Elgar" all his days, and took whatever honours came his way for her sake'. Even for a man as ambitious as Elgar, to make a positive resolve not to receive a knighthood before one had even been offered would have displayed a conceit of unbelievable magnitude. Nevertheless, the uncomfortable fact is that that was what the obituary said, and if Elgar did sanction such a remark it was a regrettable dissimulation on his part. So far as his attitude to the majority of his honours was concerned, it should be noted that prior to Alice's death he had received only a knight bachelorhood and, in 1911, the Order of Merit (at that time a relatively new addition to the honours system – it had been instituted by Edward VII in 1901), a mark of personal esteem by the king himself and one of the very few honours in the personal

6. *Alice Elgar: Enigma of a Victorian Lady.*

gift of the sovereign. So far as the OM was concerned, Elgar was in no doubt about its significance – the Order is restricted to a mere two dozen members – and on 11 July 1911, writing to Troyte Griffith from the Royal Societies Club, he revealed his attitude explicitly: 'I wish you wd write to the Worcester paper & say a little what the Order of M. really is! Some of the locals think it is a sort of degradation & quite unworthy of me. I see in the festival list ... they have put it *after* Mus.D. etc. At the Investiture Sir A. Trevelyan & I were marshalled next GCB & *before* GCMG (which is Ld Beauchamp's highest distinction!) of course before GCSI etc. It was very nice.' (Elgar was actually incorrect about Lord Beauchamp's 'highest distinction'. He was made a Knight Commander of St Michael and St George in 1899, on his appointment as governor of New South Wales, but he was never advanced to Knight Grand Cross.) The intricacies of the honours system apart, Elgar's letter hardly displays the indifference of a man whose natural inclination is to refuse honours; it is more the fussing of a provincial worthy who has thoroughly brushed up on his personal knowledge of the order of precedence and has a very clear idea of his own place within it. When he was offered the OM, Alice herself informed Troyte Griffith the very next day that it gave Edward the greatest pleasure: 'You know that this is the only thing that really delights him,' she added. Elgar certainly did not hesitate before accepting it, writing to Lord Knollys, private secretary to King George V, the very day the offer arrived, to 'accept with the greatest gratitude the Order of Merit which His Majesty the King has done me the honour to wish to confer upon me'. He went on to say, 'If it would be convenient, if not unusual, I should be much obliged if you would be so good as to convey to His Majesty an expression of my deep appreciation of the distinction and my loyalty and devotion now and at all times.'

After Alice's death, when the acceptance of honours could hardly have affected her happiness one way or the other, Elgar accepted from the state a baronetcy in spite of having no heir, and from the king personally the KCVO and eventually the unique distinction for an artist, advancement to GCVO. It is true that when offered the KCVO by George V in 1927 he wrote to Alice Stuart-Wortley (by then Lady Stuart of Wortley), 'H. M. has offered me the wretched *KCVO* (!!!) which awful thing I must accept! Alas!', though this sounds less like genuine distaste than a playful attempt at false modesty, commonly made to close friends by recipients of honours. (It was also a breach of confidence: the award was not announced officially until New Year's Day, 1928.) When Sir Walter Parratt died in 1924 Elgar actually wrote to the king's private secretary proposing himself for the vacant post of Master of the King's Music, and when, at about the same time, there was talk of a peerage for Elgar, he wrote to Lady Stuart, 'I fear it is hopeless but it wd please me.'

The idea that Elgar accepted honours simply to please Alice may have been compounded by some rather muddled accounts of various insignia being buried with her. Dorabella says that Carice told her the ribbon of the OM was buried with her mother, together with Elgar's court sword and the diploma of the Institut de France, and that Elgar later had trouble replacing the ribbon when he needed to wear the OM on 'the next state occasion'. If the story is true, it does seem significant that Elgar allowed only the ribbon of the OM to go into the grave, not the beautiful and valuable Order itself. It also seems rather unlikely that a man so acutely conscious of the niceties of the honours system and so fond of dressing up would not have realized that he could never wear the OM again without the ribbon, and that a letter to Buckingham Palace applying for a second ribbon might be regarded as rather odd. Anyone who doubts that Elgar took a personal pride in his honours should consult a photograph of him now kept at the Birthplace (Plate 30), for which he posed in 1933 at the Three Choirs Festival in court dress with the Broad Ribbon, Star and Badge of the GCVO, and no less than three decorations slung round his neck, the OM, his baronetcy badge and the Belgian Ordre de la Couronne.

Elgar's old father was now too frail to live on alone in the High Street at Worcester and he had gone to be looked after by Polly in Bromsgrove. Elgar rode over to Stoke to tell him the news about his knighthood, and one of Elgar's nieces, May, had a loaded camera handy and took a photograph of father and son (Plate 9). William, white haired and with a handkerchief in his hand, is seated beside Edward who is standing against a backdrop of bracken, all four buttons on his tight country jacket tightly buttoned up, his hand behind his back. On 5 July Elgar struggled into dress court to see how it looked, and well may he have taken extra care over his sartorial appearance, for he was, after all, about to present himself to a perfectionist in the matter of dress, a king who once remarked, 'I thought everyone must know that a *short* jacket is always worn with a silk hat at a private view in the morning.' But his receipt of the accolade seems to have gone off much as everyone else's, with King Edward saying to him, 'Very pleased to see you here, Sir Edward.' (The depth of Elgar's friendship with King Edward has been much exaggerated: he was entertained by the king and liberally encouraged and patronized by him, but by no stretch of the imagination could Elgar ever have claimed to have been a personal friend.)

Elgar's knighthood was celebrated by a move to an even bigger and more expensive house. On 1 July the family was installed at Plas Gwyn, now 27

Hampton Park Road, a mile east from the centre of Hereford. 'We are far from settled yet,' Elgar reported to Jaeger on 11 July, 'but it is very lovely here ... you must come soon.' By the end of the month, he was 'woefully short of money' and was contemplating taking violin pupils again. But, he explained to his 'dear Jagpot', 'as I have not touched it for so long, I should have to begin once more with elementary ones! Such is life & I hate, loathe & detest it.' Which was not a very cheerful start to life in a house described by Percy Young in *Elgar: OM* as a miniature mansion. It stood on four floors and probably contained ten bedrooms – today it is divided into four large flats. A wrought-iron gate at the entrance to the short drive has replaced the wooden gate the Elgars knew, and the drive is more overhung than when they lived there. Otherwise the house has altered externally very little since their time. It was built in about 1840, in a distinctive Germanic style which may have appealed to Elgar, and a Regency veranda covered with climbing roses and honeysuckle shaded a substantial study with high moulded ceilings. At the end of the drive, just past the imposing steps leading to the front door at the side of the house, stood an out-building known as 'the Ark', where Elgar played at chemistry and one day managed to bring about a substantial explosion. The Ark survived, however, and has now been shifted behind the house, where it serves as a garage.

One of the first visitors to Plas Gwyn ('the White House') was Dorabella, who was greeted by Alice with the rhetorical question, 'I think great music can be written here, dear Dora, don't you.' By the time they left, in 1912, Elgar had composed his second oratorio, *The Kingdom*, the *Introduction and Allegro* for strings, both symphonies and the Violin Concerto. Not by any means all the work on these compositions was carried out at Plas Gwyn itself, but Elgar's tenancy of the house certainly coincided with one of the most concentrated and rewarding periods of his life. He worked at Plas Gwyn using a small mahogany dining table as a writing desk, and Dorabella has left us an account of the way he functioned. 'I once watched him orchestrating something,' she writes, 'the 24-stave music paper at the bottom of his right hand, the first finger at a bar on the lowest line, the right hand and pen running up to the top to do a passage for the flutes, coming down to put something for the brass, lower for the harp, and below, a whole cascade of notes for the violins.'

Dorabella also tells us, which was true, that Plas Gwyn was 'larger and far more comfortable than Craig Lea', just as Craig Lea had been larger and far more comfortable than Forli, and she gives the lie to Elgar's plea of poverty to Jaeger by noting that, coincidentally with the move to Hereford, royalties were coming in more freely 'and ends were being met more easily'. A title, a large house and an adequate income did not however prevent Alice acquiring what Elgar used to refer to as her 'stony image' look, her face, so Dorabella remembered it, 'becoming set in an odd sort of way, her large blue eyes staring straight in front of her into vacancy'.

Carice told Dorabella that while living at Craig Lea and at Plas Gwyn it was difficult for her to find out about business affairs as 'no mention was ever made in a diary of anything disagreeable or vexing'. It seems not to have occurred to Carice that there is no reason why business affairs should necessarily be disagreeable or vexing, or even entered in a diary – in a well-adjusted family they are openly talked about. The pattern of behaviour the Elgars seem to have adopted was for Alice to clam up and for Elgar to moan in letters to friends. Only a week after telling Jaeger he was woefully short of money and hated, loathed and detested life, Elgar was writing again to say it was all very well to talk to him about writing symphonies '& all the things I *want* to do, but tell me what & who is going to keep a roof over our heads. Nobody thinks of that.' All this talk of hating life was coming from a man whose life had been transformed in the space of five years: since 1899 he had produced the *Enigma Variations*, *The Dream of Gerontius* and *The Apostles*, and from being known by merely a handful of discerning musicians in 1899, he had by 1904 had his music patronized by the royal family and performed at a three-day festival at Covent Garden, and seen his labours rewarded by a knighthood. His reputation overseas was advancing almost as rapidly as it was at home: *Sea Pictures* and the *Enigma Variations* were being played in Boston and Chicago; *Gerontius* had been heard in the USA for the first time in 1903, and performances of it were also mounted in Danzig, Darmstadt and Vienna; within twelve months of its première *The Apostles* had been sung at Rotterdam and Mainz; in June 1904 Fritz Kreisler was asking if there was a violin concerto in existence; and in the autumn of that year the *Variations* were to be played in Russia. All this was happening without benefit of wireless, television or the cinema. Not content with bemoaning his fate to Jaeger, Elgar decided to enlist the sympathy of Lord Northampton, who replied on 15 August from his Tudor home at Compton Wynyates, 'You *must* realise that you have in you a special power of bringing upon others the strongest influence for good. You have already used that power in a most remarkable degree. You have moved men's souls to the highest truths of Christianity ... I can only think of you as a musical apostle, given one of God's greatest gifts.'

Northampton's testimonial evidently did not satisfy him, for in September he decided to see how much sympathy he could extract from Schuster: 'I am still very low,' he wrote, '& see nothing in the future but a black stone wall against which I am longing to dash my hand – and that's all; a pitiful end for a "promising" youth.' Elgar's melancholic moods bore so little relationship to external signs of personal achievement, recognition and friendship that they have to be regarded as the irrational and painful outpourings of a depressive. Signs of goodwill towards him were abundant all his life, but never to any lasting effect. On 7 August, for instance, Jaeger had written to say, 'Dear old Sanford [a professor at Yale University who admired Elgar's music] is in town as nice as ever. He has a wonderful upright Steinway piano for you ... Don't rub him up the wrong way. He is a good fellow at heart & means you well. Would do *anything* for you in fact.' 'I hope I may see him & have telegraphed this a.m. I am terrified at accepting the piano,' was Elgar's response.

Elgar could often be alarmingly distant and cold. When Arthur Johnstone, music critic of the *Manchester Guardian* and one of Elgar's earliest and most consistently astute and loyal advocates, died that December at the age of forty-three, Elgar was unmoved: 'Yes, it is dreary about poor Johnstone,' he commented to Jaeger. 'One of the best fellows & *the* best critic we had.' When not emotionally involved with someone who had died, even though that person may have been a good friend in every respect, Elgar appeared to want to know as little about death as possible.

A letter Elgar wrote to Troyte Griffith on 12 December ended with one short and ominous sentence: 'I have accepted the Chair.' Having declined a professorship at Manchester only two years before, Elgar now, after a great deal of hesitation, accepted a new professorship of music especially endowed for him at Birmingham University. Once again, his benefactors' idea was to help relieve his constant financial anxieties, real or imagined, and to obtain for themselves the prestige his name would carry. Adolf Brodsky, principal of the Royal Manchester College, whose offer had so recently been declined, generously showed no resentment, and the scene seemed set fair for Elgar to become a professor and to deliver his inaugural lecture on 16 March the following year. Elgar asked that if he found his duties at Birmingham interfered with composition his tenure of the chair should be terminated after say three years; in the event he gave eight lectures and extricated himself after only two years from one of the most painful entanglements he ever got himself into.

Another characteristic waste of emotional energy was about to unnerve Elgar prior to delivering his first Birmingham lecture. Up to this point, the record of Stanford's friendship for Elgar and his practical and wholeheartedly enthusiastic professional support speaks for itself. But on 27 December something very odd happened. Alice records in her diary that Elgar received from Stanford 'an odious letter'. It is inconceivable that Alice fabricated the entry, the letter does not appear to have survived and if it was really odious it would have been natural for Elgar to destroy it. On the other hand, a letter which might to an independent observer have deserved a less drastic adjective than odious could have seemed so to Alice (and to Elgar) had it contained even the mildest criticism or apparently inadvertent or tactless comment. Whatever the contents of the letter, the two friends ceased to communicate for the next twenty years, and when they did resume tepid relations they both, like a pair of preparatory schoolboys who have had a tiff, professed ignorance about the cause of their quarrel. The real cause of their rift has remained a mystery, put down as a rule to a mere clash of temperaments. However, a clue to the nature of the 'odious' letter and the twenty-year separation that followed may perhaps be found in Arthur Benson's diaries, for the period of the *Coronation Ode*. According to David Newsome in his biography of Benson, 'Originally the invitation to write the music was extended to C. V. Stanford who objected to Novello as the publisher. He was blowed if he would write a line of music for the blackguard,' he told Arthur. 'He thinks they will come a cropper by miserliness soon; they have alienated Elgar.' Elgar, however, accepted the commission, and – according to Walter Parratt – Stanford was deeply offended that none of his music was played at the Coronation – 'simply furious ... He considers himself so much the first of all British musicians that this is to him a deadly rankling insult.'

If this is true, we may conclude that the 'odious' contents of the letter from Stanford to Elgar were occasioned by a sense of grievance for which Elgar was in no way responsible, and which had been building up for a couple of years. Elgar must have known that Stanford had turned down the original commission to write an ode, and that he himself was only Sir Walter Parratt's second choice, which no doubt rankled with Elgar. By the time *The Apostles* had been performed in 1903 Stanford must also have realized that his day as England's leading composer was over, while Elgar was far too insecure ever to be able to deal generously with a man he had overtaken. Bearing all these factors in mind, it seems reasonable to conclude that the famous separation between Elgar and Stanford arose out of professional rivalry and was simply kept on the boil by two exceptionally touchy people.

However upset Elgar may have been on 27 December, by New Year's Eve he was in generous mood, sending to an up-and-coming musician called Walford Davies, who thirty years later was to succeed him as Master of the King's Music, what he described as 'the last letter I shall write in this eventful year'. It was a note full of encouragement and congratulation, Elgar having the previous night been 'ravished' by the young composer's Christmas carol, *Rocking*. (Early in 1901 Elgar had used his influence to encourage the

Worcester Festival Committee to commission work from Walford Davies, and he did the same, at Gloucester, for Coleridge-Taylor.)

The new year, 1905, opened with distressing news. Dorabella heard on 6 January that Jaeger was to undergo three months of intensive medical treatment. She says that she mentioned this fact in a letter to Elgar but received no reply. In January and February Elgar sat for his portrait by Talbot Hughes, a painting commissioned by Schuster, and on 6 February he was in Oxford to receive an honorary doctorate of music. A week later he ended a letter to Troyte Griffith, 'Yours ever, Edward Elgar, Mus. D. Oxon'. Yale also gave him a degree in 1905, and in October his newly adopted home town of Hereford was trying to jump on the rapidly accelerating Elgar bandwagon by offering to make him mayor. Having had no experience of local government, and not even being a member of the corporation, Elgar kept his head on this occasion and very properly declined. Any mayor who takes his duties seriously will find himself out almost every night at some social function, and the offer, although well intentioned, was hardly a realistic one. Oddly enough, the man then elected mayor was Elgar's landlord.

A far more appropriate and moving local honour was conferred on Elgar in September – the Freedom of the City of Worcester. Wearing his newest academic acquisition, his robes from Yale, Elgar walked in procession through Worcester to the Guildhall, past the shop in the High Street where he had lived as a boy. His father travelled back to the city for the occasion and, too frail to attend the ceremony, he sat in the window of the shop to watch his son pass by. What can this simple, homely old man's feelings have been – this self-made artisan from Dover who had received a royal warrant at twenty-two, lost two children and fathered one of his country's greatest composers – as Professor Sir Edward Elgar passed beneath the window, looked up and raised his mortar? The ceremony was doubly nostalgic because the mayor, who was to hand to Elgar the scroll and offer him the Freedom of the City, was none other than Hubert Leicester, Elgar's old schoolfriend.

The year was to be clouded by two disappointments, one musical, the other academic. On 28 October the previous year Jaeger had written to Elgar to say he hoped he could write a short new work for the London Symphony Orchestra. 'Why not a *brilliant* quick String Scherzo, or something for those fine strings only? a real bring down the house *torrent* of a thing such as Bach could write ... You might even write a *modern Fugue* for strings.' By 26 January 1905 Elgar was telling Jaeger, 'I'm doing that string thing in time for the Sym. orch. concert. Intro: & Allegro – no *working-out* part but a devil of a fugue instead.' The outcome of Jaeger's suggestion would have entitled him to a place in musical history had he done nothing else to earn one. 'I have

133

finished the string thing & it's all right,' Elgar told him three weeks later. 'Of course it will take you some time to get used to it, but it will sound really wholesome & bring out much tone from the strings.' On 8 March the *Introduction and Allegro* for string quartet and string orchestra, one of the finest pieces of music ever written for strings alone, received its first performance at the Queen's Hall, with Elgar conducting, in a programme consisting entirely of his own works – the programme opened with *In the South*, and included *Sea Pictures*, *Cockaigne*, the *Enigma Variations* and the first performance of the *Pomp and Circumstance March* No. 3. The *Introduction and Allegro* was dedicated to Professor S. S. Sanford, the admirer from Yale, in gratitude perhaps for his gift of the Steinway piano (in anticipation, too, of the honorary doctorate Elgar was to receive from Yale University on 28 June), but its reception was cool, and once again Elgar had reason to be grateful to Richter, who conducted the work in Manchester on 7 December. The applause on this occasion was again only moderate, so Richter did a splendid thing: pretending to interpret what little clapping there was for a sign of appreciation, he swung back to the orchestra and promptly played the whole work through again. Even so, it was many years before this example of Elgar's string writing at its greatest achieved popularity with the public.

In April Elgar told Dorabella, 'Nothing better for strings has ever been done and they don't like it.' In his own programme note for the first performance, Elgar explained that three years previously he had thought of writing a brilliant piece for string orchestra, and that one day by the shore in Cardigan-shire – in fact at Ynys Lochtyn, Cardigan Bay – he had heard the sound of singing. He made a sketch from these sounds, which he revised when he heard a song in the Wye Valley, and the work had become a tribute to 'that sweet borderland where I have made my home' – in other words, to Herefordshire. Today it would be difficult for any composer to snatch such inspiration from the air, but at the turn of the century, when people still sang folk-tunes out of doors where there were no cars or aeroplanes to drown their voices, and when there was in any case a great vogue among composers for folk-songs (the English Folk-Song Society had been founded in 1898), the story of the genesis of the *Introduction and Allegro* is perfectly plausible.

The use of the word brilliant should be understood in purely musical terms, used to denote panache, perhaps, and daring, music both scintillating and complex. There is nothing more brilliant than the opening bars of the *Introduction and Allegro*, music that, as so often with Elgar, belies the nature of the man. In private life he was frequently indecisive; in the opening of most of his works he goes straight to the heart of the matter without a moment's prevari-cation. In a letter to Schuster, written three weeks before the Queen's Hall concert, he alluded to the two new works: 'The new 'Pomp & C.' is a devil & the new string thing most brilliant with a real tune in it however.'

Only eight days after the lukewarm reception accorded to the 'new string thing' Elgar faced his second disappointment of the year, the failure of his foray into academe. In preparing his inaugural lecture as professor of music at Birmingham University, Elgar displayed a good deal of moral courage mixed with a kind of self-lacerating fatalism. He felt obliged to say things he believed to be true even if he knew they were bound to cause offence. In his music he could keep his emotions under control – not for him the brow-beating, brassy appeals for sympathy of Tchaikovsky; but in life, there were times when he could not resist the temptation to make tactless, sometimes hurtful, comments. Anyone less suited than Elgar to the task of turning his emotional or even intellectual attitudes towards music into the basis for an academic debate would be hard to imagine, and in taking on the job, he had accepted a perfect, ready-made platform from which to drop a few bricks prior to running for shelter before the inevitable gale of criticism.

Rosa Burley's first-hand account of that first lecture makes painful reading. 'With its high-sounding enunciation of incomprehensible theories' it was, she tells us, 'one of the most embarrassing failures to which it has ever been my misfortune to listen. The opening was greeted with the respectful attention which Edward's eminence deserved but as the evening wore on and point after point missed its mark feet were shuffled, a cross-fire of coughs set in and one gradually realised that the day was hopelessly lost.' It is amusing, and instructive, to compare that account with the entry in Alice's diary: 'E. spoke splendidly at Birm. & looked very nice in gown & hood – Had a great reception.'

'I must go and get some strychnine. This is the end for me,' was Elgar's own predictable aside as he stepped off the platform. (It was not, however, the end for Elgar: two evenings later he was dining with the king at Buckingham Palace.) He went on to prepare another five lectures that year, three in November and two in December; a further two were delivered in November the following year. The title he gave to his second lecture, on 1 November, was 'English Composers', and it earned him a sharp rebuke two days later from his former friend and champion, Charles Stanford. Writing to *The Times*, the author of the 'odious' letter of two years before accused Elgar of casting an 'undeserved aspersion upon the taste, judgement and perspicacity of foreigners and an unjust disparagement of the influence which has long been exerted by the music of his own country'. Elgar had been reported as saying that English music was held in no respect abroad, 'that was to say, the serious compositions which up to the present time had been turned out'. Even what might have been thought a non-controversial topic – an analysis of Brahms's Third Symphony, chosen by Elgar for a lecture a week later during which he championed the concept of 'absolute' music – stirred the *Manchester Guardian* critic Ernest Newman to a laborious denunciation of what he saw as a 'rickety thesis'.

Elgar had Alice and his niece May Grafton working on his notes, and choirs, choirmasters, conductors, audiences and solo instrumentalists came in for some carefully prepared and deliberately aimed barbs. In the view of Sir Thomas Armstrong, a former principal of the Royal Academy of Music, much of Elgar's pent-up bitterness came out in these lectures.[7] Anyone wishing to plough through them and attempt to untangle Elgar's musical message and emotional state of mind at the time should consult *A Future for English Music and Other Lectures* edited by Percy Young. Just about the only people to merit praise were British orchestral players, one of whose number Elgar, of course, had once been. The fact is that by now he was, in terms of sheer originality and genius, far superior as a composer to any of his British contemporaries, and he should have held himself above the petty squabbles of the artistic world. For a man of Elgar's extreme sensitivity to criticism, it was folly to enter the arena of public debate and start flinging mud around – when some of it stuck to himself he was bound to squeal. He started to object because extracts of his lectures were published 'out of context', a regular complaint of men who enter public life in an unsophisticated frame of mind, and the price he paid for unburdening a pile of chips from his shoulder was hardly worth while. 'I am killed by the University,' he told Schuster on 29 October, exaggerating the situation as usual, and everyone was relieved, when, after collecting an honorary MA in 1907, he resigned in August the following year. Mr Richard Payton, the founder of the chair who had insisted on it being accepted by Elgar in the first instance, wrote to the university secretary on 28 August to say, 'I am pleased to think that there will be now a prospect of some satisfactory results attending the existence of a musical professorship in the University ... The actual result and virtual waste of time has, I need not say, been a great disappointment to me.'

Elgar seldom had occasion to write to Carice, who was now fifteen, but when she spent part of her summer holiday in 1905 with friends Elgar sent her news of her rabbits and of a rather hair-raising encounter he and her cousin May had suffered with a bull. He ended his letter, 'Much love, yr affec father, Edward Elgar'. It was a curiously eighteenth-century way to end a letter to a daughter, and his attachment to his surname may account for Carice's own life-long devotion to the name of Elgar (when she first married she called herself Mrs Carice Elgar Blake, and eventually she unashamedly joined the two names together with a hyphen).

7. In conversation with the author.

It was in 1905 too that Alice began sending Carice each Saturday morning, accompanied by her cousin May, to the gymnasium at Hereford High School. Carice has left an account of these disagreeable outings: 'It was absolute torture for me in those days, for I had no idea of marching time and the idea of a running jump at the horse so paralysed me with fright that I just could not do it. I used to dread Saturday mornings to which my poor cousin May always had to take me because I was not allowed to go into Hereford alone down St Owen's Street because in those days there were so many drunk people about even at eight or nine in the morning.'[8]

A year later, in a letter written on 17 July 1906, Elgar gave a rosier account of Carice's adolescent progress: 'Carice is very busy with her studies,' he wrote to Rosa Burley, '& swimming & all sorts of things & she is very strong & full of vitality & revels in any amount of work.' Carice gives a telling impression of her childhood relationship with her mother in a reminiscence relating more or less to the years spent at Plas Gwyn: whenever Elgar was away, 'One could hardly get an answer [from Alice] about anything and until his telegram came saying he was safely in London – or wherever it was – she was terribly on edge, and seemed to think that one was very unfeeling if one did not appear to be worried about the journey. If she ever allowed herself to throw off this terrible worrying, she could be the most delightful companion, but unfortunately this did not very often happen.'[9]

Much of 1905 was taken up with work on *The Kingdom*, the second part of the intended trilogy of oratorios, yet Elgar did get away from it between 15 September and 12 October when he was invited to join Schuster on a rather grand Mediterranean cruise. Although Lord Charles Beresford and Sir George Warrender were to be there with their wives, Alice for some reason did not go too. Elgar and Schuster travelled by boat and train to join the party at Piraëus. On the first night Elgar 'had a berth with a young Greek' and 'did not attempt to undress'. During the cruise they seem to have gone ashore a lot; they heard 'a pretty shepherd boy playing on a pipe', and one night, just as they were going to sleep, 'there was a shout and a crash – a sudden stoppage of engines – horrible 'scape of steam and the ship rolled'. They thought they were sinking and lifeboats were lowered. They had in fact run down two other boats and ten men, apparently Turks, were drowned. They circled around, looking for survivors, for one and a half hours. 'Then all quiet.' In the notes he kept on the journey, Elgar expresses not one word of regret or sympathy. Elgar and his friends were refreshed with rose-leaf jam and iced water, but missed an ambassadorial reception, which was 'hurriedly abandoned on acct.

8. *Alice Elgar: Enigma of a Victorian Lady.*
9. *ibid.*

of the attempted suicide of a young Greek gentleman'. Lady Maud Warrender entertained the company by singing some of Elgar's songs, which he accompanied on the piano.[10] After luncheon one day two autograph hunters boarded the ship to wait for him, and once again he got *'frightfully'* bitten by mosquitoes. The ship's band played Elgar's *Sérénade lyrique* and *Salut d'Amour*, and on 3 October there were squalls all day and everyone was ill. At Patras, on the return journey, Elgar and Schuster ordered tea, and a waiter ran into the street 'as the goats were coming in. One was caught & milked into my jug, on the tramlines.' A 'boy guide' showed them round a prison, and Elgar bought a 'roughly carved knife' from a prisoner. The next day he purchased a dagger, and the next he bought another. He got back to 'dreary civilisation' on 12 October.

Towards the end of the year Elgar was referring to Jaeger's condition – he had tuberculosis – in a letter to Schuster, written on 2 November: 'He does look well,' he reported, 'but the lung is not healed.' November too saw him busy conducting the London Symphony Orchestra in Manchester, Sheffield, Glasgow, Newcastle and Bradford, engagements that involved travel, preparation and rehearsal time at a period when he was also hard at work on *The Kingdom*. Dorabella has left us a vivid account of the creative process in respect of that composition. It seems that one day, at Plas Gwyn, he worked in his study all morning and only had 'a mouthful of luncheon'. He then 'ignored' a tea tray left outside the study door (perhaps he did not know it was there) and appeared at dinner time.

'Where's dinner?' he said rather roughly.

'It's here now, dear darling – we are just going in,' Alice replied.

According to Dorabella, Elgar then looked up and saw her on the stairs. 'Hallo, you here?' he said. 'I'm busy.'

After which he ate his dinner in total silence, looking straight in front of him 'with rather a tense expression when he wasn't looking at his plate'. She says he was very pale and looked tired and drawn. Half-way through dessert Elgar pushed back his chair, struck Dorabella's hand 'quite sharply' and left the room. He banged the study door and turned the key.

Alice explained that since having a study on the ground floor Elgar had taken to locking himself in as it made him feel safer. There, it seems, he remained, composing, until half past one in the morning, the two ladies alternately brewing tea, eating sandwiches and listening enraptured to the music as it flowed from the study, seeming in fact to come down the chimney,

10. She had a magnificent contralto voice, according to her elder son, Lord Bruntisfield, in a letter to the author of 17 December 1981; she once sang with Melba in the duet from Boito's *Mefistofele*, and she also wrote a Marching Song for the Girl Guides.

for the piano, on which Elgar was trying out his new score, stood with its back to the drawing-room fireplace. Released at last from the concentration of composition Elgar emerged as his cheerful old self, ate prodigious quantities of sandwiches, cake and biscuits, and then, notwithstanding the lateness of the hour, proceeded to play through the entire day's output with Dorabella turning over the pages. It was 2.30 a.m. when Alice went off 'to put things straight in the drawing-room', leaving Elgar to talk to Dorabella in the study. Dorabella records:

'Seeing me make for the door, E. E. called out "Oh, do stop and talk to me, Dorabella, I haven't heard half the news yet".'

Alice: ' "Yes, *do* stay, dear Dora, and talk to him; I *promise* not to carry any heavy trays!"

'Elgar opened the door for her and I remembered the sound of her quick little steps going across the hall.

' "Fancy your staying up all that time – why ever did you?" ' Elgar asks.

' "I just loved it."

' "You do look charming in that frock. When I saw you on the stairs –"

' "I wished I had brought something quieter and more ordinary – but you see I never bring –"

' "Don't you dare to bring any dingy, smoky frocks when you come to stay with me, because I won't stand it – and you only looked at me twice during dinner!"

' "Twice, was it? Well, I was terrified! I simply daren't look at you for fear of putting you off your stroke or something."

' "At first I hoped you wouldn't and then, as dinner went on, I hoped you would. Finally I went away; you'd won, and that was why I hit your hand so hard. Did it hurt? I meant it to!"

'He picked up my hand and inspected it.

' "It stung a bit at first, but there isn't much of a mark left. Here's the Lady. Do you know that it's nearly three tomorrow morning?" '

Elgar ended 1905 as he had ended 1904, by writing a letter on 31 December to Walford Davies. Musically, he told the young composer, of whom he was becoming increasingly fond (and hence increasingly prone to make use of him as a letter-box for his moans and groans), he was the same depressed being, keen for everything except his vocation, 'which I feel is not my vocation by a long tract of desert'. But he added, with reference to *The Kingdom*, 'I am working away & some of the themes are not bad.'

Early in 1906 came a political blow for Elgar: the Conservatives were routed in the general election, and a large radical majority now dominated the House of Commons. No less that twenty-nine Labour candidates were returned, and even Hereford's Tory MP lost his seat. On the brighter side, Aberdeen University gave Elgar a degree, and he found time to plan a visit to the USA to conduct *Gerontius* and *The Apostles* in Cincinnati, but the election results were still rankling when he wrote to Troyte Griffith on 17 March. 'I sail on Ap. 6 & shall make arrangements to live in the USA,' he told him. 'This country is no longer possible for respectable people.' Those who find it difficult to disengage Elgar's music from his politics were certainly given ammunition by Elgar himself, but perhaps his feelings were mild compared to those of the king, who (as Prince of Wales) had once written to his eldest sister, the Crown Princess of Prussia, to report on a 'tremendous crowd' in Hyde Park: 'The more the Government allow the lower classes to get the upper hand the more the democratic feeling of the present day will increase,' he told her.

While Elgar was in America his father died on 30 April, at the age of eighty-five. He and Anne are buried in Astwood Cemetery, on the northern outskirts of Worcester, off Astwood Road, and in October 1907 Elgar asked Troyte Griffith to suggest a gravestone, taking, if practicable, 'some Saxon thing for a model' since the family bore 'an old Saxon name'. He was careful to explain that he could not afford much 'as the living seem to have more pressing needs'.

Old William missed by five months the première of Elgar's next great work, *The Kingdom*, given at the Birmingham Festival on 3 October. At one time it seemed as if, like *Gerontius*, *The Kingdom* was doomed to an unsatisfactory start in life. On return from the States, Elgar had still not completed the score, and to make matters worse he slipped on some wet stones and suffered a bout of considerable pain and depression. He went so far as to ask the festival committee if they would accept only half the work for 1906, but he then made one of his rapid returns to health and worked at incredible speed. By 21 July he told Jaeger he was finishing the final revision, and two days later he had done so. On 7 August he was boasting, again to Jaeger, and with some justification, 'I scored 70 pages in the week,' and the orchestration was over by the end of the month. Once again it had been a close thing, leaving just four weeks for orchestral and choral rehearsals. We should not conclude from this, however, that it was only under the pressure of completing a commission on time that Elgar was able to work best. That many of his major, commissioned works were completed under this kind of pressure was more because the work of composition had to be fitted in with travel, conducting and sometimes lecturing; he had in any case an amazing capacity for working fast, as Reed's account of Elgar's method of composition in relation to the Violin Concerto will show. One of Elgar's problems was the uneven flow of energy, leaving him as dissatisfied and despondent at the end of a bout of concentrated work as it made him exhilarated and buoyant during the course of it.

Sir Adrian Boult believes *The Kingdom* to be not only superior to *The Dream of Gerontius* but that it is in fact Elgar's finest work. 'It is,' he says, 'the one extended work with no blemishes. There are several very bad weaknesses in *The Dream*, some of them only 10 or 12 bars, but they exist.'[11] Alice was in no doubt that *The Kingdom*, at the time it was written, was 'his greatest achievement'; she said so in a very priggish letter to Jaeger, designed to put the sick man and his constructive criticisms in their place. She thought it curious that the chorus, 'Oh ye priests', did not fire him: 'It works up all who have heard it to a great pitch of excitement,' she asserted, as though the poor man was not only dying of tuberculosis but was half-witted as well. She added, 'I think you might have given E. some credit for his fine literary taste & poetic feeling in his selection of words.' In the end she got so carried away she was downright rude. 'Wait to judge of the new work, & especially to *remark* to anyone on it till you have heard E. play it,' she commanded. 'All those who have, & all those who have been real musicians, think it the most original & greatest thing he has done.' Alice added that the strain of the work had been very great for Elgar, '& makes him very easily worried'. We may reasonably infer from the letter as a whole that stresses and strains at Plas Gwyn had become infectious. Alice, in her over-enthusiasm, was echoing her husband's own high opinion of his new work. He had earlier told Jaeger, 'So far it is the best thing I've done *I know*.' But he had also had the sense and humility to acknowledge the merit of Jaeger's well-intentioned and sympathetic comments ('Your remarks about those *two* bars in the intro. were quite right'); on Jaeger's part, it says much for his 'grand and noble mind' that he seems to have taken Alice's impertinent letter without offence.

In fairness to Alice, she had written to Jaeger in 1900, in connection with *The Dream of Gerontius*, to say, 'May I send a line and say how *beautiful* I think your analysis?' And in 1908 she was to make handsome amends by writing, 'Dear Mr Jaeger, I must be allowed to send you a few lines to tell you how immensely I appreciate your beautiful and valuable article on Edward's part-songs. You have shown such true insight into their depth of meaning and so truly recognise all their wonderful, poetic atmosphere like a true interpreter. Such an interpreter is a necessity between the genius and the outer world; the thoughts of a genius are always in advance of the ordinary world's under-standing, and intense gratitude is due to the one who can see the new and beautiful thing offered to the people, and reveal it to their more slowly perceiving eyes.'

Perhaps of greater interest than the subjective question of whether *The*

11. In conversation with the author.

Kingdom is a greater or lesser work than *The Dream of Gerontius* is the reason why Elgar never completed the trilogy. The most improbable reason of all was supplied by Elgar himself when he told Ralph Vaughan Williams that in writing the choral work *Sancta Civitas*, Vaughan Williams had written the third part of the trilogy for him.[12] By the end of 1907 Elgar had told Novello he had given up the idea, and he was confirming his decision to Jaeger in June 1908: 'I have no intention of completing my oratorio cycle or whatever it is,' he told him, adding 'Of course I have the thing – the biggest of all – sketched but I cannot for the sake of others waste any time on it.' Among those who tried to persuade him to change his mind were Schuster and the Marquess of Northampton. Elgar tended to claim that the financial rewards of writing a major work were inadequate inducement in view of the time and effort required. He may also have felt that the standards of choral training and singing made the effort hardly worth while. Alice's diary for June 1914 records that 'a feeling of great joy settled on us' after Elgar had seemed to give a promise to write the third oratorio for the Leeds Choral Union, but as time slipped away oratorio grew less fashionable, Elgar grew older, and the sheer magnitude of the task of writing, never mind scoring, such a major project must have seemed more and more daunting. As late as 1921 he made a valiant gesture towards returning in all seriousness to *The Last Judgement* when he wrote to Troyte Griffith, a year after Alice had died, to ask if he could find a house in Malvern so that he could be near his wife's grave and have Troyte 'not too far off', for now that he was no longer young he wanted 'to complete the great work'. Six years later his seventieth birthday concert at the Queen's Hall was to be only half filled, and a general decline in interest in his music towards the end of his life can have done nothing to encourage him. While fashion has since swung back in his favour, *The Apostles* and *The Kingdom* have become perhaps the least well known and attended of his major works.

Visits to the United States were now becoming as regular as visits to Germany had once been, part of the attraction being the desire of American universities to bestow honorary doctorates. In the spring of 1907, the year that the University of Pennsylvania made him a doctor of law, Elgar was back in America, where he reported from New York on 14 April, 'I have that dear & wonderful woman, Mrs Worthington, to speak to.' Julia Worthington lived

12. Information supplied to the author by Mr Edgar Day. *Sancta Civitas*, an oratorio for tenor, baritone, chorus, semi-chorus and orchestra, was composed in 1925 and first performed at Oxford in 1926, twenty years after the first performance of *The Kingdom*. In making his remark to Vaughan Williams, Elgar was surely complimenting his fellow composer rather than offering a serious explanation for failing to complete his own trilogy.

at 853 Seventh Avenue, New York. In 1912, recommending Tertius Noble, on his appointment as organist at St Thomas's Church on Fifth Avenue, to call on her, Elgar wrote, 'You will find her home a haven of rest if ever you feel rushed & overworked.' J. B. Yeats (the father of W. B. Yeats) had no doubt that Mrs Worthington – 'a sort of Duchess over here' – was socially clever, a friend to all the distinguished people, a very nice woman and 'an intimate friend of the musician Elgar'.[13]

It was in 1907 too that Elgar, haunted for so long by the fear of never becoming a symphonic composer (he had said in his capacity as professor of music at Birmingham, 'I hold that the symphony without a programme is the highest development of art'), and loath to be remembered simply as the saviour of English oratorio, seems at last to have begun to make serious progress on the work shortly to become his First Symphony. Dorabella began to hear Elgar playing 'odds and ends, bits and scraps', which she found 'fascinatingly interesting'. He was eventually to strike out in the first movement with one of his large and memorable tunes, much as Tchaikovsky had done in his First Piano Concerto: Tchaikovsky brought his tune to its conclusion and never returned to it; Elgar, so strongly influenced by Wagner's use of motif, stuck with his tune and wound it back into the development section, allowing it to return yet again at the conclusion of the whole work.

Since Elgar's return from America, his head had been 'full of music', Alice wrote to tell Jaeger on 7 June. 'He has been continually sketching & playing ... & now he is orchestrating another Pomp and Circumstance March a splendid one, one to rouse every spark of martial fire.' This was to be No. 4 in the series of five and Alice was right, it is a splendid piece, arguably the finest of them all. Elgar completed the work on 7 June and conducted its first performance at the Queen's Hall on 24 August. He had told Jaeger, 'The first pt of the 4th march is good: the middle rot but pleasing to march to.' Three weeks later Alice's diary entry refers to Elgar 'playing great beautiful tune', presumably the tune that opens the First Symphony.

At the same time Elgar also resurrected those youthful tunes he had written as a boy for the amusement of his brother and sisters, and the result, the first Wand of Youth suite, was conducted by Sir Henry Wood at the Queen's Hall on 14 December. It must have been an initial inability to progress beyond the 'great beautiful tune' that caused Elgar, on 6 October, to apologize to Walford Davies for depressing him and to offer as an excuse the fact that 'my future does not look interesting – and I dread that. Poverty I am used to & hard work but it has always been interesting in the best sense: but now I see nothing

13. Letters to His Son W. B. Yeats and Others, 1869–1912 by J. B. Yeats (Faber, 1954).

ahead.' Elgar's obsession with poverty (always a relative matter) was to pursue him to the grave.

He was in fact on the point of leaving for another holiday, in Italy, this time with Alice, and he was planning to stay there from November until May. In Rome, where they were 'very comfortable', Elgar told Schuster, '& [could] see over the tops of the houses across to S. Pietro with fine sunsets thrown in', inspiration came fitfully. Alice penned the most frightful poem, which Elgar felt obliged to set to music and send to friends in England as a Christmas greeting. One verse began:

> On and on old Tiber speeds,
> Dark with its weight of ancient crime;
> Far north, through green and quiet meeds,
> Flows on the Wye midst mist and silvering rime.

The poem had a recurring chorus:

> To you in the snow,
> To us in sun,
> Love is but one;
> Hearts beat and glow
> By oak and vine,
> Friends, always mine.

As further indication that Alice had not sacrificed a literary career in order to further Elgar's musical one, this poem may be compared with a previous effort, on the subject of Carice. It starts:

> Dear little ship, go forth
> High-hearted, south or north,
> Spread white and wide thy sails
> Buoyed with the Hope that never fails.
> Soon dawns the day
> When you must take your way:
> Must leave the lea
> And sail upon the sea.

Elgar's choice of verse, seldom brilliant, was not always as disastrous as when he fell back on Alice's efforts although, incredibly, his setting of Alice's poem about old Tiber and its weight of crime was chosen by Dr Sinclair for performance in Hereford Cathedral. While in Italy he also set to music as a part-song, *Go, song of mine*, what he rightly described as 'fine words' by Cavalcanti in a translation by Rossetti; his biggest part-song, it was first performed at Hereford on 9 September 1909, and it has been described by Michael Kennedy as 'superb, as imposing as Parry at his best'.

'I am trying to write music,' Elgar told Schuster, 'but the bitterness is that it pays not at all & I must write and arrange what my soul loathes to permit me to write what *you* like & I like. I curse the power that gave me gifts & loathe them now & ever. I told you a year ago I could see no future: now I see it & am a changed man & a *dour* creature.' It was hardly a letter calculated to cheer a friend at Christmas.

The music Elgar was still really trying to write, however, was the longed-for symphony. He was now fifty, seven years older even than Brahms had been when, dogged as he felt himself to be by the shadow of Beethoven, he eventually managed to write his first symphony. Elgar had been struggling with sketches and ideas since 1903 – or five years before that if the idea for a symphonic work based on the life of General Gordon is taken into account. His harping at this time on his lack of any future relates entirely to his feeling of failure and frustration in the symphonic field; once the symphony had begun to take shape his whole tone of voice changed. On 15 June 1908, not long after their return from Italy, Alice was writing to Jaeger with encouraging news: 'E. sends his love,' she said, '& he wants to say to you the "Sym. is A1". It is *gorgeous*, steeped in beauty. He is quite absorbed in it.' There is no reason to take too literally a letter from Elgar to Walford Davies of 15 July – 'I am trying to work and am covering sheets of paper to no good end' – for just four days later he was writing to Troyte Griffith, 'Do come over: I am writing heavenly music (!) & it will do you good to hear it.' By 28 August the main task of composition was over and he was scoring the work. He felt so relaxed that he allowed himself to write one of his genuinely funny notes, to Frank Schuster: 'I am resuming chemistry & made soap yesterday between fits of scoring (not scouring!) the symphony. I have been vainly trying to persuade Carice to wash with it – strange how little encouragement I get!'

By way of light relief, Elgar arranged a second *Wand of Youth* suite, and the first performance of this work, conducted by Elgar himself at Worcester on 9 September 1908, would have provided an instructive contrast between the 'light' and the 'serious' Elgar to anyone who travelled also to the Free Trade Hall in Manchester for the première of the First Symphony on 3 December. The work was completed at the end of September, and not only did Elgar dedicate it to Hans Richter – 'true artist and true friend' – but fulfilled another promise by entrusting its first performance to him. He had also fulfilled his ambition to contribute to 'the highest development of art' by writing a symphony without a programme. 'There is no programme beyond a wide experience of human life with a great charity (love) and a *massive* hope in the future,' he wrote on 13 November to Walford Davies, having heard 'with the greatest joy' that he was to write about the work. Jaeger was by now very ill, and Elgar thoughtfully sent a piano score of the symphony to the man to whom he owed so much. On 26 November, Jaeger wrote to say he had been allowed to go downstairs for the first time for a month, and had spent some 'happy quarter hours' studying the piano arrangement of the Adagio – the third movement. 'My dear friend,' he wrote, 'that is not only one of the very greatest slow movements since Beethoven, but I consider it *worthy of that master.* How original, how *pure*, noble ... It's the greatest thing you have done.' He ends, 'I must go to bed, though I know that haunting adagio won't let me sleep.'

Biased though he may have been in Elgar's favour, Jaeger was not alone in his opinions. The critic of the *Manchester Guardian* described the work as the noblest ever penned for instruments by an English composer. Among the audience at the first performance were Parry, Edward German, the nineteen-year-old Neville Cardus and, interestingly, Stanford. Jaeger, too, although dreadfully ill, managed to attend, and to record his impressions for Dorabella. He described the hall as packed and the atmosphere as electric. Newspaper accounts record the audience bursting into applause after the slow movement, and it was then, apparently, that Richter, catching on to the mood of exceptional excitement, called Elgar out to acknowledge the clapping. Jaeger tells us that at the end of the performance Elgar was called out five more times, and that he had never heard such shouting and frantic applause, with people standing on their seats to see the composer. The *Daily Telegraph* described the audience as 'almost beside itself with enthusiasm' after the slow movement, and noted hearty applause from the orchestra at the end, the players rising 'as one man to cheer Elgar to the echo'. His friends were almost beside themselves, too. Lord Northampton wrote to say, 'I hardly know what to think and certainly not what to write. That you, a mortal with whom I had just talked, had out of yourself just given the world *that* ... it is almost terrifying in its greatness.'[14]

Within a year the symphony had received over a hundred performances, in America, Austria, Germany, Russia and Australia as well as London. The work was 'making a very wild career', Elgar reported to Adela Schuster on Christmas Day. He was disappointed she had still not heard it. He told her he was receiving 'heaps of letters from persons known & unknown telling me how it uplifts them'. But of course he had to spoil the pleasure by adding, 'I wish it uplifted me – I have just paid rent, Land Tax, Income Tax and a variety of other things due today.' It sounded almost like a begging letter, from the man of whose triumphant masterpiece Richter only three weeks before had said to

14. Sir Thomas Armstrong, in conversation with the author, said, 'It is quite impossible for someone of your age to appreciate the impact Elgar's First Symphony made on young men of my generation. It was not just that we were hearing the first English symphony; it was the whole tremendous excitement of experiencing great new music.'

the orchestra as he mounted the rostrum to conduct a rehearsal for the first London performance, 'Gentlemen, let us now rehearse the greatest symphony of modern times, written by the greatest modern composer.'[15]

---

15. *Elgar* by William H. Reed. Reed also records that when Richter came to the third movement, he exclaimed that it was a real Adagio, 'such as Beethoven might have written'.

CHAPTER FIVE

'Music is Written in the Skies'

In producing, at last, an English symphony, Elgar had laid the continental demon once and for all and paved the way for other composers (less than two years later the thirty-eight-year-old Ralph Vaughan Williams was to launch his brilliant *Sea* Symphony). He was soon to start work on his first completed concerto, but soon too he would have to learn to live without the moral support and artistic encouragement of August Jaeger. In October 1907 Elgar had arranged to transfer to Jaeger some of his royalties due from Novello, a generous but belated gift. The day after the première of the First Symphony, on 4 December 1908, Jaeger wrote his last letter to Elgar, assuring him, 'The Scherzo is a real joy & one of the biggest things of the kind in all symphonic literature. And that mysterious Lento with its abysmal depths of tone colour & the astounding Finale, an overpowering outburst of optimism & joie de vivre that carries one away in spite of oneself until the superb peroration crowns the whole splendid structure.' He went on to say it was a great and masterly work, that would place him higher among the world's masters than anything he had done before. The first London performance was scheduled for three days' time, and Jaeger ended by saying, 'Ill as I am (& I feel so ill tonight that I want to go to the nearest Ry Station & throw myself under a Train to end my misery) I hope to go next Monday. I have bought a ticket & am looking forward to what I fear will be the last great ...' (the end of the letter has been removed). In order to 'economise', Elgar left once again for Italy, and it was while the Elgars were abroad that Jaeger died, on 18 May 1909. He was cremated at Golders Green and a memorial concert was held the following January, at the Queen's Hall, at which Richter conducted music by Wagner, and Parry and Coleridge-Taylor conducted works by themselves. The *Enigma Variations* were played, Muriel Foster sang Brahms's *Alto Rhapsody* and the first performance was given of three new songs by Elgar, conducted by the composer, one of which, *Oh, soft was the song*, was encored. So passed from the musical scene Elgar's 'dear colossal Moss', the man regarded by Rosa Burley as a 'lovable but rather typically commonplace little German'', and by most impartial observers today as a dedicated and selfless impresario, one of the staunchest, most loyal and astute champions Elgar ever had.

In 1909 Elgar had three projects in his mind: a gathering together of existing sketches in order to produce a second symphony, a violin concerto to replace the one he had destroyed in 1890, and an opera. He and Alice had returned to Italy in April, staying at a villa near Florence; close by in another was Julia Worthington, and it may have been her proximity at this time that led Alice to confide to Dorabella that hers was the soul eventually enshrined in the Violin Concerto (Dorabella, having promised Alice never to reveal the secret, did so when revising her memoirs in 1946).

So far as the opera was concerned, Elgar bought a sketchbook in Florence and drew in it a plan of a stage set. Immediately on his return to England he wrote, on 25 June, to Laurence Binyon to thank him for a suggestion for a libretto; but, he concluded, it was 'not for my music', and he said he was still searching. Not until the very end of his life did Elgar settle upon a libretto that satisfied him, and one reason why he does not appear to have searched particularly diligently at this time may have been the lack of any permanent opera company in London.

Once back at Plas Gwyn, the concerto began to take shape. 'E. possessed with his music for the Vl. Concerto,' Alice recorded on 19 August. The Second Symphony was also progressing, and fortunately Dorabella was on hand to help matters along. Towards the end of dinner one night she managed to make Elgar laugh, and 'the Lady looked positively grateful'. After dinner they had coffee in the study, and after coffee Alice sat back on the sofa looking nearly done. 'Shall you think it *very* rude, dear Dora, if I slip off to bed now?' she asked her younger and more energetic guest. 'I am so *very* tired!'

That left the coast clear for Elgar and Dorabella to get down to the serious business of composition. First of all however Elgar remembered his manners, opening the door for Alice and even going upstairs with her. Waiting for his return, Dorabella felt a little nervous, for so much seemed to be expected of her. 'Should I succeed as I had before?' she mused, waiting for Elgar to descend. Pulling herself together, she realized that 'nervousness would be hopeless and would wreck everything. It was an honour to feel oneself accounted one of the family, able to take a turn and be a help.'

Dorabella tells us it often used to take a long time and a great deal of patience before the mood arrived and Elgar felt inclined to touch the subject of music. 'Of course,' she says, 'I never mentioned the word, or work of any sort. I just listened and sympathised and laid myself out to be amusing and a distraction from worry generally.'

It seems she laid herself out that night with her usual degree of sympathy, for before long Elgar had shaken off his depression 'like a sort of cloak' and was his old self again, and she remembered hearing a lot of music that night, both old and new, including the first movement of the Second Symphony.

At some unearthly hour in the morning Elgar exclaimed, 'My giddy aunt! Look at the time! Cut along, child, I *shall* catch it.'

'As I went slowly upstairs,' Dorabella recalled, 'I realised that I was dead tired, but what a triumph it was. I had done it again.'

At breakfast, her cup must have overflowed, for before Elgar appeared Alice told her she had 'lain awake for an age' and then, hearing the piano, was 'so glad and thankful ... and went to sleep quite soon after that'.

'Poor little dear!' says Dorabella. 'One can quite easily understand how the anxiety and worry of it all would get on her nerves.' The wonder of it really is that Dorabella herself did not get on Alice's nerves.

In July, at a gathering in Bournemouth of all the leading British composers of the day, there had been a sad incident when Stanford 'fled when he saw E.', according to Alice's diary. In October, for the Three Choirs Festival, the Elgars rented Harley House in Hereford rather than risk their guests catching scarlet fever from Carice, and on 28 October Thomas Beecham, then aged thirty, condescended to conduct Elgar's First Symphony at the Victoria Hall in Hanley. The result was a travesty, judging by an account of the proceedings in a letter to the *Musical Times* the following month from the composer Havergal Brian. 'The first movement was cut down one half,' Brian wrote, 'part of the "exposition" and the whole of the "development" were cut out, and some minutes were sacrificed in the succeeding movements. Those who know the symphony will be astonished to hear that the actual time occupied in its performance was only 38 minutes! It was an insult to the composer and also those responsible for the concert.'

As the normal playing time of the First Symphony is about fifty-five minutes, Beecham seems to have chopped off some seventeen minutes. An anecdote is told in a privately printed booklet, *In Memory of William Henry Reed*, of how at the beginning of a tour a certain symphony took forty-five minutes to play and at the end only fifteen, and in an annotated copy of the booklet which he has since presented to Elgar's Birthplace, Sir Adrian Boult has identified the work as Elgar's Second Symphony and the conductor involved in the butchery as Beecham. According to Beecham's biographer, Alan Jefferson, Elgar 'protested in a mild fashion' after the 1909 Beecham performance of the First Symphony, with the result that when the symphony was again due for rehearsal with him, Beecham said to the orchestra, 'Gentlemen, the composer of the immortal masterpiece we are now about to rehearse again has written insisting that we play it as written. So now, gentlemen, if you please, we'll play it *with all the repeats*!' Alan Jefferson also tells us that Beecham dismissed Richter as an ass, and held a generally ambivalent view of Elgar's music. 'On the whole,' he writes, 'he found it too German by half, although he played *Cockaigne* and found it went down well abroad. He played the *Enigma Variations* infrequently, conducted the cello concerto only once, and cut the First Symphony to pieces at a Hallé concert because he found it far too long-winded.'[1] If it was at a Hallé concert that Beecham behaved like this he had taken no notice of Elgar's 'mild protest' or Havergal Brian's letter, for it must have occurred after the Hanley performance. Small wonder that, on meeting Beecham during the war, Alice noted in her diary that he was 'very phantas-magoric and not appealing to us at all'.

In December, a song written in Italy to words in the Tuscan dialect and dedicated to Alice Stuart-Wortley was sung at the Mansion House, and on the ninth anniversary of Queen Victoria's death, 22 January 1910, an elegy, *They are at rest*, with words by Cardinal Newman, was sung at the Royal Mausoleum. The queen had been of a decidedly low-church inclination – she thought that to receive Holy Communion more than once a month was excessive – and her views on a commemorative dirge by two Roman Catholics might have been interesting.

At home at Plas Gwyn, in addition to conducting mildly dangerous chemical experiments, Elgar had taken to throwing boomerangs around, and at about this time Billy Reed first noticed in him a habit common to a number of gifted eccentrics. He tells us he began to notice how a sentence, however frivolous, or perhaps only a word, would run in Elgar's head endlessly, just as a fragment of a tune might do. Once, it seems, Elgar heard someone describe some trashy music as 'jossy'; this became a word that Elgar cottoned on to and kept repeating. ' "Jossy," he would say, and then clap his hands on his knees and roar with laughter.' Reed recalls that when they were playing the Violin Concerto 'and I waxed enthusiastically about any passage, he would say, "I don't mind what you think about it as long as you don't think it jossy." '

Elgar had first met Billy Reed in 1902, and Reed has left a patchy account of episodes from Elgar's life, his character, behaviour and methods of working, in an engaging if at times slightly inaccurate, and always wildly partisan, book entitled *Elgar As I Knew Him*. Written in 1936, two years after Elgar's death, it covers more or less the last quarter-century of the composer's life, for it was not until about 1909 that Reed came to know him well.

Billy Reed was born in 1875, joined the Three Choirs Festival Orchestra in 1902 and was leader from 1910 to 1938; he was also for many years leader of the London Symphony Orchestra, and he became an examiner at the Royal

1. *Sir Thomas Beecham: A Centenary Tribute* by Alan Jefferson (Macdonald & Jane, 1979).

College of Music. He played in the first performances of Elgar's Violin Sonata, his String Quartet and the Piano Quintet. He became a living repository of musical folklore, and in the days when archbishops of Canterbury made imaginative use of their right to confer honorary degrees he was given a Lambeth doctorate of music; he must also have been one of the few leaders of an orchestra to have received from the sovereign the MVO. He composed tone poems, and played under such legendary figures an Nikisch, Richter, Weingartner, Mengelberg and Koussevitsky. When he died, in 1942 at the age of sixty-five, *The Times* called him the kindest man in the world and an invaluable friend to amateur orchestras, 'whom he licked into shape with the gentle firmness of a mother cat performing her kittens' toilet'. It added that the Three Choirs Festival, 'that delightful but somewhat haphazard institution', depended on him for life itself. His ashes are interred in Worcester Cathedral.

This then was the man who tended to claim an exclusively intimate friendship with Elgar. Elgar was just old enough to be his father, both were orchestral players in their time, both were musicians to their finger tips, and there is no doubt that they were very fond of one another. Reed saw Elgar on his deathbed, and it was Bernard Shaw who encouraged Reed to write an account of their relationship. Another Shaw (T. E. Lawrence) read the book in manuscript.

When Elgar and Reed first met, Elgar had been rehearsing the Funeral March from his incidental music to *Grania and Diarmid*, a play by Yeats first performed at the Dublin Gaiety Theatre in 1901. The Funeral March was due to be performed at the Queen's Hall on 18 January 1902 by Henry Wood, to whom the work was dedicated. Reed, an impressionable young man of twenty-five, was among the first violins. After the rehearsal, Reed pursued Elgar through the curtains and up the stairs, to ask whether he gave lessons in harmony and counterpoint. 'My dear boy, I don't know anything about these things,' was the polite brush-off, and for the next seven years they do not seem to have more than smiled and exchanged a few words whenever Elgar conducted an orchestra in which Reed was playing, until, in the spring of 1909 when the Violin Concerto was being written, they bumped into one another in Regent Street. By this time Elgar had a flat at 58 New Cavendish Street (in addition to Plas Gwyn), and realizing instinctively that he could talk about the problems of writing for the violin quite unselfconsciously with a professional violinist, one of the 'members of British orchestras' to whom *Cockaigne* had been dedicated, he invited Reed to the flat to ask his advice about bowing and 'certain intricacies in the passage work'.

On arrival at New Cavendish Street, Reed found Elgar striding round with loose sheets of music-paper, arranging them in different parts of the room. Some were already pinned on the backs of chairs, or stuck up on the mantel-piece. Elgar told Reed he had become dissatisfied with the concerto and had put it aside after playing the early sketches through with Leonora von Stosch, the wife of Sir Edgar Speyer, but that now, although he was using the same themes, he was treating them in a new manner. Elgar often said to Reed, 'If you have a good idea, don't waste it; make the most of it.' While he could be absurdly disparaging about his achievements in general, his individual com-positions often gave him unaffected pleasure: as far as the Violin Concerto was concerned, Reed tells us 'There was no false modesty about his joy in hearing the solo violin boldly entering in the first movement with the concluding half of the principal subject instead of with the beginning, as if answering a question instead of stating a fact. Several times we played that opening, to his infinite glee at the novelty of the idea.'

Sir Adrian Boult refers in his autobiography to the 'real thrill on the first night' experienced on hearing the first entry of the solo violin, 'in the heart of the texture in the middle of a sequential passage'. The concerto, he says, also 'broke new ground in the way the cadenza grew out of the final movement and gathered up material from the whole work, making use of an absolutely new colour in the string accompaniment'. On the subject of Elgar's sense of orchestral colour, Boult says that only Strauss could compete with him.

Reed saw something of Elgar the perfectionist at work. 'He would write a phrase many times,' he recalled, 'with a slight alteration in each version, or make such drastic harmonic or rhythmic changes as to alter the entire character of the theme as originally conceived. He loved to present his ideas in all moods and then consider them from every aspect. It was never too much trouble to write a passage again and yet again, if he were not satisfied with it, as if, with his characteristic restlessness, he had started a new hare.'

Reed illustrated Elgar's 'characteristic restlessness', and the sheer speed at which he was able to work, when writing about progress on the finale. At Plas Gwyn, with Reed playing the fiddle and Ivor Atkins at the piano, 'Sir Edward strode about the room, listening and rubbing his hands excitedly. He would dash up to us with a pencil and scratch something out, writing an alternative in the margin, or add an "allargando" or "tenuto" over a certain note to make it stand out; always trying every possible effect in tone gradation, slurring or detached bowing, harmonics or natural notes. He was untiring in his efforts to explore all the possibilities in his music, and bubbling over with enthusiasm when the quest was ended and he had found what he had been seeking.'

We also see something of Elgar the individualist in Reed's account. He tells us the composer kept a potato on his desk, to clean his pen. When Reed asked him why he used a steel pen instead of one of the many fountain pens he had been given, Elgar replied, 'So that I shall have to keep going forward to dip it in the ink instead of keeping my hand in the same position the whole time. Do you think I want to get writer's cramp!'

Another account of Elgar's working methods at this time is given by Vyvyan Holland, younger son of Oscar Wilde, who was living in Hereford while working for a firm of solicitors between September 1909 and April 1910. Holland was twenty-four at the time, and he may have been introduced to Elgar by Robert Ross, Wilde's literary executor and 'the first boy Oscar ever had', as he told Frank Harris.[2] The Elgars took to inviting Holland to Sunday lunch. Writing his reminiscences[3] at the age of eighty, Holland recalled that Elgar also used to take him for walks by the Wye, when Elgar 'always carried small sheets of music paper about with him, and from time to time he would take one out of his pocket and jot down notes of some theme that had come into his head, humming to himself as he did so'. He once told Holland that he had musical day-dreams in the same way as other people had day-dreams of heroism and adventure, and that he could express almost any thought that came into his head in terms of music. Holland describes Elgar as 'a tall man [he was in fact six feet tall] overflowing with energy and nearly always in a hurry'; but although he appears to have visited the Elgars frequently over a period of six months, Holland unfortunately records nothing about Alice, the house or their domestic life.

When staying in the new London flat, Elgar took the opportunity of attending '*all* the first nights', as he told Troyte Griffith, reporting that he had seen plays by Barrie, Shaw and Granville-Barker. He had some caustic comments on them: 'The two things that produced most laughter,' he told Troyte, 'were when one man said he was brought up a Baptist (this convulsed the house both times I saw the play): in the other case a man said "I belong to the Ch. of England" this also produced roars of laughter! Curiously nothing was done or noticed when someone said he was a R. Catholic. Can you make this out? It cannot be explained in a few words but its very curious.'

The previous occupant of the flat (Arthur Strong, a former professor of Arabic at University College, London, and at one time librarian at the House of Lords) had it seems left some of his possessions behind. 'I wish you could

2. Elgar had probably met Ross through Frank and Adela Schuster; a letter from Wilde to Robert Ross of 1897 however makes it clear that Wilde had known Schuster a long time prior to 1897, so Elgar could have met Wilde's children through Schuster himself. Another possibility is that he first met them through his close friendship with the Ranee of Sarawak, with whom, it will be recalled, he had once played *Faust* as a piano duet. The ranee had a wide circle of friends, who included Henry James and H. G. Wells, and according to her daughter-in-law, the future ranee, it was Oscar Wilde who was 'the man who had been her dearest friend'; when Wilde was arrested, the ranee gave a home to his wife and children.

3. *Time Remembered* (Gollancz, 1966).

come before we leave this flat,' Elgar wrote to Troyte. 'The library here is immense ... You really should see the books – they're in all langwidges. The "pictures" also are interesting & the furniture & cups & saucers nice.' The lease on the flat expired in May 1910 and Elgar took a service flat in Queen Anne's Mansions, near St James's Park Station. His reference to the interesting pictures at 58 New Cavendish Street is a little surprising in view of corroborative accounts we have, from Reed and Dorabella, of his eccentric behaviour with regard to other people's pictures. Elgar also rented in 1910 a house in College Green, Gloucester, formerly a cookery school, and it was here, at a piano run-through of the Violin Concerto, with Ivor Atkins playing the treble and Elgar the bass, and with a crowd of friends sitting on the arms of chairs, on the floor and on the stairs, that Dorabella arrived to find all the pictures turned to the wall. Reed tells us that in many of the houses Elgar borrowed or rented, the pictures were either turned round the wrong way or covered over with some hanging material, even newspaper. 'No comment was ever made,' says Reed, 'about the odd effect produced in the room. He just didn't want these family portraits, or whatever they were, staring at him.'

In April, Elgar enjoyed a ten-day tour of Devon and Cornwall, leaving Alice at home, and it may have been while on this tour, with 'east winds mostly but glorious sun', that his ankle was so badly stung that it kept him indoors in London, in May, 'anxious to correct all I can'. It was the proofs of the Violin Concerto that he was correcting. In May too he had cause, in a letter to Schuster of 8 May, to describe the times as 'too cruel and gloomy', lamenting the death of 'that dear sweet King-Man' who 'was always so "pleasant" to me'. Grossly overweight, his body hopelessly punished by food and tobacco, Edward VII had nevertheless been receiving visitors until a few hours before he died, and his death on 6 May came as a genuine surprise and shock to the country. Elgar indeed had reason to be grateful for the king's patronage and hospitality, and he was fortunate, in view of Edward's evil temper, to have seen only the sweet side of the 'King-Man'. In the same letter, Elgar told Schuster the concerto was well in hand, in fact, that it was '*good*! awfully emotional! too emotional but I love it'. He went on to complain of having a cold, explaining that this was the reason he had not been down to The Hut: 'I have a cold & cannot face the winds,' he wrote. 'So I did not venture to Bray today although I ventured to Cough.' Alice Stuart-Wortley had been to tea and had had 'a dose of the Concerto which beseemingly she liketh well', and Lady Maud Warrender had called the day before, also for tea and to hear the concerto, so in his service flat, laid up as he was with a swollen foot and a cold, Elgar was not being neglected by his friends. The king's death was however a good excuse to remind Schuster that heaven will never be attained this side of the grave: 'We are dismally gay – walk like ghosts & eat like ghouls,' he ended. 'Oh! it is terribly sad.'

On 30 May Elgar wrote to Billy Reed – still addressing him as 'Dear Mr Reed' – to say that he did not know how to thank him sufficiently for his kind help and most beautiful playing. He was anxious to send the first movement to the printers '& am only waiting for the final "flourish" '. He said he was enclosing 'a truly diabolical effort' for him to look at: 'Any wisdom you may have to spare will be thankfully received by your very grateful friend Edward Elgar.'

Despite 'fine rows going on over the 1st performance', and being 'desperately annoyed at several things', as he reported to Schuster on 29 June, Elgar remained in exuberant mood over his first concerto. 'Good Mr Reed comes tomorrow,' he went on to tell Schuster, 'to fiddle thro' the 1st & last movements: the IIIrd is now good and strong ... This Concerto is *full* of romantic feeling.' And with a sense of absolute self-confidence he added, 'I *know* the feeling is human & right.' Elgar was of course writing for his own instrument, and the result is perhaps one of the half-dozen most original and beautiful violin concertos ever written; but in need of sympathy none the less, he opened this letter by complaining that he had been working too hard and was tired, and – 'as usual' – the weather was 'too awful'.

By August the concerto was finished. It was dedicated to Fritz Kreisler, who gave the first performance with the Royal Philharmonic Orchestra in the Queen's Hall on 10 November; according to Dorabella, Kreisler came on to the platform looking as white as a sheet. Elgar conducted the performance, and clearly felt guilty for not entrusting the task to Richter, to whom he had written a gushing and ungrammatical letter the day before: 'I have feared,' he began, 'that you may have felt a little annoyed over the first performance of the Concerto being given here.' Fine rows, he had told Schuster, had been going on over the first performance, and Elgar explained to Richter that 'things were not quite in my hands regarding this'. Some day, he promised, he would explain. Meanwhile, the German maestro would have to be content with effusive protestations of love and gratitude. 'It is wonderful to me to know that I have your real friendship,' Elgar told him. 'Perhaps, no not perhaps, that I have your love. My dear friend, you have from me all the love and reverence one man can feel for another. I feel a very small person when I am in your company, you who are so great and have been intimate with the greatest. I meet now many men, and I want you to know that I look to you as my greatest and most genuine friend in the world. I revere and love you ... The man you befriended long ago, be assured this man will never forget your kindness, your nobility, and the grandeur of your life and personality.' Three months later, his eyesight having failed, Richter retired from the rostrum.

Fritz Kreisler was not the only one in a state of nerves. Dorabella says that Elgar, when he came on to the platform, was 'very much strung up', but 'the ovation at the end was tremendous'. An explanation for the state of everybody's nerves, and for the fine rows which Elgar had told Schuster had been going on, is given by Basil Maine, at one time music critic of the *Daily Telegraph*, in *Elgar: His Life and Works*. The concerto had apparently been promised to the Royal Philharmonic Society when Novello sent a copy of the score to the Queen's Hall Orchestra, who naturally tried to secure the first performance. Both Novello and Kreisler favoured the Queen's Hall Orchestra while Elgar was determined upon the Royal Philharmonic, and according to Maine the climax of the quarrel was reached when Elgar actually tore to pieces the last movement of Kreisler's copy of the score. After the performance Schuster gave a supper party at Old Queen Street, where the guests sat at three tables in the music room, with a menu on each table headed with a theme from each of the three movements of the concerto. One of the guests was the twenty-one-year-old Adrian Boult, who recalls Elgar going up to Claude Phillips, Keeper of the Wallace Collection and a fellow-guest from time to time at The Hut, and saying, 'Well, Claude, don't you think that was a work of art.'[4]

A typically Elgarian enigma hangs over this particular work. Five days before the first performance, Elgar wrote to Nicholas Kilburn, a distinguished amateur musician with whom he had been staying near Durham when news of his knighthood arrived at Malvern, to say, 'Here, or more emphatically *in here* is enshrined or simply enclosed – buried is perhaps too definite – *the soul of* . . . ? The final 'de' [Elgar's inscription on the score is a quotation from Le Sage's preface to *Gil Blas* which reads, '*Aqui esta encerrada el alma de . . .*'] leaves it indefinite as to sex or rather gender. Now guess.' Elgar was playing games again, just as he had over the 'enigma' of the *Variations*. Michael Kennedy's reasons for believing the soul enshrined to have been that of Alice Stuart-Wortley, argued in his book *Portrait of Elgar*, seem convincing. He cites a number of letters from Elgar to Alice in which Elgar refers to 'our own concerto'. Elgar called her 'Windflower', and while working on the concerto he wrote to her to say, 'I have been working hard at the windflower themes – but all stands still until you come and approve.' In a letter to Schuster, Elgar referred to Alice Stuart-Wortley and added, 'I want to end that concerto but I do not see my way very clearly to the end so you had best invite its stepmother to The Hut too.' He wrote to Alice herself, before the first performance, to say, after mentioning a spare ticket, 'I wish I could use it and you might conduct – but you *will* be conducting the concerto wherever you are.' According to Kennedy, a sheet of Alice's notepaper has even been found with the Spanish

4. Sir Adrian Boult, in conversation with the author.

quotation in Elgar's handwriting. Perhaps more intriguing is why Elgar should have wanted to conceal the sex of the person who had inspired the concerto. He tended to idolize women and to love men, and perhaps the puritan in him felt a sense of guilt for dedicating so personal and intimate a work of refined beauty to a woman, as though it would be taken as evidence that he and whoever the woman happened to be were lovers. There is no evidence to suggest that in the physical sense Elgar ever had a lover (of either sex or gender, as he would have said). In his day platonic expressions of affection between men were not frowned upon as they often came to be later in the century, but on the other hand, infidelity between married people was officially taboo, and divorce, although obtainable at law since the year of Elgar's birth, remained the ultimate social scandal until long after his death.

Siegfried Sassoon, while on convalescent leave in 1916 in Liverpool, his mind at that time much occupied with religious imagery and the horrors of war, heard the concerto for the first time, and according to his book *Siegfried's Journey, 1916–20* (Faber, 1982) it was for him an emotional experience which his after-thoughts impelled him to report in terms that bore little relation to the music. He noted in his diary, 'In all the noblest passages of this glorious work I shut my eyes, seeing on the darkness a shape always the same – the suffering mortal figure on a cross. And around it a host of shadowy forms with upraised arms – the souls of men, agonised, and aspiring, hungry for what they seek as God in vastness and confoundment.' That first encounter with the Violin Concerto also inspired Sassoon, who in old age was himself to become a Roman Catholic, to write in his diary a poem in what he was later to describe as 'a fine – and perhaps foolish – frenzy'. It was not included in his *Collected Poems*:

> *I have seen Christ when music wove*
> *Majestic vision. Storms of prayer*
> *Deep-voiced within me marched and strove.*
> *The sorrows of the world were there.*
>
> *A god for beauty shamed and wronged,*
> *A sign where faith and ruin meet*
> *In glooms of vanquished glory thronged*
> *By spirits blinded with defeat,*
> *His head for ever bowed in pain,*
> *I feel his presence plead above*
> *The violin that speaks in vain*
> *The crowned humility of love.*
>
> *O music undeterred by death*
> *And darkness closing on your flame,*
> *Christ whispers in your dying breath*
> *And haunts you with his tragic name.*

While composing his Violin Concerto, Elgar had not been neglecting his Second Symphony. In seeking to obtain permission to dedicate it to 'the memory of His Late Majesty King Edward VII' he may have done himself a disservice, helping to fix his music in the minds of later generations as irredeemably 'Edwardian'. The work in fact has far less of the martial confidence of the First Symphony, but for some reason the slow movement, the 'lament for King Edward and dear Rody ... and all human feeling', as Alice described it, is sometimes taken to be a sad farewell to a glorious age. Elgar was not clairvoyant, and in 1910 he could not possibly have foreseen the holocaust about to overwhelm Europe; moreover, King Edward and the Edwardian era were still very much alive when he sketched the symphony. At its first performance in the Queen's Hall on 24 May 1911, just a month before the coronation of George V, the Edwardian audience itself was less than wholeheartedly enthusiastic, perhaps because they did not feel the new music from the composer of *Land of Hope and Glory* any longer reflected the glory of their age. While there was plenty of applause, the hall – surprisingly for an Elgar première – was not sold out, and Elgar sensed that the clapping was for him, not for his new composition. Alice as usual had no doubt where the fault lay: 'Dull and undiscriminating' was how she described the audience in her diary. Elgar, conducting, was even more direct: 'What is the matter with them, Billy?' he hissed at the leader, his new friend Billy Reed. 'They sit there like a lot of stuffed pigs.' It was the beginning of the end of the public's instant acclamation of anything Elgar wrote; indeed, the first performance of the Violin Concerto had been the last occasion on which a major work of his was to be received with real excitement. Elgar was to write many more works, only one of them incontestably great, and he still had twenty-three years to live.

Writing about the Second Symphony in his book *Elgar*, Billy Reed confirmed Alice's understanding that the slow movement constituted a 'lament for King Edward' when he wrote that it expressed the deep feeling and grief experienced by the people on their national bereavement. He seems to have known, and to have disagreed with, Alice's linking of 'dear Rody' with the king, for he added, 'There is no personal note in the profound sorrow and grief.' Not only was the king still alive when the work was sketched, but there could hardly be a more deeply felt cry of anguish than that which almost screams from the slow movement of the Second Symphony, and both Alice and Reed were surely missing something, especially in the light of Elgar's behaviour and correspondence at the time of Alfred Rodewald's death in 1903, in attributing its inspiration to the demise of the sovereign. It was without doubt for 'dear Rody', and no one else, that this broken-hearted lament was written.

Nevertheless, Elgar did make rather a meal of dedicating the whole work to the memory of King Edward. Sir Arthur Bigge, private secretary to King George V, told Elgar on 16 March 1911, 'Your request to dedicate to the memory of King Edward a Symphony which you composed shortly before the death of His late Majesty has been brought before the King, and I am commanded to inform you that His Majesty has much pleasure in granting the desired permission.' Not content with such a straightforward response, Elgar sent, on 22 March, no less than three possible versions of the precise wording of the dedication, together with a sprawling three-page letter, and a postscript asking for a reply before sailing for Canada – this at a time when the royal household was trying to cope with the aftermath of King Edward's death while making preparations for the new king's coronation.

'Dear Sir Arthur Bigge,' Elgar wrote, 'I have received your letter kindly conveying His Majesty the King's precious permission to dedicate my symphony to the memory of His late Majesty King Edward and I shall be very grateful if you will be good enough to convey to His Majesty a simple expression of the gratitude I feel for the permission and my deep sense of the honour.

'I am very sorry to trouble you further but the wording of this dedication is necessarily somewhat unusual and I should be extremely obliged if you could tell me if either of the forms which I enclose would be suitable and correct. I am very sensible that I am troubling you in a very small matter as regards my symphony but you will readily and very kindly understand that I am anxious that the dedication, to which I attach the highest importance, should be absolutely agreeable to His Majesty the King. Believe me, Yours very faithfully, Edward Elgar. PTO. PS, I have to sail for Canada on Saturday and it would be delightfully convenient if it could be possible for me to have a reply before sailing.'

The reply Elgar received, dated 24 March, could have been neither more prompt nor more brief: 'Dear Sir Edward Elgar, The King approves of the proposed wording of the dedication of your Symphony, which I have marked with a cross. Yours very truly, Arthur Bigge.' Elgar acknowledged the king's choice of wording from on board the Cunard ship *RMS Mauretania* on 25 March.

In coronation year the Elgars rented another London flat, this time at 75 Gloucester Place. In April, Elgar toured Canada and the Mid-West of America, where he wore a bowler hat and claimed that every nerve was shattered by some 'angularity, vulgarity and general horror'. On 17 June he received a letter from Buckingham Palace offering him the Order of Merit in George V's Coronation Honours List, and that meant the time had come for Sir Edward Elgar, OM, and Lady Elgar to take their proper place in Society. Clearly a permanent home in London was called for. The 'sweet borderland' where he had made his home, with its over-hung lanes and bird-filled hedges, the River

Severn and the River Wye, not to mention Plas Gwyn itself, were all to be sacrificed. Clubs in the West End and a huge house near Hampstead Heath were now the order of the day, and by July they had fixed upon an imposing property called Kelston, at 42 Netherhall Gardens. The architect was none other than Norman Shaw.[5]

Until the emergence of Sir Edwin Lutyens, Shaw was perhaps the most famous architect of his day, an 'alert and versatile genius' in the opinion of Sir Robert Ensor.[6] One of his most famous buildings (although not perhaps his most successful) was New Scotland Yard, built in 1889, two years after he had designed Kelston for the painter Edward Long. Elgar renamed his enormous new home (the first he had ever owned – though, alas for his self-esteem, it was on a mortgage) Severn House. The square, mahogany-panelled entrance hall boasted a floor paved with Carthaginian mosaics said to be over 2,000 years old. A picture gallery sixty feet long (a strange feature for the home of a man who liked to hang pictures facing the wall) led from the entrance hall to a second inner hall, followed by a dining-room twenty-eight feet by twenty-five and a heated conservatory with a vine. The entire house was centrally heated. There was also a billiard room, for which Elgar purchased a billiard table, and on this, Billy Reed tells us, he would lay out his microscopes but seldom finish a game of billiards.

On the first floor, in eighteenth-century fashion, there was the drawing-room, twenty-nine feet by nineteen (supplied by Frank Schuster with French Empire furniture), a half-panelled studio, measuring no less than thirty-six feet by twenty-four, which Elgar used as a music room, an Oriental Room and a library, fitted with book-cases with movable shelves. There were also five principal bedrooms, three bedrooms for servants, stabling and a garage. The garden however was fairly small because after eight years Edward Long had become bored with the house and had commissioned Shaw to build him another one in the back garden.

'I ape royal state,' Elgar confessed in a letter to a friend, Canon C. V. Gorton, before he had moved in.[7] In May workmen were still swarming about, and during what he called 'the trouble', Elgar told Troyte Griffith he had shifted his muse into his dressing room, where he could only hear 'a dull thud

5. Kelston was to be demolished in 1937, when it was just fifty years old, for no better reason than to build four new houses on the site. A plaque has been placed on the present No. 42 Netherhall Gardens, but a more accurate siting of the original house is believed by some to be where the present No. 44 Netherhall Gardens stands.

6. Sir Robert Ensor, writing in *England 1870–1914*. Readers interested in the work of Norman Shaw should consult *Richard Norman Shaw* by Andrew Saint (Yale University Press, 1976), in which further details about the house can be found.

7. Canon Charles Gorton was chairman of the Morecambe Music Festival Committee and had met Elgar when the composer was adjudicating at the festival. Elgar frequently consulted him on matters of theology and church history.

occasionally'. He was at this time engaged on *The Music Makers*, begun some eight years before. Apart from this work and the symphonic study *Falstaff*, no music of any consequence was written actually under the roof of Severn House during the nine years Elgar lived there, although much inferior music was, and there can be little doubt that it was written to pay for the cost of running a place described by Sir Adrian Boult, a regular visitor to the house, as 'so absolutely pretentious it wasn't funny'.[8]

The Elgars were invited to the coronation ceremony on 22 June, to which Elgar contributed a March, one of his less inspired occasional pieces, and an Offertory for chorus and orchestra, *O harken thou*. The new king in whose honour he had composed these works was very different from Elgar's previous royal patron. While Edward VII had been idle and unlettered, in diplomacy as well as literature, unfaithful to his wife but quick to take offence if he thought himself in any way slighted, George V came to typify everything that was worthy, conscientious, honourable – and dull. Not particularly bright or imaginative (it took some persuasion by the Dean of Westminster before he would consent to the burial of the Unknown Warrior), and in artistic matters even less well tutored than Edward, George was also a harsh and repressive father where his own father had been indulgent and loving. In time he came to identify himself exclusively with his own repressed and ageing generation, to which Elgar (but not Edward VII) also belonged.

Shortly after the coronation, William Strang, a disciple of Whistler who was to be elected to the Royal Academy as an engraver a few months before his death in 1921, and who had in 1909 drawn a portrait of King Edward's fifteen-year-old grandson, Prince Edward, was commissioned by the king to draw a portrait of Elgar to hang at Windsor Castle. Elgar sat for Strang in profile, and the result is a strong, serious and imposing head and face, made all the more impressive by the light, almost incidental treatment of the shoulders and suit, a few deliberately indecisive pencil marks fading away to the bottom of the drawing.

The cumulative strain of work on the Violin Concerto and the Second Symphony, the excitement of the coronation, the receipt of the OM and the move to Hampstead, may have prompted Elgar to seek some relaxation (as well as some instant remuneration with which to meet the running costs of Severn House) by accepting for a short period the post of principal conductor with the London Symphony Orchestra. It was in 1912 that Reed became its leader, and he and the other players with whom Elgar toured enjoyed one another's company, swopping tales on trains of musical events and en-counters, Elgar 'rubbing his hands together gleefully', according to Reed,

8. In conversation with the author.

'entirely forgetting the pessimistic moods and the despondency that sometimes overtook him'.

As a conductor, Elgar was generally considered more successful with his own works than with other people's. Reed in fact thought that during Elgar's lifetime the finest performances of his works were those he conducted himself. 'He had something quite magnetic about him when he took his place at the conductor's desk,' he recalled. 'He had the power to hold everyone with his glance; and when his sensitive hands – with those long, delicate fingers – were raised, the atmosphere was tense, the mood established.' Reed says that Elgar conveyed all his meaning without effort, and had the rare gift of showing his innermost feelings by his facial expression alone. His early experience as an orchestral player, Reed adds, had taught him the most valuable lesson, of 'allowing the orchestra to play'. His innate sympathy for players is illustrated by a comment Richter made about Elgar's scoring of the First Symphony, to the effect that he scored accurately for each instrument with the dynamic marks needed for each player, whereas most composers put their signs in from the point of view of the conductor.[9]

Often, when conducting his own music, Elgar's 'expressive hands hardly moved' while he obtained 'fire, passion, serenity, and above all, spirituality' from the players. As a conductor of other people's works, however, Reed thought he was 'naturally very diffident and restrained . . . and this hampered him in many ways, so that he could not obtain that spontaneous expression that he nearly always elicited from his own works.'

Sir John Barbirolli recalled playing in the cello section at the first post-war revival of the Three Choirs Festival in 1920, when Elgar – 'radiantly happy among his friends in the cathedral precincts' – conducted *The Dream of Gerontius* from memory. 'Although he could not be called a great conductor by the highest professional standards,' Sir John has written, 'it was extraordinary how he could make you feel exactly what he wanted if you were in sympathy with him.' Barbirolli's own conducting of his music was to be appreciated by Elgar at the end of his life, although they met very seldom, the last time being about six months before Elgar's death when Barbirolli went to see the composer at Marl Bank, his last home in Worcester.[10] Barbirolli later

9. *My Own Trumpet* by Sir Adrian Boult.
10. 'I know that Mr Barbirolli is an extremely able youth and, very properly, has ideas of his own, added to which he is a remarkably able conductor,' Elgar wrote to Compton Mackenzie on 6 July 1928. After Barbirolli had conducted the Second Symphony for the first time in December 1928 Elgar wrote to him to say, 'I hear splendid accounts of your conducting the symphony concert on Monday last; for your kind care of my work I send you my sincere thanks. I should have sent a word before the concert had I known of it, but I was quite unaware that anything of mine was being given.' It was perhaps just as well that Elgar had been unaware: originally the symphony was due to be conducted by his *bête noire*, Beecham, who had to withdraw four days before the concert owing to a leg injury.

recalled to his wife that Elgar was very warm, gave him a hug and told him how much he liked the way he interpreted his music. When Barbirolli left, 'Elgar embraced him again with great warmth and affection'.[11]

During 1911, while the king had gone off to India to be crowned emperor and to kill animals, Elgar had patched together various old sketches to produce a popular suite for a masque called *The Crown of India*. A contralto and bass soloist share with chorus and orchestra such numbers as the 'Dance of the Nautch Girls', the 'March of the Mogul Emperors', the 'Rule of England', a 'Warriors' Dance' and of course a 'Crown of India March'. Elgar conducted the entire run of the masque at the London Coliseum, opening on 11 March 1912. Elgar explained to Frances Colvin, whose husband Sidney was at the time Keeper of the Department of Prints and Drawings at the British Museum, that as a reward for writing *The Dream of Gerontius* he had been obliged 'to starve and go without fires for 12 months', whereas 'this small effort allows me to buy scientific works I have yearned for and I spend my time between the Coliseum and the old bookshops'.

In other ways, however, his bout on the rostrum did not pay off: by 25 March Elgar was reporting to Canon Gorton that he had been trying to keep engagements 'between rather severe attacks of gout'. He must have been better a month later, for on 27 April he went for a walk on Hampstead Heath (the Elgars had moved into their new home on New Year's Day), where, he later reported to Frances Colvin, he came upon 'two excellent anti-socialist lecturers'. He was back on the Heath on 19 June, having that day completed his setting of Arthur O'Shaughnessy's *The Music Makers*, an ode for contralto or mezzosoprano, chorus and orchestra, to be first performed at Birmingham on 1 October that year. The work makes use of quotations from previous scores – the *Enigma Variations*, *Sea Pictures*, *The Dream of Gerontius*, the Violin Concerto and both symphonies – and is regarded by some as one of Elgar's few seriously undervalued compositions. His own reaction to its completion on 19 June was a wail of self-pity, sent up the following day in a letter to Alice Stuart-Wortley. He had had 'the most awful day', he told her, 'which inevitably occurs when I have completed a work'. Having promised himself 'open air and sympathy', a day 'with lovely weather', it had turned out bitterly cold. Alice and Carice were away, so he had wandered alone on the Heath, wrapped in a thick overcoat, and had sat for two minutes with tears streaming out of his eyes, loathing the world. He had then gone back indoors, only to find the house empty and cold, so out he had gone again, back to the Heath – a good twelve minutes' walk, across Fitzjohn's Avenue, probably down Lyndhurst Road, across Rosslyn Hill and down Pond Street. Having returned to the Heath, he

11. Letter from Lady Barbirolli to the author dated 31 May 1980.

shivered and longed to destroy his latest creation; fortunately for posterity, he had just sent the last pages to the printer.

Another work begun much earlier (it had probably been in Elgar's mind since about 1902), the symphonic study *Falstaff*, was also resurrected and finished within eighteen months of the move to Severn House. On 22 July 1913 Elgar reported to Troyte Griffith that *Falstaff* was 'immense' and wanted a 'gigantesque orchestra'. He took the manuscript with him on holiday to North Wales, to a house called Tan-yr-allt ('Under the Hill') at Penmaen-mawr, where he scored the work in time for the 1913 Leeds Festival. Landon Ronald, to whom the work was dedicated, told John Barbirolli that he could not make head nor tail of it, and the audience at the first performance on 1 October was equally unenthusiastic.[12] In 1931, however, when Eric Fenby, Delius's amanuensis, met Elgar at the composer's favourite London hotel, the Langham, and told him he thought *Falstaff* 'the finest piece of programme music ever written', Elgar responded by telling him he actually thought it was his best work.[13]

Fenby's high regard for *Falstaff* was shared by Bernard Shaw, who wrote to Elgar in 1921 to say, 'I never heard Falstaff before. It's magnificent, and perfectly graphic to anyone who knows his Shakespeare. All the other geniuses whom I venture to admire let me down one time or another; but you never fail.' Shaw went on to suggest that *Falstaff* was a more successful work than Strauss's *Till Eulenspiegel* and *Don Quixote*, indeed, that it ought to be played three times to their once.

With Severn House to fill with guests, it can safely be assumed that Alice was in what Jaeger would have called her seventh heaven of happiness. She soon established a sort of musical salon; callers and diners included the great Russian bass Chaliapin, whom Elgar had heard in *Boris Godunov* on 24 June 1913, describing him a month later to Troyte Griffith as 'a fine man & glorious artist', Paderewski, the Polish pianist, composer and statesman, Siegfried Wagner, the composer's son, and Hamilton Harty. For Elgar the distractions of life in Town were piling up: attending the Royal Academy private view (it took only fifteen minutes by cab into the West End); paying visits to friends in Kensington; lunching with fellow-clubmen in St James's Street; or spending a quiet afternoon in the London Library. The gay social whirl was only disturbed by news that Julia Worthington was dying of cancer, and both she and Lord Northampton, who had invited Elgar to stay with him only two weeks previously, died in June, within a week of one another.

The purchase of Severn House, the award of the Order of Merit and entry

12. *Barbirolli* by Michael Kennedy (MacGibbon & Kee, 1972).
13. *Delius As I Knew Him* by Eric Fenby (Bell & Sons, 1936).

into London life seem to have precipitated in both Elgar and Alice an acute attack of *folie de grandeur*. 'Pray it may be given to E.,' Alice noted in her diary after discussing with a friend possible candidates for the Nobel Peace Prize. On arriving at a Royal Academy dinner to which he had been invited, and after inspecting the seating plan, Elgar decided he had not been given a position worthy of a holder of the OM, and stormed out.[14] At the Three Choirs Festival he rigged himself out, not for the last time at a musical event, in court dress in order to be photographed with Saint-Saëns. While living in Hereford, Elgar had already had printed a card that read: 'SIR EDWARD ELGAR is absent abroad; your communication shall be laid before him on his return', and he had once told Dorabella, perhaps half in jest, 'Don't you know yet that "England" is sufficient address for me?' (According to Sir Compton Mackenzie, writing in his autobiography *My Record of Music*, Elgar did once receive a postcard from a South Sea island addressed 'Edward Elgar, England', which had given him great pleasure.) Now, on purchasing Severn House, he submitted to the Post Office a palindromic telegraph address made up of his current honours: 'Siromoris'. The truth is that both Elgar and Alice, even with her upper-middle-class origins, tended to behave as what they undoubtedly were – parvenus. They both referred to their titled friends (and social equals) by their titles alone; in letters, Elgar referred to Alice as Lady Elgar, and when she died he even had her title, with her father's, engraved on her tombstone. He would take hours redrafting letters to celebrities until he was satisfied he had the correct usage under control, and it is sad to find him at seventy, Master of the King's Music and one of the most eminent Roman Catholic laymen of his day, commencing a letter to the Archbishop of Canterbury 'My Lord Archbishop', and signing it 'With every respect, Believe me to be, Very sincerely & affectionately, Your Grace's obedient servant'.

Elgar's stay in London was to coincide with the gradual collapse of the world on which all his values were based, and although increasingly garlanded with honours, he was to find himself stepping further and further out of tune with the times in which he lived. His formative years had run parallel with the transformation of England from an agricultural into an industrial nation, and for a composer who was a country boy and drew his inspiration exclusively from nature this mad rush to intensive industrialization and mass production must have had an enervating effect. It was the industrial revolution which had created a whole new prosperous middle class and made possible an unprecedented degree of social mobility; while most men who achieved increased

14. The Royal Academy dinners were at that time serenaded by a choir. Sir Thomas Armstrong recalled to the author going as a choirboy to one of these dinners and attempting, through an intermediary, to obtain Elgar's autograph; Elgar 'made a most ungracious fuss' about it.

social status did so through hard work in industry or commerce, Elgar had been notably assisted by his marriage, and he never showed any sympathy or understanding for those whose success had been achieved by real struggle, hardship and hunger. All Elgar's deprivations were emotional, and it is not difficult to see how trade unionism, or radicalism in any form, struck him not as a reasonable and legitimate means of fulfilling the aspirations of others less fortunate than himself, but merely as a threat to his own social stability.

The Elgars were on holiday in Scotland when war was declared on 4 August 1914. Alice immediately entered into the prevailing madness of the time and after watching soldiers leaving Inverness and Edinburgh to be slaughtered in France, she noted that 'a glorious spirit seemed to pervade all'. On returning to London she 'embarrassed us by going into the local shops and asking how many recruits they had', according to Carice, and then flung herself into war work, making use of her linguistic abilities by teaching French to a group of fifty private soldiers in Chelsea Barracks. Carice took up censorship, and Elgar lost no time in joining the Special Constabulary, soon becoming a staff inspector. 'I am sure others cd do the work better,' he told Schuster on 25 August, 'but none with a better will.' After informing his patron of his absolute financial ruin, and regretting being too old to be a soldier, he assured him also that he was cheerful and would die 'a man if not a musician'.

In the same letter he gave off a lamentable shriek about sending horses to the front (a number of the First World War generals believed for a long time that the matter could be settled by cavalry, and the artillery made use of horses throughout the war). 'The only thing that wrings my heart and soul,' he told Schuster in a flight of hysterical fancy which was bizarre and unconvincing even by Elgar's standards, 'is the thought of the horses – oh! my beloved animals – the men – and women can go to hell – but my horses; I walk round & round this room cursing God for allowing dumb beasts to be tortured – let him kill his human beings but – how CAN HE? Oh, my horses.'

The idea that God was to blame for the army transporting horses to France was poor theology, and despite his posturing as a country gentleman, any suggestion that Elgar cared for animals other than his own dogs is humbug. He may have ridden his father's pony when he was a boy, but putting money on race horses as an adult hardly made him an animal-lover: on the contrary, he hunted otters, thrashed other people's dogs and catapulted shoes at cats. As to the men and women he preferred to see killed, few people in public or artistic life had been more generously treated than Elgar, and it is difficult to guess what gigantic grudge he thought he was justified in holding against the millions about to die in order that he might go on living in luxury at Severn House. Sir Adrian Boult might well have had this ludicrous and distasteful letter in mind when he said of Elgar, 'He had a very stupid mind, in some ways.'[15]

Various forms of mental derangement were gripping people on the outbreak of war. Hans Richter, while claiming the hours he had spent with his English friends had been the happiest of his artistic life, lost no time in shedding his honorary English degrees. German music became as unthinkable at concerts as dachshunds in Green Park, and Elgar could hope no more for performances of *The Dream of Gerontius* in Düsseldorf. The king himself saw fit to change his surname from Hanover to Windsor, in case it was thought that a man with so much German blood in his veins, even if he were king, might prove a traitor; and Queen Mary's brother, Prince Alexander of Teck, who was directly descended through his mother from George III and had married Queen Victoria's granddaughter, Princess Alice, renounced his royal title in exchange for an earldom. Prince Louis of Battenberg, First Sea Lord, was actually sacked because of his German origins, and became a marquess; and even the Bechstein Hall was renamed the Wigmore.

Apart from his duties in the Special Constabulary, and later in the Hampstead Volunteer Reserve, to which he transferred in 1915, Elgar was to devote the first three years of the war to writing patriotic music. The first Promenade Concert of the season, held only eleven days after the war had been declared, saw the première of *Sospiri*, a miniature piece for strings, harp and organ, dedicated to Billy Reed, and the orchestra also played the *Pomp and Circumstance March* No. 1; Benson's words and Elgar's music proved an irresistible combination for the times, and *Land of Hope and Glory* quite simply became a second national anthem. *Follow the Colours, Carillon, Polonia, The Spirit of England* (dedicated 'To the memory of our glorious men, with a special thought for the Worcesters'), a song called *Fight for the Right* (for the 'Members of the Fight for the Right Movement') and a setting of four poems by Kipling, *The Fringes of the Fleet* (this was dedicated to Elgar's old friend Beresford, now an admiral and a baron) are some of the musical offerings that kept Elgar busy and audiences happy until increasing depression and ill-health drove him, towards the end of 1917, to the peace and quiet of Sussex and back to his last brief phase of serious composing.

Quite apart from the outbreak of war and the opportunity it gave Elgar to parade his talents as Master of the King's Music long before that post fell to him (a post for which, as few musicians ever are, he was admirably qualified), 1914 stood as a watershed in his and Alice's lives in a number of ways. At the very start of the year, Elgar commenced his association with the recording industry, an association that was to fascinate and amuse him until the very

---

15. In conversation with the author.

end of his life. He and Alice celebrated their silver wedding anniversary, and Dorabella – now, as Alice had been on the eve of her marriage, a spinster of forty – decided that the time had come to stop flirting with Elgar and to face up to reality. It was time, too, for Elgar to acknowledge that his sweet Dorabella was no longer a child. She became engaged to a man called Richard Powell, whom she brought to meet Elgar shortly after their marriage in January, and from that moment, the nineteen-year-long relationship ceased. By her own account, during the years that she knew Elgar, Dorabella had been 'a good deal taken up with both parish and town activities in Wolverhampton, helping with entertainments, sales and bazaars, and attending countless committee meetings'. She also ran a string orchestra and sang with the Wolverhampton Choral Society, and no doubt these worthy provincial activities had helped to keep her mind off marriage during the years when she felt such fascination for Elgar and was so flattered by his friendship and attention. But he was now fifty-seven, and 'the Lady' seemed to be managing rather too efficiently to run her new, grandiose establishment in London without sending for help every few minutes. Elgar, in any case, was no longer the local celebrity who nipped off on a bicycle for a couple of hours or flagged down a carriage if he wanted to go shopping; he was a member of the establishment, who lunched at the Athenaeum and for whom cars were sent by recording companies. One way and another it was obvious that the relationship had served its time.

Dorabella had seen Elgar at work and at play over the entire period of his greatest inspiration, and she had been a catalyst to some extent in both. She tells us she danced round the room while Elgar played, and no one with Elgar's fiery temperament would have tolerated such conduct from anyone of whom he was not especially fond. She was willingly made use of by Alice, and she became so familiar with the family that she took to using many of the virtually meaningless expressions that clutter the pages of Elgar's letters (when staying at Forli on one occasion, she recorded in her diary that Troyte Griffith had been to dinner: 'Great larks' was her illuminating comment on the evening). While much of what she recorded about the Elgar household so long after the events has to be taken with a pinch of salt, some of her musical reflections are valuable. Her description of Elgar playing the piano, 'not like a pianist, he almost seemed to play like a whole orchestra', is illuminating. 'It sounded full,' she said, 'without being loud and he contrived to make you hear other instruments joining in.' The evidence she provides of Elgar's likes and dislikes, however, has to be disentangled. While living at Craig Lea, Elgar began to receive unsolicited manuscripts from aspiring musicians hoping for free advice. One score through which Elgar and Dorabella were thumbing one day contained a melody which Elgar said was straight out of Beethoven, and

Dorabella, somewhat tactlessly, responded by suggesting that Elgar had himself quoted in *Gerontius* from Chopin's *Polonaise Fantaisie*. 'I know nothing about pianoforte music,' Elgar is alleged to have snapped. 'I hate the piano as an instrument and I don't care for Chopin and I have never heard the piece you mention.' This sounds like an over-reaction to the suggestion that he had consciously cribbed someone else's tune, and is interesting more as a record of Elgar's touchiness than as a literal commentary on his musical preferences. In telling Dorabella he hated the piano as an instrument, if indeed this is exactly what he did say, he must have meant he hated to play it in public for he did not play it well. In response to a suggestion made to him in 1925 by Compton Mackenzie that he should play the piano part in a recording of his Piano Quintet, Elgar wrote, 'I never play the pianoforte. I scramble through things orchestrally in a way that would madden with envy all existing pianists. I never did play really. I must not begin now.' Elgar never composed at the piano, and he never played the instrument professionally, but he did teach the instrument, and of course he used it to try out his compositions from manuscript or to run through his scores with intimate friends or fellow musicians. No one who hated the piano as an instrument in the sense that Dorabella conveys would have written a piano quintet or toyed for years with the idea of writing a piano concerto. As for Chopin, Elgar based his symphonic prelude, *Polonia*, composed in 1915 for the Polish Relief Fund, on a Chopin Nocturne, and in 1933, as one of his very last musical tasks, he transcribed the Funeral March from Chopin's Sonata in B flat minor; it received its first performance on 25 February the following year, at his own Royal Philharmonic Society memorial concert.

The position Elgar had now attained as a prominent member of the establishment, and not just within the musical world, was pointed up when he was approached in 1914 to sign, along with nineteen others, a letter to *The Times* protesting about the government's intention to grant Home Rule to Ireland. He is said to have hesitated before signing because he had religious scruples, but in the end he agreed, on the telephone on the evening of 2 March, and the letter appeared the next morning. Among his co-signatories were the Duke of Portland, Lord Roberts, Lord Balfour, the Dean of Canterbury and Rudyard Kipling. It could be suggested that he joined a company more notable, on this occasion, for its eminence than its wisdom, for the declaration incorporated in the letter, to which he and the others invited people of like mind to subscribe, was in fact an exhortation to anarchy: 'If the Bill is so passed,' it read, 'I shall hold myself justified in taking or supporting any action that may be effective to prevent it being put into operation, and more particularly to prevent the armed forces of the Crown being used to deprive the people of

Ulster of their rights as citizens of the United Kingdom.' Just how Elgar, Kipling and the others thought they were going to hold back the armed forces of the Crown is not clear, but more than one million people signed the declaration, civil war broke out, Ireland was partitioned and the bloodshed has never ceased.

Much more constructive was the initiative of Fred Gaisberg of the Gramophone Company (producers of the His Master's Voice records) in acquiring in 1914 the prestige of Elgar's name and patronage. F. W. Gaisberg, one of two brothers who pioneered the recording of music in this country, was to become a major collaborator with Elgar; indeed, his initiative in recording Elgar's interpretations of his own works probably gave him more satisfaction than anything else he did. He was the kind of romantic adventurer who, having signed up Caruso in 1910 to record ten songs for a fee of £100 only to receive a telegram from London reading 'Fee exorbitant forbid you to record', was capable of ignoring instructions, paying the tenor himself, and in the process making £1 million for Caruso and £2 million for his own company. Born in 1873 in Washington, DC, Gaisberg sang as a boy in Sousa's choir and was awarded a piano scholarship by the city, but it was essentially as an impresario that he was to flourish, for he had an extraordinary gift for dealing with artists with tact and sympathy.[16] His brother, W. C. Gaisberg, was gassed while recording in the field the last weeks of the Great War and died in 1918, just six days before the Armistice was signed. He and Fred, who lived until 1951, are buried in Hampstead Cemetery.

The English branch of the Gramophone Company had a top-floor studio in London at 21 City Road. Landon Ronald, the conductor, was the company's musical adviser. He was due to conduct the first performance on 15 February 1914 of a new short work for small orchestra by Elgar called *Carissima*, and it occurred to him that because of its length it would make an ideal test piece for the recording studio; if they hurried, it might also be on sale before the first performance. So on 20 January, Elgar having written a 'wonderful part-song' in the morning, according to Alice's diary, he and Alice set off on the first of many journeys by car to the studio. The weather, we are told, was 'very cold and grey', but they were 'much amused' by the excursion. Elgar would have known most of the musicians who had been recruited for the occasion from a variety of London orchestras, and with them he conducted his first recording. By 24 January the company had also presented him with his first gramophone, and for the next twenty years they were to treat him like a star. Nothing would be too much trouble: cars would be sent to collect him from his home, new

16. His book, *Music on Record* (Robert Hale, 1946), is a fascinating history of the recording industry he had done so much to promote.

gramophones delivered to match the colour of his own furniture, piles of records would be dispatched whenever he requested them. From Elgar's point of view, conducting his own works for the gramophone gave him an entirely new interest just when his creative powers were beginning to wane; after the death of Alice in 1920, and with the virtual certainty that he would never write another masterpiece, his connections with the Gramophone Company were a godsend. He had always been intrigued by mechanical gadgets, and in the early years of this century one had to be very sophisticated indeed not to believe that some form of magic was at work in reproducing the sounds of an orchestra or a human voice on a disc. His visits to the studio kept him in touch with the musicians whose company he enjoyed more than anyone else's, the sales of his records ensured for his music a far wider audience than it would have enjoyed had it been restricted to the concert hall, and the retainer he was paid by the company became a valuable addition to his income. The one major disadvantage, the initial necessity to cut drastically and to rearrange long works in order to accommodate them on four-minute records, does not seem to have bothered him in the least.

In the early days of recording a great many composers and performers were deeply sceptical about the quality of reproduction it would eventually be possible to obtain through gramophone records, but Elgar was thrilled with the whole process right from the start. On 24 January, the day their first gramophone arrived, the Elgars listened to it most of the afternoon, and thought Chaliapin as Boris 'the most wonderful'. Next day found 'E ... still pleased with gramophone', and on 26 January, 'Gramophone Co. sent man to see colour of wood to match E.'s room better.' Although 'deep in his part-songs', he was 'playing gramophone very often'. Alice Stuart-Wortley came to tea, heard the new toy, and was 'much astonished by it'. Only a week after being recorded *Carissima* arrived: 'Most lovely and exquisite record,' Alice enthused. 'Pray it may go on.' That evening a new, unpolished gramophone was delivered, but the Elgars were not satisfied with its tone and had it sent back. By April, when the record of *Carissima* was not only on sale but received a favourable review in the *Talking Machine News*, Elgar was under contract with the company and Alice's prayer had been answered.

Elgar's patriotic period was launched on 10 October with the first performance at the Albert Hall of *Follow the Colours*, an adaptation of an earlier Marching Song. He followed this up by a recitation with orchestra called *Carillon*, of which Elgar conducted the first performance at the Queen's Hall on 7 December. For the next two years Elgar was to involve himself in an arbitrary sort of way with an odd diversity of projects. In 1915 he was persuaded to collaborate on a play for children called *The Starlight Express*, for which he wrote the incidental music, but which ran for only four weeks. *Polonia* had its première on 6 July that year. In 1916 Clara Butt gave the first performance of Elgar's setting of Laurence Binyon's poem *For the Fallen* part, of the larger work, *The Spirit of England*. This was not performed as a whole until the following year, when the king and queen and Queen Alexandra went to hear it. He was also at work on the score of a ballet, *The Sanguine Fan*, incorporated in March 1917 in a review called *Chelsea on Tiptoe*.

In 1916 he went on a tour with the London Symphony Orchestra that crammed into less than a week engagements in Birmingham, Liverpool, Manchester, Newcastle, Glasgow and Edinburgh, and shortly after the tour, on his way to stay with his sister Polly, Elgar suffered an attack of giddiness on the train and was rushed to a nursing home where he was kept under observation for three days. The cause of this collapse may have been a combination of emotional and physical stress. He had no relatives or close friends engaged in the war, and in many ways he was under less strain than many people; on the other hand he had no major work in progress to absorb his nervous energy, no focal point of artistic striving about which to write to friends. By composing a great deal of trivial stuff he was in his own way making some sort of war effort, but that was no substitute; no doubt he just wanted the whole meaningless period through which both he and the entire nation were living to stop.

It has been suggested that Elgar was suffering, like Julius Caesar, Martin Luther and Dean Swift, from Menière's Disease, named after Prosper Menière who first described it in 1861. It is a condition usually confined to middle age and is slightly more common in men than in women. The symptoms are often deafness and intermittent attacks of giddiness, and a sudden attack of intense giddiness can follow an initial deafness in one ear. Elgar certainly seems to have suffered an unexpected attack of giddiness, but there is no record of any deafness, and his condition seems to have cleared up without the necessity of an operation.

Another possibility is that Elgar's collapse on the train had been to some extent a psychological protest at living in London. He and Alice certainly had very different tastes so far as the countryside and even the provinces were concerned. 'So nice to be in London again after Bradford's very local atmosphere,' Alice patronizingly noted in her diary on returning to Severn House in June after a visit to stay with friends. Elgar however had lost no opportunity to slip away to the Lake District (from whence he wrote to Schuster in October to say he was sick of towns), to go down to Worcestershire to see Ivor Atkins or to stay with the Graftons; the following summer he was to settle something in his mind by renting a cottage in Sussex in much the same manner as nineteen years before he had rented Birchwood Lodge. It was to prove an equally inspired move.

Having already rescued some of the effort that had gone into the ill-starred *Starlight Express* by recording extracts from the score in February 1916, in November that year Elgar set about cutting his Violin Concerto for the recording company and writing in a part for harp. The extent of the cuts required was far more drastic than any mutilation carried out by Beecham on the First Symphony, and fascinated though he may have been with the technical problems associated with recording, there can have been only one reason a man of such fastidiousness should have been prepared to slash a work he loved: he needed the money to run Severn House. What was left of the concerto was recorded on 16 December. Shortly after nine o'clock in the morning, the Gramophone Company's car arrived, and the Elgars set off for the studio in 'frightful fog'. On the way, a cart ran into them, and on the way back they just managed to avoid a smash with a Red Cross car, apparently travelling on the wrong side of the road. They did not get any lunch until a quarter to three, by which time Elgár was suffering from a headache and was feeling very tired. The concerto, however, all twelve minutes of it, sounded 'lovely'.

In January 1917 the company launched their own magazine, the *Voice*, and just three years after having made his first recording, Elgar was writing for the first issue to describe the gramphone itself as 'perhaps the most remarkable of all home instruments', and the records of his own compositions as 'remarkably faithful reproductions of the originals'. It is hard to judge how sincere these comments were; he was, after all, under contract to the company, and it was in his interests to promote the records commercially.

The death on 12 February of George Sinclair left a gap in the list of those associated with the *Enigma Variations* (his dog, Dan, had died in 1903 and was buried in the garden of the Conservative Club in Hereford); only twelve days later his old uncle Henry died too, creating another rift with the past, and a further reminder of his own advancing years.

The final flowering of Elgar's genius in a last concentrated burst of creative energy coincided with the renting in 1917 of Brinkwells in Sussex, a tiny thatched cottage standing at the end of a cart track in countryside extraordinarily reminiscent of the Malvern Hills; two miles outside the village of Fittleworth on the A283, and half-way between Petworth and Pulborough, it is within easy motoring distance of Brighton and Chichester. The cottage had an open log-fire in the sitting-room, an earth closet in the garden (which still remains), only three bedrooms (one, of course, being reserved for the maid), and a garden studio (since removed) where Elgar worked. Alice must have loathed it, but here Elgar was able once again to indulge his fantasy of returning to nature. Those who would argue that this was no fantasy should remember that it was real for Elgar only in so far as he drew his musical inspiration from the countryside; he was always torn between his creative vocation and his social ambitions, and the rustic walker needed to dress up every now and again in frock-coat, court dress and decorations.

Brinkwells was surrounded by acres of chestnut trees, among which was a ghostly copse of dead trees once struck by lightning and left with gnarled and twisted branches, to which Elgar was repeatedly drawn and which Reed believes had a profound influence on the chamber works Elgar wrote while staying at Brinkwells. In particular the 'mystical and fantastic' theme of the second movement of the Violin Sonata, the 'rather oriental and fatalistic themes in the Quintet', and 'the air of sadness in the Quartet' reminded Reed of the wind 'sighing in those dead trees'.

There was a servant attached to Brinkwells called Mark, a countryman of few words with whom Elgar slid instinctively into the intimate relationship that exists only between the English upper middle class and their staff. Mark's dour comments on life in general and on the visitors to Brinkwells in particular, many of them famous and all of whom totally failed to impress him, became a part of the family's folklore.

In April, Elgar had told Sidney Colvin, 'I cannot do any real work with the awful shadow over us.' War has inspired great music, literature and painting in others, but it would be wrong to conclude that Elgar saw it as an excuse for having failed to do any 'real work'. The shadow, in Elgar's case, was a personal as well as a national one, and once he had taken the cottage at Fittleworth it lifted. His health improved (less than a month after recording the Violin Concerto, the Gramophone Company had heard that Elgar was too indisposed even to see friends), and on 7 June he was writing to both Schuster and Troyte Griffith, to tell Schuster the place was 'divine', and Troyte that he was walking about all day in a shirt and underpants.

Serious composition still had to wait until the basic cause of Elgar's intermittent ill-health was cleared up, even though, at Brinkwells, he was able for once to make light of the matter. Writing to Schuster on 25 November, he ends, 'My love to you – Oh! I forgot; I've been ill for ten days. The old trouble – better now.' The old trouble, as he called it, had never in fact been labelled, but eventually infected tonsils were diagnosed and on 15 March 1918, at the age of sixty, Elgar underwent an operation for their removal. He had a good deal of pain, and stayed at The Hut to recuperate. On his return to Brinkwells he wrote to Carice asking her to contact Alice's cousin, William Raikes, a barrister (and under the terms of a second codicil to Alice's Will, signed on 3 May 1905, appointed, along with Frank Schuster, a guardian to Carice), in connection with Alice's trust fund. He now wished to have the fund handled by the Norwich firm of solicitors Hansell & Hales – because, so he told his daughter, 'I want to leave things nicely for you'. As a matter of passing interest, the Hansell partner was a brother of that sadly incompetent Mr Hansell hired by King George V as tutor to the future Edward VIII. (One wonders why, barring the tenuous royal connection, Elgar suddenly wanted his family affairs directed from a firm in Norwich.)

Following his operation and visit to Bray, Elgar now settled down to a long period of rest at Brinkwells with a splendid excuse to remain in the country indefinitely. Writing on 12 May to Alice Stuart (the former Alice Stuart-Wortley – in 1916 her husband had been raised to the peerage as Baron Stuart of Wortley), Elgar gave precise details of his daily time-table: he rose at about seven, and worked for an hour or so before dressing and having breakfast. After breakfast he smoked a pipe, and then he did more work until lunch at half past twelve. After lunch, another pipe and an hour's rest, with more work, only interrupted by tea and yet another pipe (having just undergone an operation on his throat, his addiction to a pipe can hardly have commended itself to his doctors). At half past seven, he changed for dinner, and by ten o'clock he was in bed. The woods, he told her, were full of flowers, and he was looking forward to her coming to stay 'with acute joy'; the food was good and plentiful and there was 'much beer!'.

'We are still in this lovely cottage in the woods,' Elgar wrote on 2 June to Percy Hull, Dr Sinclair's successor as organist at Hereford Cathedral, 'high above the world in peace, plenty of quietness and I am trying to get well and strong to do something useful again.' One of the things he did, which presumably he thought useful at the time, was accept a commission from the Ministry of Food to set to music a poem called *Big Steamers* for the magazine *Teachers' World*; meanwhile, inspired by the copse of dead trees, what he was really working on was to make up at last for the dispiriting trail of unfinished chamber works of his youth. While in hospital he had begun to make sketches for a string quartet, and by 6 September he was able to report to Sidney Colvin, 'I have been writing much music & I had Mr Reed with his violin here for a clear day.' Elgar had actually asked Reed to stay for a week, for once again he wanted his advice about writing for the violin; this time, it was not a violin concerto but a sonata for violin and piano, the first of three chamber works he was to complete in the space of a few months, an achievement for which he has never really been given adequate credit. On 28 September he told Colvin the Sonata was finished. Adrian Boult, who had received the seal of approval from Alice in February when he called at Severn House for tea ('Quite a nice quiet man'), learned of the Sonata's existence and asked if the newly formed

British Music Society might have the first performance. The Sonata was played privately at Severn House on 15 October, and on 24 November Boult received a letter from Elgar telling him the work was not yet completely engraved and that he feared he could not let the British Music Society have the *'first'* performance. The fact that Elgar underlined the word 'first' indicates that he regarded the private performance as the première, but he did allow the work to be played at a meeting of the society on 13 March the following year, eight days before its first public performance – with Billy Reed playing the violin part – at the Aeolian Hall.

While at work on the Sonata, Elgar had well in hand the String Quartet in E minor, which he had begun in hospital, and the Piano Quintet in A Minor, one of his very finest works. But domestic problems, and hence distractions, were never far away. In December, Severn House was burgled by what turned out to be two former policemen. Someone else was trying to forge Alice's cheques, and in the aftermath of war she found much else to grumble about. The railway workers – 'traitors who ought to be shot' – were 'worse than the worst enemies'. A manservant recommended by one of her friends turned out to be clearly not the sort one could have relied upon before the war: he went so far as to put up his fists and offer to fight with Elgar. 'An end of A.'s experiment,' the affronted master recorded with justifiable irritation. 'An entire and utter failure & lamentable expense. Entirely A.'s doing.' Once again, nerves were becoming frayed, and the Elgars seemed to be drifting, if somewhat prematurely, in the direction of a plot for an Evelyn Waugh novel. One day Elgar repaired to his club, the United Services, for a spot of peace and quiet only to find the place in a state of turmoil, a member having committed suicide on the premises. At the same time as the house was being broken into, the Elgars had begun to realize that they could no longer afford to run it, perhaps because the supply of lucrative wartime commissions for patriotic songs and reviews had dried up, and once again they seemed unlikely to resolve their conflicting love of town and country. On 3 December Elgar had written to Schuster from Brinkwells to say, 'Poor dear A. is not well & of course is bored to death here while I am in the seventh heaven of delight.' He foresaw a return to London as 'another interruption', and added, 'It seems that if I have to live again at Hampstead composition is "off" – not the house or the place but *London* – telephone etc all day and night drives me mad!'

On returning to Severn House in the new year, however, and in spite of burglars, forgers and Alice's ill-health, Elgar did seem to find it possible to carry on with the chamber works. He wrote from Hampstead to Sidney Colvin on 12 January 1919 to tell him he was 'hard at it' – hard at work, in fact, on the Quintet. One cannot escape noticing that if Elgar did not necessarily thrive on interruptions, once he had the bit between his teeth interruptions failed to stem the flow of inspiration, for he was working simultaneously not only on the Quartet and Quintet (which were both premièred at the Wigmore Hall on 21 May 1919), but while composing these fine and somewhat neglected works Elgar was striving to sum up a whole world of feeling in what was to prove to be his last great work, the Cello Concerto.

Writing of the Piano Quintet, during the composition of which he had been of assistance to Elgar, Reed says of the slow movement: 'It opens with a sublime melody entrusted to the viola. It abounds in finely shaped and polished phrases; and, with its warmth of expression and inspired moments, it appears to have grown like some work of nature, without the help of human hands. Only a hopeless pedant would attempt a technical analysis of such a piece of music, which expresses all the higher emotions of which humanity is capable. It expresses them so truly, and goes so much further into the hidden meaning of things than any mere words, that it seems to be a message from another world.'

Bernard Shaw's estimation of the opening of the work, according to a letter from Alice to Troyte Griffith, was that there had been nothing like it since *Coriolan*. Shaw was to become a major champion of Elgar's music during the composer's years of widowerhood, and he greatly admired both the man and the musician. Shaw had first met Elgar the previous year at lunch at the house of Madame Lalla Vandervelde, wife of the Belgian socialist statesman, and it seems to have been one of those meetings that prove an instant success, where two people are immediately attracted to one another and start talking as though they had many years of separation to catch up on. It transpired that as far back as the 1880s Elgar had read and enjoyed articles Shaw had written in the *Star* under the pen-name of 'Corno di Bassetto', and he was able to quote jokes from the articles that even Shaw had forgotten. So animated was their conversation that they both allowed their food to get cold (so the story goes, but as Shaw was a vegetarian his food may have been cold in the first place). The conviviality of the gathering was however somewhat upset when Roger Fry, a founder member of the Bloomsbury group, remarked in a voice described by Shaw as 'beautiful, like the *chalumeau* register of a clarinet', that there was only one art, the art of design. Design was certainly something Fry knew about (it was he who opened the Omega workshop) but he was essentially a Renaissance figure, a connoisseur of early Italian painting; no sensible, sophisticated person could have seriously doubted that Fry's remark, coming from such a man, was the sort of deliberately provocative comment people make at parties to stimulate conversation and the flow of ideas. According to Shaw, however, Elgar was stimulated to the degree of emitting a threatening growl from the other side of the table: 'His hackles were all out and we had not long to wait for the explosion. "Music is written in the skies: that's where it comes from," Elgar spluttered furiously. "And you compare it to a damned imitation!" '[17]

Shaw many years later gave a slightly different account of his first meeting with Elgar (which was also his first meeting with Roger Fry), in a letter he wrote to Virginia Woolf on 10 May 1940, which is quoted in the third volume of Leonard Woolf's autobiography[18]: 'Elgar,' he told Mrs Woolf, 'talked music so voluminously that Roger had nothing to do but eat his lunch in silence. At last we stopped to breathe and eat something ourselves; and Roger, feeling that our hostess expected him to contribute something, began in his beautiful voice (his and Forbes Robertson's were the only voices one could listen to for their own sakes), "After all, there is only one art: all the arts are the same". I heard no more; for my attention was taken by a growl from the other side of the table. It was Elgar, with his fangs bared and all his hackles bristling, in an appalling rage. "Music", he spluttered, "is written on the skies for you to note down. And you compare it to a DAMNED imitation."

'There was nothing for Roger to do but either to seize the decanter and split Elgar's head with it, or else take it like an angel with perfect dignity. Which latter he did.'

There was one romantic postscript to the war which in a way affected all those, including the Elgars, who were friends of Frank Schuster and *habitués* of The Hut. Walking round a hospital named after Lady Astor, Schuster's eyes lighted on a handsome young New Zealand captain, Leslie Wylde. Having fought with the Anzacs he came to be known as Anzy. He had lost a leg in the Dardanelles, but it was not so much this that attracted Schuster as the similarity of his name to Oscar Wilde's, his 'hooded' eye, a feature he apparently had in common with the dead playwright, and, according to the painter Wendela Boreel, whom Wylde was later to marry, 'his manner and looks'. Miss Boreel has recorded that Schuster 'came almost to adopt him, leaving all his money to him on his death'.[19] Schuster did virtually adopt Leslie Wylde, buying for him a Rolls-Royce specially adapted so that he could drive it with a hand-clutch, and a yacht moored at Cannes, although Wylde was to inherit only a small part of the entire estate; Schuster left some £24,000 in individual legacies, including £7,000 to Elgar, but to Wylde he did leave The Hut. The Wyldes had one son, but they can hardly be said to have lived happily ever after, for Anzy took to the bottle and died in 1935.

Severn House was put on the market in 1919. Whether all the social

17. *Bernard Shaw: His Life and Personality.*
18. *Beginning Again,* Hogarth Press, 1964.
19. Parkin Gallery catalogue, 1–18 October 1980.

gatherings that had taken place there since 1912 had been an unqualified success remains a matter of opinion. Rosa Burley thought they had not: 'The training and outlook of the Elgars were of course such as to make an un-buttoned mood very difficult for them except when they were strictly en famille,' she has written, 'and the effect was a little chilling. Parties were given but their stiffness hardly ever relaxed into anything like joviality and the guests rarely felt wholly at ease. An odd feature was that music, which might have been expected to form the main attraction, was seldom heard on account of Edward's dislike of performers.' While prospective purchasers were being shown round, Elgar either made a pretence of escaping out of a side door, or else he was in rural retreat at Brinkwells, 'frantically busy writing', as he told Sidney Colvin on 26 June, in a letter announcing that he had nearly completed a concerto for violoncello and asking permission to dedicate it to Sidney and his wife. He described it as 'a real large work & I think good & alive'. He went on however to disparage his achievement in a mild sort of way: 'I cannot say the music is worthy of you both (or either!) but our three names wd be in print together even if the music is dull & of the kind which perisheth.'

The Cello Concerto has certainly never perished and few could think it dull. Many people have come to regard it as a conscious farewell to both a historical age and a personal life, but there seems to be no evidence to suggest that, at the time he wrote it, Elgar regarded it as a final achievement. Sir Adrian Boult certainly does not share the view that it was designed as such: 'With the Cello Concerto he struck a new kind of music, with a more economical line, terser in every way,' he has said. 'He was rather good at it, and having written the Cello Concerto it is extraordinary he didn't get bitten by the new style.'[20]

During the summer of 1919 Elgar was up at four o'clock each morning working on the Concerto (he had actually jotted down the opening theme in the nursing home shortly after his operation for tonsillitis), and according to Alice's diary entry for 2 August, Felix Salmond, who was due to give the first performance at the Queen's Hall on 26 October, was 'thrilled with the thought of playing the concerto for the 1st time & wildly excited about it'. Six days later she walked the four miles to and from the post office at Fittleworth to dispatch the score. Elgar was to conduct the Concerto in a programme including works by Scriabin and Borodin, these to be conducted by Albert Coates. Coates kept Elgar and Salmond waiting an hour at the rehearsal, which was also attended, under the notorious deputy system, by the young cellist, John Barbirolli. The concert itself was not sold out, and the *Musical Times* considered the work under-rehearsed. Wistful and sad as the music is, it can have done little to raise the spirits of a new generation of concert-goers, members of a generation who

20. In conversation with the author.

preferred to do the knees-up on the beach at Filey or smoke themselves to death at the Embassy Club, who wanted to forget the war, not to be reminded of it.

In his reminiscences, *Music on Record*, Fred Gaisberg says that Elgar regarded Albert Coates as a bit of a mystery, and he recounts two anecdotes illustrating Elgar's benign aloofness towards him. On one occasion Coates started to tell Elgar he intended to clothe the old classics with new raiment, to which Elgar responded by saying, 'Don't put new coats on them.' Even more witty, bearing in mind Coates's Russian origins, was Elgar's riposte when Coates, priding himself on his musical discrimination, handed him a piece of paper saying, 'What do you think of this programme?' 'Programme!' exclaimed Elgar, 'it looks to me more like a pogrom.'

Like her diary entry about the striking railway workers, Alice's comment on Coates's conduct at rehearsal betrayed a streak of scarcely suppressed hatred that had come to sour her last years. 'An insult to E. from that brutal, selfish, ill mannered bounder A. Coates,' she recorded. After the first performance, she was again on the rampage: 'Still furious about rehearsals – *shameful*. Hope never to speak to that brutal Coates again.' Her hopes were not in vain. Just a week after the première of the Cello Concerto she became unwell. The date was 2 November, and it was a date that Elgar was able to recall quite distinctly when writing to Laurence Binyon on 14 January 1920 to tell him she had been for a short walk the day before, the first time she had been out of the house 'for 10 weeks'. Even Alice's headaches never lasted that long; she was clearly very unwell indeed.

Despite its cool reception in the concert hall, plans were in hand by the end of the year to abridge and record the Cello Concerto, and a recording was made on 22 December; it was the first occasion on which Elgar had travelled to the studio, now at Hayes in Middlesex, without Alice. At the beginning of 1920, Reed tells us, Alice was often listless and would creep up close to the fire, looking fragile; every time he saw her she seemed to be getting smaller. No one seems to have realized that she was slowly dying. Elgar went on his own to lunch on 6 January with Bernard Shaw and his wife at their house in Ayot St Lawrence. On 5 February he was telling Sidney Colvin he was overwhelmed with emotion at having been elected to the Literary Society, a select group of painters, writers and politicians who met to dine together once a month.[21] Colvin was president at the time, and Elgar's fellow members included Maurice Baring, Geoffrey Dawson, E. V. Lucas, John Murray, G. M. Trevelyan and Hugh Walpole. 'What a gorgeous crowd,' Elgar told Colvin. As a footnote to his letter

---

21. Elgar's election to the Literary Society was of course a mark of personal esteem rather than in recognition of any literary achievement. Sir Sidney Colvin, to whom, with his wife, Elgar had just dedicated his Cello Concerto, had no doubt used his influence.

of thanks, he mentioned that his 'poor A. does not rid of the tiresome cough'.

On 3 February, the day Elgar heard about his election to the Literary Society, he also received a diploma granting him membership of the Accademia in Florence. Two days later he learned that he had been elected to the council of the Royal College of Music, and on 18 March he became a member of the French Académie des Beaux Arts. Alice was able to share in all these successes, and on 24 February she had recovered sufficiently to make what was to be her last visit to Hayes, despite it being 'cold and vy foggy'. Perhaps it was the knowledge that royalty was to be in the recording studio that afternoon that encouraged her to venture out. When Queen Victoria's granddaughter, Princess Alice, and the Crown Prince of Romania entered, Alice remained seated, something she would never have dreamed of doing had she been well enough to stand. She also dragged herself along to the Queen's Hall on 16 March to hear Boult conduct the Second Symphony. However ill she may have been feeling, the effort was well worth while: 'Wonderful performance of the Symphony,' she recorded afterwards. 'From beginning to end it seemed absolutely to penetrate the audience's mind & heart.' Alice wrote to Boult the following day: 'Dear Mr Boult, I must send you a few lines to thank you from my heart for your wonderful performance last evening. I cannot describe the delight to me of hearing that great work so splendidly rendered. You made it so clear & irresistible that I feel sure it penetrated straight to the minds & hearts of numbers who had failed to understand it – I rejoiced in your triumph & hope it will be succeeded by every possible success for you – I only hope you are not quite exhausted by the tremendous demands of the work. I know that you will like to know that Edward was *so* happy & delighted it has done him so much good – Thank you – Yours very sincerely, C. A. Elgar.'[22]

Revelling to the very end of her life in her husband's music – the vindication of her own unswerving belief in his genius – and deeply grateful to others who understood and appreciated his work and who thus made him happy, she took to her bed. The date was 25 March. Even then no one seemed to realize just how ill she was, although ten days later, Alice's condition having deteriorated rapidly over the Easter weekend, Elgar wrote to Schuster to tell him 'the poor little dear one' was inarticulate and could understand nothing. 'Pity *us* more than her even,' he added. The same day, 6 April, he was told by the doctor that Alice was beyond help; on the morning of 7 April, now recognized to be *in extremis*, she received Conditional Absolution and Extreme Unction, and in the evening she died. She was seventy-one.

22. John Ireland was in the audience on this occasion and afterwards he too wrote to Boult, to congratulate him on his 'splendid performance of Elgar's truly noble Symphony'. and to say, 'We owe you so much for so clearly demonstrating that the greatest music of the present time is by a Briton.'

Myrrha Bantock, the daughter of Sir Granville Bantock, recorded in 1971 a visit paid by the Elgars to her parents shortly after the Bantocks' marriage in 1898 (the anecdote was of course second-hand, having been passed on to Myrrha by her mother): 'Elgar was somewhat delicate,' she wrote, 'and many arrangements were necessary for his comfort, including an apparatus for his nightly tea-making. Elgar's wife was absolutely devoted to him and surrounded her husband with a ring-fence of attention and care which was almost pathetic. The composer himself depended upon his wife to a surprising extent ... my newly-wed mother was, I am sure, awed by Mrs Elgar, with her array of rugs, shawls and cushions, extra body-belts and knitted bedsocks for Edward's comfort. One evening Helena [Helen von Schweitzer, Bantock's wife] noted with astonishment no less than seven hot water bottles being filled for his bed, on the occasion of Elgar complaining of a slight chill.'[23]

Much criticism has been levelled at Alice for fussing over her husband. 'She really did worship him with a blindness to his faults ... that seemed almost incredible,' Rosa Burley has written. One should however remember that Alice was eight years Elgar's senior, and that by the time she married him she was old enough to have been a mother for twenty years; part of her desire for marriage was clearly so that she could fulfil towards him a maternal role. This was not such a very unusual arrangement, and only seems pathetic to those whose marriage takes another form. In the area of snobbery and social ambition, where some degree of criticism of Alice may be more justified, her obsession with Elgar's worldly success was in fact no greater than his. It would be impossible to prove, and quite unfair to suggest, that Alice ever did anything to hinder her husband's career, and even if Rosa Burley's somewhat harsh assertion, that 'many of the friends whose wealth had dazzled Edward in the later years had barely concealed their contempt for Alice', was true, there is no evidence that his social career was in any way impaired by his marriage. Alice tastefully furnished fine town houses in which to entertain, and when Elgar needed the countryside in which to write, friends lent them their homes or he and Alice rented country cottages. She may have smothered him with the seven hot water bottles, but she was also content to prepare his sheet music, correct his manuscripts, proof-read his scores, post his parcels and, according to Dorabella, contrive that he should meet the right people, be saved from troublesome interviews and be kept from worries generally.

There are people – politicians and church leaders – for whom a mollycoddling wife spells disaster; these are people who need to be exposed to the world, not shielded from it. Composers do not fall into that category, since the primary need of any artist is to be free to live a selfish life, to have around him

23. *The Elgar Society Journal*, May 1980.

people whose criticism or encouragement can be called upon at will or ignored. It is in the artistic field that Alice's association with her husband has perhaps been most misunderstood, and Billy Reed surely had the situation in perspective when he wrote that she was not able to criticize him technically but that she had 'unerring judgement and aesthetic sense'. Some twenty-seven years after the event, Elgar recalled to Reed an occasion, probably at the time of the composition of the Violin Concerto at Plas Gwyn, which reveals very clearly this aspect of their relationship. It seems that one evening Elgar played to Alice some of the music he had written during the day. Elgar told Reed, 'She nodded her head appreciatively, except over one passage, at which she sat up rather grimly, I thought. However, I went to bed leaving it as it was. But I got up as soon as it was light and went down to look over what I had written. I found it as I had left it, except that there was a little piece of paper, pinned over the offending bars, on which was written, "All of it is beautiful and just right, except this ending. Don't you think, dear Edward, that this end is just a little . . . ?" Well Billy,' Elgar went on, 'I scrapped that end. Not a word was ever said about it. But I rewrote it, and as I heard no more I knew it was approved.'

Many years before, Elgar had drawn attention to the encouragement he received from Alice when he wrote to Jaeger on 27 April 1899 to say, 'Oh! I am so anxious to be done with the whole art – it's only my wife who begs me to go on.' As far as Alice was concerned, she had found in Elgar the perfect partner. His career gave her an over-riding mission in life, and he was someone she could mother. He provided her with a title and, where she did not already possess it in her own right, the entrée to a glamorous world of musicians, actors, writers, politicians and wealthy patrons. She took a major gamble in marrying him, and in terms of his achievements it was a gamble that paid off handsomely; the suggestion that Elgar owed everything to her is only true if one is also prepared to say that she owed everything to him. Rosa Burley was convinced, however, that the marriage was a failure: 'Throughout his life,' she has written, '[Elgar] had been at immense pains to maintain a façade of married bliss.' Beside this assertion needs to be set a letter sent from Elgar to Jaeger on the occasion of Jaeger's engagement: 'I am just in and find your good letter,' Elgar wrote on 21 December 1898. 'I will not say a word now. This is only coming because I cannot get away alas! – to wish you again *everything* & may you be as happy together as I & my dear one have been and are.'

Elgar received 208 letters and telegrams, including condolences from the king and queen, after Alice's death. What Elgar was able to make of the tribute from Fred Gaisberg heaven knows: 'Little did I think that your dear lady would leave you so soon,' he wrote. 'Our hearts are sad today and mine is full of sympathy and pain at the departure of one of the sweetest spirits that God has given during the terrible days of the war. As Lady Elgar's presence influenced me for the good and upon all others who knew her were inspired we know well.' This was signed, 'From your humble worshipper.'

Alice was buried on 10 April at St Wulstan's Roman Catholic Church in Little Malvern, just down the road from Craig Lea, her grave tucked away into the wall, guarded by fir and yew trees, where blackbirds sing today undisturbed in the quiet, uncluttered peace. During the service, Billy Reed and three others played the slow movement of the String Quartet in the gallery. As Reed was moving off afterwards for the interment, someone placed a hand on his arm and said, 'Tell him I had to come. I dare not go to the graveside as I am not well, and my doctor absolutely forbids me to stand bareheaded in the open air. But I felt I must come. Do tell him for me.' So saying, the man burst into tears and hurried away. It was Stanford.

Elgar discovered eight days later that Stanford had been present. His natural paranoia stiffened by grief, he wrote to Schuster, 'I only regard it as a cruel piece of impertinence ... His presence last Saturday was a very clever "trick" to make it appear that after all he is really a decent fellow.'

Elgar and Carice remained in Malvern after the funeral, Elgar seeming at first to be stunned into a sense of peacefulness, and his letters are unbearably sad. He wrote frequently to Schuster. On 12 April he said he could see the little grave in the distance, '& nothing cd be sweeter & lovelier only the birds singing & all *remote* peace brought closely to us'. He told Schuster that Alice had chosen the spot for her burial 'long years ago'. The blossoms were white all round, and 'if it had to be – it could not be better'.

Elgar then went to stay with his sister Polly at Bromsgrove. 'Here,' he wrote to Schuster on 17 April, 'my dear A. never came so I can bear the sight of the roads & fields.' His bereavement had come on top of other family troubles, for Polly, now a widow, was about to be turned out of the tied house her husband had occupied as manager of the salt works (they had lived there for thirty-seven years), and Lucy, sixty-eight and stone deaf, had also apparently had her house 'bought over their heads'. With time on his hands in which to brood, Elgar admitted that he was 'plunged in the midst of ancient hate & prejudice'; he was referring to the disapproval his marriage had incurred in Alice's family, and to the loss, as a result, of a certain amount of family money. He recalled to Schuster 'poor dear A.'s settlements & her *awful aunts* who cd allow nothing to descend to any offspring of *mine* – I had forgotten all the petty bitterness but I feel just now rather evil that a noble (& almost brilliant) woman like my Carice should be penalised by a wretched lot of old incompetents simply because I was – well – I.' He ends by saying that Polly's dog Juno presses his nose against him, '& says a walk is near'.

Two days after writing to Schuster (to whom he must at some time have recounted the early family squabbles), Elgar also wrote to Troyte Griffith, whom Alice had always liked, and told him, 'I do not know how I shd have got through the awful lonely time without your friendship & care. As the days go by ... the "blank" seems greater and unbearable.' Troyte had helped, with Schuster, to take care of the funeral arrangements, and had many years before designed the gravestone for Elgar's parents. Elgar's mind was now turning to his own death: 'I wish you would see if the *next space* to the little lonely grave is to be had & if so secure it for me,' he wrote. 'I shd like to know this at once & shd be glad if you wd have a simple edging of stone put round the graves or the grave & unoccupied space – if the latter is secured.'

On his return to Brinkwells in July, Elgar still had to wind up Alice's affairs. For probate purposes she left £2,280 3s. 8d. (which probably represented the deposit she had paid on Severn House), and her address, oddly enough, was registered in Somerset House as No. 40 Netherhall Gardens, although the Elgars had always written from No. 42, the number by which Severn House was known both before they bought it and when it was sold by Elgar. Thanking Schuster, who was a trustee of Alice's estate, for taking the trouble to go to Lincoln's Inn (Field, Roscoe & Co., Elgar's solicitors, were at 36 Lincoln's Inn Fields), Elgar told him on 2 July that he and Carice now had 'a comfortable two hundred a year' on which to live, 'and anything I can make'. This figure need not be taken too seriously: Severn House was expected to fetch £7,000, he had his royalties, paid by his publishers quarterly, and an annual retainer from the Gramophone Company, and this alone, by the end of 1921, stood at £500.

Four months after Alice's death, lonely and with no one but Carice for company, Elgar wrote from Brinkwells to Billy Reed. 'My dear Billy: I was delighted to get your letter: we are still here – very, very sad – but lovely – if you really could bring yourself to consider a few days here we shall be delighted – we go up to London for the Wor: Festl. rehearsals on the 20th Monday & shall be here till then: so, if you can bear to rough it I shd be overjoyed to see you. There are all the old "works" to be done & we might fish again. I am not very well & have lost all interest in life & I fear nothing will ever revive it – the wrench was too severe & I have lost too much as you know to ever recover.'

CHAPTER SIX

'Everything Buttoned Up'

Like any busy man in any walk of life who is suddenly confronted by bereavement, Elgar found himself with engagements in his diary made before Alice died, and these he sensibly fulfilled. They were mainly engagements to conduct, and involved a certain amount of travel at a time when he might have been tempted to sit at home and brood. They also offered the easy companionship of fellow musicians. As for thoughts of composing, however, Alice's death handed to Elgar a ready-made excuse for indulging in the kind of self-pity to which he was always prone – self-pity and pessimism tinged with a certain agreeable surprise at the discovery that life goes on. To Sidney Colvin he wrote from Fittleworth to announce the dramatic news that his one short attempt at life had been a failure; nevertheless, he noted, 'inscrutable nature goes on just the same – young larks six in a nest on the lawn and many other birds; nightingales sing; but I miss the little gentlest presence and I cannot go on.'

Adrian Boult was treated to similar sentiments. Writing to him on 5 August 1920 Elgar said, 'I am lonely now and do not see music in the old way and cannot believe I shall *complete* any new work – sketches I shall make but there is no inducement to finish anything; – ambition I have none.' It was a prophetic letter so far as completing any major compositions was concerned. Boult was due to conduct *Cockaigne* for the first time in November, and three weeks later Elgar added a postscript to another letter, thanking him, but reiterating that he could not bear the thought of new music.

Severn House had still failed to find a purchaser, and towards the end of 1920 Elgar was making a brave attempt to stay on there. Writing from Brussels on 12 October, he told Billy Reed, 'We are going to try to live at S. House and you must come and cheer me a little. You are always a ray of sunshine.' And on 9 November he told Boult he hoped that he too would come and see him soon. 'Carice and I are trying to start life again here,' he wrote from Hampstead, 'but (you will easily understand) it is sad, sad work to gather up the threads.'

There were certain threads, however, which, if Rosa Burley is to be believed, he did not intend gathering up. After nearly thirty years of intimate friendship, she found, following Alice's death, that when she chanced to meet Elgar face to face at music festivals, she was completely ignored. The explanation she offers is 'that an overmastering sense of guilt towards Alice led him to shun the society of those who had been allowed to look behind the façade of happiness and were thus regarded as having in some measure connived in his disloyalty to her'.

Miss Burley does not explore this ambiguous statement, but it was a view to some extent shared by Ernest Newman when he made an equally ambiguous comment in a letter to his wife, written on the day that Alice died: 'Whatever people may say,' the critic wrote, 'to a man of his fine and sensitive nature the severance of a long tie like this must inevitably mean much bitterness and suffering, much dwelling in the past and self-reproach. We always seem heavy debtors to the dead; we feel they have not had their chance and that life has given us an unfair advantage over them.'[1]

As far as 'disloyalty' is concerned, we can dismiss any idea of infidelity: Rosa Burley had in mind something far more fundamental. Describing Elgar in the early days when he lived at Forli and taught at The Mount, before he had achieved fame through the *Enigma Variations*, she refers to him as shy and rather morose, and while prone to fluctuations of mood, 'the prevailing mood appeared to be one of acute unhappiness'. Telling her one day about his early life, he apparently brought his story to a close at the age of thirty-two: ' "And then," he said, as if it were the climax of his misfortunes, "I married." '

The guilt Elgar felt was surely to some extent related to the lack of passion he felt for Alice in contrast to the passion he felt for his friends and was able to translate, as a result of those friendships, into music. The 'Nimrod' variation, the Violin Concerto and the slow movement of the Second Symphony are all examples of passionate, romantic, heart-felt music directly inspired by his love for other people. Elgar's love was consummated through his art, and Alice's role had essentially been that of housekeeper, a perfectly honourable role and one which seems to have satisfied Alice; it was a tragedy that Elgar too could not have accepted in tranquillity the nature of his own emotions.

Rosa Burley ends her account of her relationship with Elgar by telling us that at Christmas 1932, after he had 'resolutely cut her' for many years, she received a card from him. Pondering on this sudden resumption of correspondence, Miss Burley wondered, 'Could it be that he hoped by reviving an old friendship to recapture some of the youthful urge towards composition of past years?'

1. *Ernest Newman: A Memoir* by Vera Newman (Putnam, 1963).

In seeking an explanation for any sense of guilt or self-reproach that may have clouded Elgar's years of widowerhood, one also has to consider the question of class and money. It is never easy for a man to depend on his wife for a private income, and money can be a far more destructive element in a relationship than physical incompatibility. Elgar, however, was obsessed by money, or at least by what he regarded as a lack of it; rather than resenting his financial dependence on Alice, did he really feel indignant that she was not wealthy enough, wealthy in the manner of men like Schuster, Rodewald and Northampton, whose beautiful homes and lavish hospitality were far beyond anything that Alice could supply?

Alice was, by all accounts, a typical product of a rigid Victorian upbringing appropriate to the daughter of an Indian Army general knighted in the service of his country. Rosa Burley tells us it was two years before she met Alice, although they lived in the same town and Elgar was music master at her school, and when eventually they did meet it transpired that the impediment had been Alice's excessive concern over the niceties of etiquette. According to Miss Burley, Alice said she had long wanted to call but had not been sure which of them had settled in Malvern first: 'She of course had been connected with it longer but thought I had actually moved into The Mount before she and her husband had taken their present house. The responsibility for the first call had therefore been difficult to allocate.'

It seems that Alice was incapable of flexibility in her concept of correct social behaviour. The first time Miss Burley, whose own social graces have never been questioned, went to dinner at Forli (which was a very modest family house), she was unprepared and surprised to find the Elgars in full evening dress; Elgar had even been trained by Alice to go through the pretentious ritual of taking Miss Burley in to dinner on his arm. Even allowing for changes in domestic customs, a modern visitor to Forli would find such conduct in such an establishment risible. Elgar was, of course, socially ambitious and would have been a willing participant in the charade, but while he had no objection to climbing up the social ladder, nothing could obliterate the fact of his lower-middle-class birth; his father was a tradesman, and Elgar had the choice of resenting either his parents or his upper-middle-class wife. She must have been for him a constant reminder of a whole caste of people whose company he longed to join but who despised people like his parents, and would have despised him too had he remained an assistant in his father's shop.

Alice seldom if ever paid a visit to Elgar's parents, and she never even went to see his favourite sister or the nephews and nieces of whom he was also fond. He must have been distressed by this behaviour, a distress that could have done nothing but build up resentment. At the same time, he leaned on Alice for permanent companionship, an orderly house and the routine of life. She gave him all that, she gave him unstinted praise, she instinctively sided with him against critics of any kind and she believed implicitly in his genius. If, then, he felt towards her a hostility aroused by her obsessive snobbery and gentility – if, indeed, one half of him quite strongly disliked one half of her – he would indeed have been more than likely to have felt guilt and remorse after her death.

In the spring of 1921, six days after the first anniversary of Alice's death, Elgar sent £1 to Troyte Griffith to cover the cost of some flowers for the grave. On 24 April he completed a transcription of Bach's Fugue in C Minor, first performed on 27 October at the Queen's Hall with Elgar conducting. In May he conducted *The Apostles* at Newcastle, and then he toured South Wales with the London Symphony Orchestra. In June he received the Ordre de la Couronne from the Belgian Ambassador. He declined an invitation to attend a reception for Sibelius, but on 17 June he took the entire company of the Hampstead Everyman Theatre to lunch at the Café Royal. Elgar seems to have enjoyed playing host in public; in the autumn of 1922 he gave a luncheon party at the United Services Club, for Richard Strauss, John Ireland, Bernard Shaw, Eugene Goossens, Arthur Bliss, Adrian Boult and Arnold Bax among others, when, according to Billy Reed, 'champagne flowed and Sir Edward made a most excellent speech ... and we had a very jolly party'.

In February, the Columbia Graphophone Company had tried to woo Elgar away from the Gramophone Company with a tempting offer which he refused, and on 20 July 1921 he opened new premises for the Gramophone Company at 363 Oxford Street. Presumably reasoning that if they could afford to move to Oxford Street they could now afford to pay him more, he wrote to them in November to say he was aware that as a commercial proposition the records he made for His Master's Voice could not compete with the popular records; that he hoped his name was of some value to them in the more serious side of their artistic work; that he had had rather tempting offers to go elsewhere; that he had always been very happy with everyone connected with the Gramophone Company; that he had no intention under any circumstances of accepting another offer; that the directors might not think he was worth more than they were paying him now; that he left the matter entirely in their hands, and if they decided that the present arrangement must continue he would accept the decision cheerfully and continue to do his best for the company as he had during the past years. He was not, he concluded, a businessman and did not pretend to treat the matter merely from a business point of view. Although a review of the sales of his records over the past five years, set against the royalties and retainers paid to Elgar, revealed a net loss to the company of £55 13s. 5d., it was agreed that 'his name would be of inestimable value to any other Company', and his contract was therefore renewed for a further three years at an annual retainer of £500, which was not too bad an outcome for someone who was not a businessman.

In the early autumn of 1921 we catch two contradictory glimpses of Elgar's consideration for other people. On 1 September, *Falstaff* and the Violin Concerto were performed at the Queen's Hall at a concert for which Frank Schuster dashed back from the continent, enduring a hair-raising journey in the course of which he lost his luggage in Brussels. He only arrived at the concert in the middle of the first movement of the concerto. According to an account he gave to Adrian Boult in a letter two days later, 'Elgar had a tremendous reception ... and took his calls with that appearance of sulkiness which would do for any composer of less commanding genius.' After the concert, Schuster went on to tell Boult, he went round to recall for Elgar 'what I had done and encountered to be present', and was greeted 'with the *coldest* of handshakes. I could have slapped him (and very nearly did).' Schuster's account of Elgar's off-hand behaviour at the concert is confirmed by Siegfried Sassoon, who had accompanied Schuster to the Queen's Hall, and who recorded in his diary six days later that Elgar 'scarcely glanced at poor old Frankie'. The incident prompted him to add, 'There is no doubt that E. is a very self-centred and inconsiderate man'. And yet, three weeks later, remembering the embarrassment he had felt when he had been unable to afford academic robes in which to receive his honorary doctorate at Cambridge, Elgar was writing to Percy Hull to offer to help with the purchase of his.

Severn House was at last sold at auction, and giving up Brinkwells too, Elgar moved into a flat (No. 18) at 37 St James's Place ('just sittingroom, bedroom, bathroom, etc', he explained to his niece, Madeleine Grafton). He became more of a clubman that ever. One Sunday he sent, again to Madeleine, a pathetic note from Brooks': 'I have rolled in here and am very lonely ... so I thought ... as there are only 10 footmen and 26 candlesticks of silver – I would write to you.' And one week after moving into the flat, he wrote to Troyte Griffith on 22 October, 'I have at last realised that my dear wife and beloved companion has left me; until about two months ago I always felt ... that she *must* return as of old.' A vital period of his mourning had passed. Some sort of delayed shock as a result of bereavement must however explain a letter he was to write on 13 December to Sidney Colvin, for otherwise it was a letter of almost unbelievably calculated ingratitude: 'As a child,' he solemnly declared, 'and as a young man and as a mature man no single person was ever kind to me.'

Carice was married in January 1922 (to Samuel Blake, a farmer, who was to die in 1939). In the autumn, at the Gloucester Festival, the famous row with

Stanford petered out, although it was never satisfactorily resolved. During the festival a memorial tablet to Parry was unveiled in the cathedral, and it was on this occasion that Granville Bantock contrived to bring about a meeting between Elgar and Stanford. Stanford held out his hand and said, 'Let's forget all about it.' Elgar pretended not to know what he was talking about, but shook hands. Later a group photograph was taken. The conductor Hugh Allen called out, 'Now then, Elgar, don't have your coat all buttoned up like that', to which came the retort, 'Ah, I always keep everything buttoned up in this company'.[2]

Elgar's increasing bitterness and sense of isolation from people and events may to some extent have resulted from a decline at this time in public interest in his music. Bernard Shaw, after a performance of *The Apostles* at the Queen's Hall in 1922, wrote, 'I distinctly saw six people in the stalls, probably with complimentary tickets . . . The occasion was infinitely more important than the Derby, than Goodwood, than the Cup Finals, than the Carpentier fights, than any of the occasions on which the official leaders of society are photographed and cinematographed laboriously shaking hands with persons on whom Molière's patron, Louis XIV, and Bach's patron, Frederick the Great, would not have condescended to wipe their boots . . . I apologise to posterity for living in a country where the capacity and tastes of schoolboys and costermongers are the measure of metropolitan culture.'[3] Eight years later, Shaw could have been forgiven for including among the schoolboys and costermongers Professor E. J. Dent, who in the 1930 second enlarged edition of the *Handbuch der Musikgeschichte* gave sixty-six lines to Parry, forty-one to Stanford and sixteen to Elgar.

Shaw was to describe Elgar, in public, as a greater man than himself, but it may be doubted that Elgar realized this was an example of the monstrous and deliberate conceit that made Shaw such an amusing commentator. Shaw's attraction to Elgar and his music is easy to see. Both men were romantics (and in the pursuit of romantic ideals were often very silly), but while Elgar was able to express himself in his music Shaw remained in his writing bogged down in intellectual ideas. Elgar, with his love of pomp, ceremony and the monarchy, celebrated quite openly all the old-fashioned values which the kind-hearted Fabian Shaw, for all his championship of Communist Russia, found rather attractive himself. Elgar was to dedicate his *Severn Suite* to Shaw and, according to Hesketh Pearson, he described Shaw as 'the best friend to any artist, the kindest and possibly the dearest fellow on earth'.

Writing to Lawrence Binyon on 31 January 1923, Elgar said that since his

2. Sir Thomas Armstrong recalled (to the author) Hugh Allen saying that whenever he heard Elgar's Violin Concerto he felt like washing his hands. It may be that Allen was not too well disposed to Elgar himself, too, and enjoyed annoying him.

3. *Bernard Shaw: His Life and Personality.*

'dear wife's death' he had 'done nothing', and he feared that his music had vanished. This was not quite true. The previous year he had followed up the transcription of a fugue by Bach with a transcription of Bach's Fantasia in C Minor, which he conducted at the Gloucester Festival, and for Leeds he supplied orchestration for Parry's *Jerusalem*. In 1923 the Worcester Festival was to hear another transcription, of Handel's Second Chandos Anthem and a setting of a motet by Wesley, and Elgar also wrote a couple of part-songs and some incidental music to Lawrence Binyon's *King Arthur*. Sparse though his musical output may have been at this time, there was in Worcester no slackening of respect for their local celebrity. In February 'a few fellow citizens of the great composer' presented to the town corporation a portrait of him by Philip Burne-Jones, 'to place on record their admiration and appreciation of his brilliant musical genius'. The painting, an intimate, domestic study of Elgar standing in profile beside a piano, his hand gripping the lapels of his jacket, hangs in the Guildhall at Worcester, facing a far larger, more ponderous and conventional painting of his schoolfriend Hubert Leicester, mayor in the year that Elgar received the Freedom of the City, and again from 1911 to 1916.

At the end of 1923 Elgar decided to go on a cruise, choosing – of all places – the Amazon. He sailed from Liverpool in a 'cabin de luxe No. 2' aboard the Booth Steamship Company's 7,000-ton *Hildebrand*, which immediately ran into the worst seas experienced in the Atlantic for a decade, and the pilot, normally put off at Holyhead, had to be kept on as far as Madeira. The cruise entered calmer waters when it reached the mouth of the Amazon and Elgar travelled 1,000 miles up river as far as Manaos, reporting home from so unlikely a setting on an opera house apparently regarded by the local people as the most important building in town.

Earlier in the year Elgar had, while retaining the flat in London, found at last the perfect setting for the pose he had so long cultivated as a country gentleman. It was Napleton Grange, a charming half-timbered eighteenth-century country house near the hamlet of Kempsey five miles outside Worcester and just off the road to Tewkesbury. The owner, Lord Dudley, from whom Elgar rented the property, lived next door. The house stands in the heart of open country, with a massive cedar on the lawn, and casement windows that open on to two acres of sheltered garden. In the fields around, Elgar took to walking behind the local farmer's tractor, accompanied by his dogs, Marco, a black-and-white spaniel, and Mina, a cairn, both of which Elgar loved extravagantly, encouraging them to sit at the table at meal-times to be fed.[4] According to Lord Dudley's daughter, Lady Dudley, who remembers Elgar from her childhood, whenever he received an invitation to dinner he would pretend to himself that

4. Marco and Mina are buried together in the garden of Elgar's Birthplace.

the dogs too had been invited. 'I would have said he was upper-class but not in the least bit pompous,' Lady Dudley has recalled. 'One day he invited me into the house to listen to some music. I forget after all these years what it was, but I remember he suddenly said, "I'm terribly sorry, I'm afraid I shall have to take that record off." I suppose it was something that had upset him.'[5]

Elgar was, like many artists, by nature partly solitary and partly gregarious; as he grew older, composing less and becoming less in need of solitude, he grew increasingly dependent upon friends for company. 'I am quite alone here and very lonely,' he had written to Alice Stuart from Napleton Grange on 12 September 1923, adding however a jaunty postscript that gives the lie to any suggestion that his worldly ambitions were at an end: 'The Kingdom, Gerontius and For the Fallen are not bad,' he reminded Lady Stuart. 'I think I deserve my peerage now when these are compared with the new works!!!' All those exclamation marks could tempt us into dismissing talk of a peerage as a joke, but it was not. With the death of Sir Walter Parratt, Master of the King's Music, Elgar returned to the topic in another letter, written from the London flat on 16 April 1924, to Alice Stuart (who, it should be noted, was the wife of a former member of the House of Commons now raised to the peerage himself, and who might well be expected to understand the workings of the honours system). Elgar began by telling her that he had written to Lord Stamfordham (the king's private secretary, formerly Sir Arthur Bigge) after hearing rumours that the post of Master of the King's Music was to be abolished, urging Stamfordham that it should be retained. Its suppression would give a very bad effect abroad, he had told him, 'where the effacement of the last shred of connection of the Court with the Art would not be understood'. Elgar's assumption that on the continent anyone knew or cared about the post of Master of the King's Music, or if they did that they imagined the post entailed any serious patronage of the arts by the Court, was a fanciful one. It seems too that Elgar's knowledge of who was who at Court was shaky: 'It was not S.'s department,' he told Alice Stuart, 'so it was turned over to S. Ponsonby.' He meant Sir Frederick Ponsonby, Keeper of the Privy Purse, and got his initial wrong. Sir Frederick wrote to Elgar to confirm that it had long ago been proposed that the office should cease. 'I wrote again,' Elgar told Lady Stuart, offering myself (honorary) – *anything* than that it should be publicly announced that the old office was abolished. No reply. Colebrooke [Lord Colebrooke, Permanent Lord-in-Waiting to George V] wrote to the Lord Chamberlain – but as far as I can make out the three departments simply quarrel over these things; no grit, no imagination – *no music*. No nothing except boxing, football and racing.'

5. In conversation with the author.

Elgar had enjoyed going to football matches as a young man, and following form on the turf gave him many hours of pleasure in later life. His noble efforts to keep alive a sinecure may have done him credit, but his castigation of the Court for following the sports of kings and commoners seems a little unfair. The post carried a nominal salary of £100 per annum, and was therefore to all intents and purposes already an honorary one, and his offer to accept it on an 'honorary' basis rather than see it abolished was somewhat disingenuous. But what followed was downright blatant: 'As to any peerage,' he added, 'I fear it is hopeless, but it wd please me.'

The peerage and the post of Master of the King's Music were not all Elgar had on his mind. He went on to tell Lady Stuart he had caught a glimpse of Frank Schuster 'in the back of a smart car ... with a "*bit of fluff*"!! in flamboyant *pink* on the front seat'. If the 'bit of fluff' was really worthy of gossip, it seems odd that she was on the front seat and not beside Schuster in the back. In view of Schuster's partiality for the company of young men rather than 'bits of fluff', not to mention the flirtatious nature of letters Elgar was prepared to write to women, including Alice Stuart, the tone of stricken horror with which he rounds off the episode is quite absurd: they did not see him, he says, and he was glad, 'for I should have been thoroughly ashamed'.

At the end of this letter he reverted once again to more important matters. 'Tell me what you do about the peerage!' he pleaded. 'It would be interesting to find out how the idea would be received.' In other words, he was inviting Lady Stuart, through her husband and influential friends, to sound out Downing Street on the possibility of going to the Lords. If they followed up his request they evidently failed in their mission, and Elgar chalked up for himself one more unnecessary disappointment.[6]

His importuning of the palace in the matter of the Mastership of the King's Music did, however, pay off, for on 26 April he received a letter from Sir Frederick Ponsonby. 'Dear Sir Edward Elgar,' Ponsonby wrote from Windsor Castle, 'I am commanded by the King to offer you the appointment of Master of the Musick. Although the King's Band has been abolished, His Majesty is anxious that this historical post, which dates back to Elizabethan times, should be kept in existence. It is proposed to give you a nominal salary of £100 per annum and your chief duties will be to advise the King on all questions relating to music.

'In case you should have seen in the newspapers that the appointment was offered to Sir Walford Davies, I must explain that there was no truth in this

---

6. In Elgar's day the peerage was reserved almost exclusively for politicians, businessmen and members of the armed forces. The Order of Merit and a knighthood would have been regarded as more than adequate recognition for a composer at that time.

statement. Sir Walter Parratt happened to combine the post of Organist at St George's Chapel with the Master of the King's Musick and it was the former only that was offered by the Dean of Windsor. The Press, however, assumed that these two posts went necessarily together and so a wrong impression was given by the newspapers.'

Elgar replied by telegram on 28 April from Bromsgrove, where he was staying with Polly: 'Regret absence from London caused delay in replying to your letter proposal gratefully accepted letter follows.' The telegram was entirely superfluous, for later the same day he found the time to have a letter of acceptance typed and sent, saying he was much honoured, trusting it might be possible for him 'as a servant of His Majesty' to help the cause of British music when fitting opportunities occurred, that he would be obliged if Sir Frederick would be so good as to convey 'a simple expression' of his sincere thanks 'for the continuation of this historic appointment' as well as assuring 'His Majesty the King of his loyalty and devotion at all times . . .' In a somewhat incongruous postscript he told Sir Frederick he quite understood about the error in the press.

In July it must have dawned on Elgar that he did not really know what was expected of him, so he wrote again to Ponsonby asking for 'instruction and advice' and a 'very brief interview as soon as may be convenient'. He was referred to the Lord Chamberlain, who saw him and supplied him with some remarkably ugly writing paper headed St James's Palace.

Elgar was the obvious choice for Master of the King's Music, not only because of his pre-eminence as a composer but because of his undoubted gift for turning out good occasional music. As far back as 1904, in an interview he gave to the *Strand Magazine*, he was reported as saying, 'I like to look on the composer's vocation as the old troubadours or bards did. In those days it was no disgrace to a man to be turned on to step in front of an army and inspire the people with a song. For my own part, I know that there are a lot of people who like to celebrate events with music. To these people I have given tunes. Is that wrong? Why should I write a fugue or something which won't appeal to anyone, when the people yearn for things which will stir them?'

Elgar's new appointment coincided with the Empire Exhibition, held at Wembley and opened by the king on 23 April – St George's Day. Elgar had been commissioned to write a march, which he conducted wearing an overcoat. Reporting on the event afterwards, he told Percy Hull that the march was short and brilliant – 'If you want a bright $4\frac{1}{2}$ mins it is there!' – and he gave wholehearted credit to the senior director of music, 'for a thrilling experience when he conducted the Imperial March which I had the honour to compose for the Jubilee of Queen Victoria in 1897; the body of tone, aided by the true military precision of rhythm, was sensational.' That account contrasts sharply with his impressions of the rehearsal, conveyed to Alice Stuart: '... overwhelmed with etiquette and red tape ... the K. insists on Land of Hope ... everything seems so irredeemably vulgar at Court'. The vulgarity of the occasion itself was evidently not redeemed, in the eyes of Siegfried Sassoon, by a rendering of Elgar's orchestration of Parry's *Jerusalem*, for it inspired one of his more satirical poems, *Afterthoughts on the Opening of the British Empire Exhibition*:

> *But when Elgar conducts the massed choirs something inward aspires;*
> *For the words that they sing are by Blake; they are simple and grand,*
> *And their rapture makes everything dim when the music has fled*
> *And the guns boom salutes and the flags are unfurled overhead ...* [7]

According to Sassoon's diary, Elgar had revealed in no uncertain terms his feelings about the king's philistine attitudes some two years before. The poet has recounted that one Sunday in June 1922, at The Hut, the conversation at luncheon got around to a project then in hand to present a doll's house to Queen Mary (which is now on display to the public at Windsor Castle). The subject, which may well have been brought up owing to the presence of Lady Maud Warrender, who had been helping to encourage contributions from manufacturers of games and sporting equipment, provoked an outburst from Elgar, for he 'delivered himself of a petulant tirade which culminated in a crescendo climax of rudeness aimed at Lady M.'. Sassoon goes on to report that Elgar said, 'We all know that the King and Queen are incapable of appreciating anything artistic; they've never asked for the full score of my Second Symphony to be added to the Library at Windsor. But as the crown of my career I'm asked to contribute to – a DOLL'S HOUSE for the QUEEN!! I've been a monkey-on-a-stick for you people long enough. *Now I'm getting off the stick.*' Elgar informed his fellow lunch guests that he had written – to the organizers of the appeal, presumably – to say he hoped they would not have the impertinence to press the matter on him any further. He considered it an insult for an artist to be asked to mix himself up in such nonsense.

Later in 1924 Elgar was again displeased. At Hereford, at the Three Choirs Festival, Adrian Boult told Elgar he was planning to conduct *The Dream of Gerontius* in Birmingham, but because of expense he was proposing to do so with a reduced body of woodwind.[8] Elgar was evidently horrified, and despite the fact that Boult paid to make up the full complement of players out of his own pocket, Elgar allowed the incident to escalate into one of his famous rows. For the next seven years he had nothing further to do with the conductor who

---

7. *Collected Poems* (Faber, 1947).
8. *Music and Friends: Letters to Adrian Boult*, edited by Jerrold Northrop Moore.

was not only a brilliant exponent of his work but was prepared to go on conducting it when it was out of favour. Left to his own devices Elgar would in all probability have taken no initiative to heal the breach, and it might never have been healed at all had not Boult become director of music at the BBC, and felt obliged to make plans to celebrate Elgar's seventy-fifth birthday when it fell in June 1932. In 1931 he asked Billy Reed to act as honest broker. The result was a typical response from Elgar: emotional, exaggerated, self-pitying and determined upon self-justification. 'My dear Adrian,' he wrote on 12 April 1931, 'I need not tell you that I am delighted to be allowed to address you in the old way: I learned from dear Billy Reed that you would like things to be as they were long ago; I will refer to the ancient matter for one moment now and never again. My feelings were acute; I have never had a real success in life – commercially, never; so all I had (and have now) was the feeling that I had written *one* score which satisfied R. Strauss, Richter and many others; it was the discovery that no one in that very wealthy city [Birmingham] – which always pretended to be proud of the production of Gerontius – cared a straw whether the work was presented as I wrote it or not; *there* at least I hoped to be recognised. Now let us forget it.'

The strength of Elgar's reaction in 1924 to the suggested orchestral reduction, and the effect his anger could have upon someone equally sensitive, can be judged by Boult's reply. 'I can't tell you what a thrill it was to see your writing again on an envelope addressed to me. Your letter only caught me up here [Newbury] this morning [15 April] and I must write to thank you for it with all my heart. Willie [Billy Reed] told me it was coming, and this was an added pleasure. He will have told you *my* feelings about it all, so there is nothing more to say about it, now that the expression of want of confidence which hurt me so much (coming as it did after such enormous kindness from you) is effectively and permanently washed out.'

In 1924 Elgar made some half-hearted attempts to regain interest in *The Last Judgement*, the projected third part of the trilogy of oratorios. Reed reports that he played some of it at the piano, and then 'the old light would come into his eyes as he worked himself up and began grunting away to himself, his hands meanwhile flying about ... He never could sustain the mood, however. He apparently had it all planned but could not face the drudgery of putting it on paper.' It would have proved a massive task at any time of life, and Elgar was now sixty-seven. He would also have been in no doubt about the improbability of the flippant, sophisticated post-war generation flocking in any great numbers to hear yet another religious work by a man whose music they regarded as celebrating a world now blown apart. He ended the year by telling Schuster on 30 December that he had had a very quiet Christmas – 'Troyte and a dog or two'. And he added, 'I fear you will have nothing more from my pen – but if that's all to look forward to you will not miss much. Music is dying fast in this country.'

Elgar's friends and contemporaries were dying fast, too. The year had seen the death of Fauré, Puccini and the man whom Elgar had overtaken so dramatically and quarrelled with so unnecessarily, Charles Stanford. In 1925, the year he received the Royal Philharmonic Society's Gold Medal, his eldest sister, Lucy, died.

At the end of 1925, Elgar's contract with the Gramophone Company was again renewed, this time for four years, and while his annual retainer stayed at £500, he received a further £500 bonus on signing the contract. He now began to have dealings at the company with Trevor Osmond Williams, who was forty-one when Elgar first met him, a man described in the *Voice*, after his death, as having a vivid and charming personality, worshipped by artists and idolized not only by his staff but 'by all who were fortunate enough to come into contact with him'. In the four years that Elgar knew Williams the younger man came to play the role of the son Elgar never had. Elgar was rather good at being a father figure, the paternalistic fount of wisdom to whom Billy Reed had been drawn many years before, and whose erudition, wit and breadth of interest, not to mention his achievements, would now be bound to prove attractive to an intelligent man like Williams, anxious to gain experience and an understanding of the past.[9] Elgar was becoming increasingly lonely; his only child was married and there seemed no prospect of grandchildren (in the event, there were none). During the course of the next four years Williams not only concerned himself with Elgar's recording activities, but took him out to dinner, arranged visits to the theatre and to concerts and generally made a fuss of him. It may be far-fetched to suggest that it was as an immediate result of his meeting Williams that Elgar took on a new lease of life, but the fact remains that on 29 April 1926 he was able to report to Schuster, 'It is curious that I do not tire now – 3 hours solid rehearsal Sunday; – the like Monday and the concert; early on Tuesday 3 hours HMV (large orchestra) Wedy afternoon also Dinner on Tuesday and Theatre last night and I am 69!!'

Elgar was less sanguine later in the year, when he again wrote to Schuster, this time about the state of singing in the country. 'There is not a single voice coming on in the solo world,' he announced, 'and young people have given up choral work and the distressingly *thin* physique of the modern boys and

---

9. Another who enjoyed a relationship of this kind was Mr Wulstan Atkins, the son of Sir Ivor Atkins. He was Elgar's godson, and he described Elgar to the author as being a 'second father' to him. Elgar was also, in the last year of his life, affectionately attracted to the sixteen-year-old prodigy Yehudi Menuhin.

girls who *do* try to sing makes their voices so frail and metallic that the general tone is miserable.'

The Gramophone Company decided to mark the year of Elgar's seventieth birthday, 1927, by granting him a contract for life. Such signs of esteem gave him little comfort, as is shown by one of his sillier letters that year, to Charles Volkert of the publishing firm of Schott & Co., whom he had met as a young man while taking violin lessons from Pollitzer. 'I have had some satisfaction and even pleasure in my life,' he managed to admit, 'but have no pleasant memories connected with music.' The letter was not only silly but ungrateful; three months before he wrote it, a concert had been arranged in Manchester to celebrate his birthday, at which the famous, generous and now seventy-five-year-old violinist and former president of the Royal Manchester College of Music, Adolf Brodsky, paid him the compliment, on behalf of his overseas admirers, of playing the Violin Concerto. The programme also included the *Enigma Variations*, *Sea Pictures*, *In the South* and the early overture *Froissart*. If we are to believe Elgar, the occasion gave him no pleasure.

In June, Frank Schuster, with only six months to live and an imaginative patron to the end, arranged a performance at his house in Bray of the three chamber works. 'Dear old Frank was radiant and, as usual, a perfect host,' Elgar told Alice Stuart afterwards. 'I *hope* I behaved as becomes an old visitor.' Twenty-two years later, Osbert Sitwell wrote, in the fourth volume of his high-flown autobiography,[10] an account of the occasion, to which he, along with his brother Sacheverell, William Walton, Siegfried Sassoon, Arnold Bennett and many others had been invited. Considering that Sitwell prefaces his report by saying that, in spite of his genius, the music of Elgar is obnoxious – 'so full of English humour and the spirit of compulsory games' – one wonders why he bothered to attend unless to sneer. 'I seem to recall,' he tells us, 'that we saw from the edge of the river, on a smooth green lawn ... through an hallucinatory mist born of the rain that had now ceased, the plump wraith of Sir Edward Elgar, who with his grey moustache, grey hair, grey top hat and frock-coat looked every inch a personification of Colonel Bogey ... Was it, can it have been, a delusion? Am I imagining it?' Sitwell, who was thirty-four at the time, was not imagining anything. 'One could almost hear, through the music, the whirr of the wings of the Angel of Death,' he went on. What Sitwell was doing was seeing off the 'floccose herds of good-time Edwardian ghosts' whom he loathed and detested as he loathed and detested everything and everybody connected with the generation of his wildly eccentric father.

In October Elgar found himself on the move once again because Lord Dudley wanted to move back into Napleton Grange. For a short time he rented

10. *Laughter in the Next Room* (Macmillan, 1949).

Battenhall Manor in Worcester, and it was here, in December, that he received news of Schuster's death, at 19 Lansdowne Place in Hove. Schuster left Elgar £7,000, having originally made a Will bequeathing 'To my friend Sir Edward Elgar, OM, who has saved my country from the reproach of having produced no composer worthy to rank with the Great Masters', £10,000 subject to death duties; in a fourth codicil to his Will, signed on 13 September 1925, Schuster increased a legacy to a godson from £2,000 to £5,000, and the £3,000 needed to do this came from Elgar's original £10,000. (Siegfried Sassoon recorded in his diary that Schuster was incessantly 'fussing about dividing bills, and money in general'.) Another godson received £10,000, his sister Adela, who presumably had resources of her own, received £1,000, and in all, Schuster left individual legacies amounting to about £24,000. For probate purposes, he left a total of £47,063 0s. 7d. (if Sassoon was correct in reckoning Schuster's income to have been about £10,000 a year in 1922, however, the real value of the estate must have been considerably greater). The Hut, his cars, his Steinway piano and the residue went to Anzy, the original manuscript of *In the South* went to the Royal Academy of Music and a fine bust of Elgar went to the National Portrait Gallery. 'I send you my deepest sympathy and regard,' Elgar wrote, somewhat stiffly, to Adela on receiving a telegram telling him of Schuster's death. 'By my own sorrow, which is more than I can bear to think of at this moment, I may realise in some measure what this overwhelming loss must be to you.' As a testimonial to a man who had lavished so much time and patience, not to mention money and hospitality, upon him, it was not perhaps one of Elgar's more effusive notes. Bernard Shaw, never one for half measures, leant the other way by suggesting that Schuster should be buried in Westminster Abbey.

Not content with having his gramophone overhauled by the Gramophone Company and receiving from them a gift of a new electrical machine – 'I am delighted with it and thank you a thousand times,' he wrote to the company on 8 December – Elgar was cadging new records off Trevor Williams on 14 December: 'I would be so much obliged if I might have a few good piano solos … I also require Overture Mignon, Pomp & Circumstances Nos. 1 and 2, Fantasia & Fugue, &, if complete, Overture Oberon.' He added that he had been quite laid up for nearly a month with a chill, 'or I had hoped to have suggested a theatre to you'.

An astonishing display of ecclesiastical suspicion greeted the company's plans in 1928 to record in Gloucester Cathedral. The Dean of Gloucester, in spite of Trevor Williams's assurances to the contrary, actually believed that structural damage to the cathedral might result if he allowed recordings to be made in it, and although Elgar himself wrote to the dean to add his authoritative reassurance, the dean stuck to his quaint and inconvenient theory.

In the New Year Honours List for 1928, Elgar was made a Knight Commander of the Royal Victorian Order, and the king followed up the honour by inviting Elgar to dine with him on 23 March. Not long afterwards, Elgar's brother Frank died. Still without a permanent home in which to end his own days, Elgar now rented Tiddington House at Stratford, where his manservant Dick rowed him up and down the Avon, and where, in the manner of monied people who have never had to fend for themselves, he discovered 'the best sausages in England', on sale twelve miles away, at Leamington, and took to sending over for them once a week.

Although Elgar had always fancied himself as a country gentleman he had no serious interest in country pursuits other than walking and fishing, and as he grew older he was also less inclined to travel around the country conducting. Composing the occasional part-song or arranging a motet by Purcell was all his creative activity consisted of at this time, and had it not been for his recording sessions at the Gramophone Company he might well have died of boredom. He still retained his London flat, to which a car would be sent to bring him to the studio, and the business of arranging recording sessions, discussing artists and requesting records for his own collection gave him new scope for correspondence now that so many of his old friends had gone. He did not always behave very graciously towards his benefactors, however, as an account of one session in November 1929, given in Jerrold Northrop Moore's *Elgar on Record*, shows: 'Elgar could hardly have been more withdrawn; he conducted with the barest movement of his stick and very little discussion with the orchestra. Having to deal with Elgar that day was rather like trying to make friends with a large and distant mastiff which gazes steadfastly into the middle distance whatever overtures one makes.'

Just five days later Elgar was writing to ask for Mozart's G Minor Symphony ('mine is worn out'), together with the *Prague* Symphony ('which came last week and which has met with an accident'). Elgar's explanation for the need to replace the latter may have been something of a euphemism, judging by an amusing account given to Northrop Moore in 1974 by the son of one of Elgar's friends, who spent an evening playing records with him in 1931. He says he was scandalized by Elgar's treatment of records. 'There they were, piled on top of one another, without their envelopes. He grabbed them as though they were cheap crockery, and when he wanted to hear a favourite passage again he just jabbed the pick-up down until he found it!' According to their age, the relationship they enjoyed with Elgar and the circumstances under which they met him, different people picked up very different impressions, and it is interesting to note another well-drawn picture of Elgar offered to Dr Moore, again in 1974, by Bernard Wratten, who as a young employee of the Gramophone Company knew the composer in his sixties and seventies. Wratten remembered Elgar as 'an extremely conventional man, a survival from an even more rigidly conventional era when convention ruled everything from our manner of speech and the degree to which we revealed our thoughts or feelings to our appearance and the clothes we wore. Against the still fairly conventional standards of the late 'twenties, Elgar seemed almost excessively correct and reserved in his manner.'

At the end of 1929, Elgar at last found a house to his liking, on Rainbow Hill, a steep road to the north-east of Worcester leading to the cemetery where his parents were buried. The area is now a run-down and depressing part of the city, and the house, Marl Bank, a substantial three-storey Victorian property with ivy-covered walls, has been demolished. In its place stand, disgracing their name, two blocks of flats called Elgar Court. The grounds once included a kitchen garden and an eighteenth-century courtyard, its walls lined by pear and apple trees. A few nineteenth-century terraced houses still stand on Rainbow Hill opposite the site of Marl Bank, but it is impossible today to gain any impression of the spot as it was chosen by Worcester's most famous son in which to spend the last few years of his life.

Elgar had been installed for only a short time when he became embroiled in the kind of domestic details so often associated with moving home but more usually reserved for the kitchen or the bathroom. In Elgar's case the problems, not all of them of a purely technical nature, centred around his gramophone. On 11 December he wrote a petulant little note to Fred Gaisberg: 'When is that Marconi wireless affair coming along?' he wanted to know. 'You see I am in my new home and will not have the old aerial fixed until I know; another thing – can't I have one of the new gramophones like my friend Walford Davies has – a later pattern than my more-than-two-year-old one?'

The matter was handed over to Trevor Williams to sort out. He told Elgar two days before Christmas that the management 'had consented' to lend him one of their latest electric gramophones, and he knew what satisfaction this would give him. Before dispatching it, however, he would need to know the following particulars of the electric current in his house: what the voltage was, and whether it was alternating or direct. 'You will also need a wall plug or lamp socket available near the machine,' Williams explained, 'so as to form a connection with the electric circuit.' If Elgar would give him these particulars, he would have the machine sent off at once.

On Christmas Day, Elgar told Williams he was overjoyed to hear about the new instrument and would send on the information about the electric current 'as soon as the holidays will allow confirmation to be obtained'. He added that he hoped Williams might honour 'this funny little house' some day with his 'esteemed presence'. Christmas holidays being conveniently brief in those days, Elgar was able to write on 27 December, 'The electric expert tells me to report that our supply is AC 200V, 50 cycles.' Instructions for the 'machine' to be dispatched were issued the next day. On 30 December, Elgar was nevertheless preparing himself for all eventualities. He wrote to Williams, 'I propose, with your assent, to hold the gramophone which you sent to me two years ago in case the new instrument is not suitable to the house. I have no doubt the gorgeous new inst. will be "at home" here but it may possibly be too sonorous. After a trial I will return the old one.' He again hoped that Williams would come to 'this cottage' one day.

All was well, however, and on 6 January 1930 Elgar was able to exclaim, 'The new gramophone is here and is a marvel! Can there be a better inst.' A new gramophone of course deserved new records, particularly after the rigours of moving house, so on 24 January Elgar wrote again to Williams: 'I hope you are well. If it comes within the compass of the generosity of HMV may I have D1409 D1614–5 which were damaged in moving house. I *should* like the Chopin *Ballades*.'

George V had the previous year suffered his first serious illness, and Elgar had celebrated the king's recovery by writing a carol. He sent copies, describing the work as a 'trifle', to Sir Frederick Ponsonby on 11 December, and was acknowledged the following day. 'My dear Master of the Music,' wrote Sir Frederick, dropping for once the 'k' on 'Music', 'The King desires me to thank you for the copies of the Carol which you have been good enough to write on His Majesty's recovery. The King is taking these copies down to Sandringham and intends to ask the choir to sing your carol.'

Elgar's first summer at Marl Bank was clouded by the sudden and premature death of Trevor Williams. Williams had gone in July to Vienna, 'in what appeared to be excellent spirits', as Elgar was later told by Alfred Clark, chairman of the Gramophone Company. It seems that on 24 July Elgar read of Williams's illness, in a newspaper presumably, and he sent a telegram to Clark saying he was deeply concerned and anxious for news. The company cabled back, 'Deeply regret inform you Captain Williams condition very grave stop he is lying at Vienna where he is receiving best possible medical attention.' The telegram was followed up the same day by a letter from Clark, telling Elgar that shortly after arriving in Vienna Williams had become very ill. 'The cause,' he said, 'is somewhat obscure, but it appears to be some internal poisoning. He has had the very best Viennese doctors, but there appears to be no hope of his recovery and the telegrams and telephone messages that we are constantly receiving seem to give worse and worse news. You will, I know, realise how deeply distressed we all are.' Williams died the next day. He was forty-four.

On 6 October Elgar suffered a 'sudden and ferocious' attack of lumbago. The next day he could 'just sit up', but 'locomotion was not possible'. In writing to Clark to explain all this, and to apologize for having been obliged to postpone a recording session for the First Symphony, he made his first reference to Williams's death, more than two months after the event. 'I cannot yet feel I can write about dear Trevor Williams: – I think you know what I feel – I cannot get over the loss.' It was not until 13 January 1931, when Williams had been dead five months, that Elgar felt able to unburden himself. It was to Clark again that he wrote. 'On looking over the year just closed I find the greatest (and bitterest) sensation was the death of Trevor Osmond Williams; his going has left a blank in my life and a pain which nothing can soften. He had become my greatest friend. At my age old acquaintances fail and depart with appalling rapidity and young friends are not easy to find. Trevor was always ready to look after me – a dinner, lunch, theatre – anything pleasant and helpful. You knew his charm and most delightful company and can realise what a loss his death made.

'I cannot claim any acquaintance with the family. I knew (as a golfer only and fellow clubman) his father in the nineties and was delighted to find that Trevor was the son of that striking and *very handsome* man.[11]

'But he has gone and I am left lonely. All this seems to be mere selfishness, but somehow I cannot help having a feeling (a feeling I am not going to attempt to analyse or excuse) that I want *you* to know how I have felt it, and if you think any of his near relatives would like to know, to tell them.

'I met Trevor's sister once and that is all I know of the present generation.'

For once, Elgar's incurable need to exaggerate ('he had become my greatest friend') can perhaps be overlooked. Elgar had known Williams scarcely four years, and while it is true that very close friendships do not necessarily take a long time to form, it is difficult to believe that Williams had become a greater friend than, for example, Troyte Griffith or Billy Reed, whom Elgar had by now known for a quarter of a century. But the letter was a painfully honest exposé of his position, and it takes courage for an old person to admit to loneliness and dependence upon a younger generation. His desire for Williams's family to be told how much Williams had meant to him is a clear indication of his love for the younger man, and of his need to have his love recognized; indeed, his reaction to Williams's death bears all the hallmarks of genuine bereavement, in contrast to his hysterical outburst when Rodewald died. On this occasion he took time for reflection, and when he came to write about his grief, his letter

11. The *'very handsome'* man whom Elgar had known and found so striking was Sir Osmond Williams, a baronet, whose eldest son and heir, Trevor's brother, had later been killed in the Great War.

was both dignified and moving. It elicited a consoling response from Clark, who wrote to say, 'Your intimate and kindly letter has touched me deeply. I knew of the bond of friendship between you and Trevor and was proud of it for his sake. He often spoke to me of it and of his affection for you and I am happy that his short life – short as we count now – was brighter by it.'

Billy Reed tells us that Elgar's lumbago had been so bad during the Three Choirs Festival in 1930 that he had to be helped on and off the rostrum, and he conducted sitting down. He says that at this time, too, Elgar suffered from nettlerash. Nevertheless, 1930 saw the completion of some of the more enduring later works, in particular the fifth of the set of five *Pomp and Circumstance Marches* dedicated to Percy Hull and conducted for the first time by Henry Wood at the Queen's Hall on 20 September. Earlier sketches, some of them going back half a century, were resurrected and transformed into the *Severn Suite*, in four movements, at first scored for brass band; dedicated to Bernard Shaw, this was given its first performance at the Crystal Palace Brass Band Festival on 27 September, and two years later Elgar arranged the suite for orchestra, conducting the first public performance of that version at Worcester on 7 September 1932.

Perhaps under the stress of pain, Elgar let fly at Fred Gaisberg over what he regarded as undue delay in releasing a recording of the new *Pomp and Circumstance March*. 'I am awfully disappointed about P & C No. 5,' he wrote on November 25. 'Your business side does not know its business alas! Here is the most "selling" thing we have had ... and it is idiotically held up for nearly six months – I get nothing from it meanwhile: it is really desperately annoying.'

By 13 January 1931 he had recovered his equilibrium sufficiently to tell Gaisberg he had revelled in the records of Verdi's *Requiem*, 'which work I have always worshipped', and to inquire about the 'the basso, Pinza'. His phrasing, Elgar said, was the finest he had heard. Needless to say, within a couple of days Gaisberg had furnished Elgar with a curriculum vitae and a list of all the records Pinza had made for the company over the past ten years, with an assurance that the company would be only too delighted to send any of Pinza's records Elgar might like to possess. Elgar promptly ordered four.

In the spring there followed a brief and unintentionally funny correspondence between Elgar and Gaisberg concerning an injury to Elgar's leg. On 13 April, Elgar wrote to say, 'I am so sorry I could not manage to be with you on Friday. I hope to be able to travel soon: I have broken a tendon (or something) in my *leg*.' To which, the following day, Gaisberg responded by echoing Elgar's letter, and his dubious medical terminology, word for word.

'We were very sorry indeed,' he wrote, 'to hear that you had broken a tendon, or something, in your leg ...' The injury cannot have been too serious; a month later Elgar was asking permission from the Gramophone Company, to whom he was of course under contract, to conduct in Hyde Park.

Elgar was now becoming increasingly preoccupied with the past. The *Severn Suite* was followed by the *Nursery Suite*, another conscious harking back to childhood and youthful music; the opening Aubade actually makes use of a hymn tune Elgar composed in 1878. Plans to record the suite, later described by the *Daily Telegraph*, perhaps a little too enthusiastically, as a masterpiece, were under discussion early in 1931, and in a letter written to Gaisberg on 10 January, Elgar floated the idea that the Duchess of York might be induced to attend a recording session. Elgar had written to Sir Frederick Ponsonby on 11 October 1930 seeking permission to dedicate the 'four little childlike (not childish) movements' to the duchess and her daughters, Princess Elizabeth and Princess Margaret. (Eventually the suite consisted of seven movements.) But as late as 25 May, Elgar was suggesting 5 or 6 June for a recording session, and he was asking Gaisberg to let him know an exact date so that he could 'communicate with the Duchess with a view to her presence'. Elgar seems to have been unaware that most royal diaries are normally full up to two years ahead, and in the event he was fortunate in arranging not only for the duchess but for the duke as well to attend the recording studio at just four days' notice. The duchess was perhaps one of the few members of the royal family in recent years to have actually enjoyed music, and either out of genuine appreciation or her accustomed spontaneity she asked Elgar, sitting at the rostrum, to repeat the fifth movement, 'The Wagon Passes'.

This pleasant occasion coincided with another state honour for the grand old man of English music; having failed in his quest for a peerage he did now at least receive a hereditary title (with no one to pass it on to), a baronetcy, which was gazetted the day before the recording. It was an honour in the gift of the prime minister, but Elgar decided that the sovereign deserved a word of thanks all the same. So on 2 June he wrote to Sir Frederick Ponsonby to say, 'I do not know if it is permissible to send personal thanks to His Majesty the King; but if it is allowed, I shall be grateful to you if you find it possible to convey to His Majesty an expression of my sincere thanks for the honour that I am informed by the Prime Minister is to be bestowed on me. This continues the happy memories I hold of recognition by the Royal Family. As long ago as 1891 Her late Majesty Queen Victoria sent several messages of appreciation to me by my old friend Sir Walter Parratt, my predecessor as Master of the Music; since that time the kindly interest of King

Edward was very precious to me, and the present honour to be conferred by His Majesty fills me today with a gratitude which I cannot help wishing might be made known to the King.' On the subject of his relations with the royal family and the honours list generally, Sir Frederick could have been forgiven had he allowed the thought to flicker across his mind that Elgar was becoming a bit of a bore.

Among Elgar's fan mail as a result of recording the *Nursery Suite* was a letter from Cordelia Mundahl, aged ten, daughter of the Middlesbrough stipendiary magistrate, as she was careful to point out, in case Elgar might think she was a mere nobody. 'Dear Sir Edward, I am writing this letter to congratulate you upon composing The Nursery Suite,' wrote the precocious Cordelia. 'I love it, the Wagon Passes is my Favourite tune. I think it is wonderful how the violin goes to such a high note. I am not very good at music, but I love listening to music Especially the Nursery Suit. I have heard that you wrote the Nursery suit for Princess Margaret Rose. I think she will love it.' Somewhat ironically she ends, 'I wish you could ask Sir Thomas Beecham to play it when he comes to Middlesbrough.'

In November, Elgar inaugurated yet another new studio for the Gramophone Company, this time at 3 Abbey Road, St John's Wood, when, according to a letter from Gaisberg to Elgar of 4 November, it was originally intended to give a luncheon, but many objections having been raised to the idea, 'There will therefore be available various drinks, such as Champagne, Whisky, Lemonade and Orangeade.' It seems to have been a strange form of economy, if economics lay behind the decision not to provide lunch, to have instead gone to the expense of laying on champagne. Among those denied lunch that day were Bernard Shaw (not that he would have cared), Cedric Hardwicke, Landon Ronald, Walford Davies and Barry Jackson.

No sooner was Elgar back at Marl Bank than he was embroiled yet again in correspondence over his gramophone. 'Please tell me if Spark & Co. can put the gramophone right,' he wrote to ask Gaisberg on 13 November. 'It is going very badly and hums. I have had a new set of valves costing vast sums!' Gaisberg replied the next day; 'I am arranging for an Expert to be sent to overhaul your machine. He should be there some time during Monday.' Alas, on 19 November, Elgar had to report, 'The engineer came from Birmingham and worked at the gramophone for a long time but it is just as bad as ever and not usable on account of the "hum" so I am reduced to silence.' This elicited a telegram of sixteen words when six would have done: 'Sending engineer with new machine stop arriving at your house about four o'clock tomorrow saturday afternoon.' Elgar duly received the new gramophone, 'mercifully, on Saturday'.

On 2 January 1932, Elgar celebrated the year of his seventy-fifth birthday by putting his signature to one of the most dramatic documents even he had yet dreamed up, a new Will. It opened, like so many of his most inspired musical works, with a grand flourish: 'I regret,' he began what was in effect a testament more to his state of mind than to his bank balance, 'that owing to the sudden collapse of everything artistic and commercial I have found it necessary to revoke the Will which I had previously made and to make this present Will. I leave nothing to any charities as I have given everything possible during my life and I much regret that it is now necessary for me to cancel the legacies which it had been my purpose to leave to servants and friends and institutions.'

There were two exceptions, however: Richard Mountford, described in the Will as his chauffeur and by some of Elgar's friends as his valet, received a less than generous legacy of £50; and Mary Clifford, his housekeeper and secretary, received an annuity of £50 for life. Elgar owned a little house in Worcester, 2 Waterworks Road, of which he left the 'free use for life' to his brother-in-law, Charles Pipe. To Carice he left his books, manuscripts, furniture and motor-cars, as well as the residue of his estate (which came to include very substantial royalties) to be held on trust, not for any children she might have borne, but for Frank Elgar, the son of his brother Frank, for Gerald, Roland, May, Madeleine and Clare Grafton, five of the six children of his second sister, Polly, and for their children. The sixth child, Vincent, was excluded on the grounds, apparently, that he was 'the black sheep of the family' and not a Roman Catholic.[12] Whether Elgar would have altered his Will to leave his estate on trust for his grandchildren had any been born during his lifetime we shall never know, but he never made any provision for the possibility of grandchildren being born after his death. Carice was forty-two when he drew up the Will, and he may have considered it unlikely that she would now have any children.

While he could not at that time have foreseen the eventual popularity and therefore commercial success of his music, he must have known that his estate would not be meagre – in fact, only two years later, he was to leave a total of £13,934 6s 9d. On account of a more than usually severe attack of paranoia when drawing up his Will, his loyal and devoted friends were not considered, and he did not trouble to leave even a small memento to the closest of his friends – Alice Stuart, Troyte Griffith and Billy Reed. His godson, Wulstan Atkins, did not get so much as a pair of cufflinks. Carice, at the time of her death in 1970, had accumulated £70,000, and in a deliberate move to make sure her first cousins once removed did not get a

12. Letter of November 1980 (undated) from Jack McKenzie, curator of Elgar's Birthplace, to the author.

penny more than the royalties bequeathed to them by her father for the remaining fourteen years of copyright, she left practically her entire fortune, in a Will dated 20 December 1968, to Hilda Russell, a friend with whom she lived, 'in appreciation of our friendship and in gratitude for all that she has done for me'.[13]

The 'sudden collapse of everything artistic and commercial' had not prevented Elgar, two days before signing his last Will and Testament, from beginning a letter to Fred Gaisberg, 'A Happy New Year to you All'. However, just to maintain the illusion that all was really for the worst in the worst of all possible worlds, he ended another letter to Gaisberg, on 7 May, 'I am glad to hear that Richard Strauss is so prosperous: I am penniless, starving and fading away.'

A seemingly incongruous but apparently successful encounter occurred earlier in the year at the recording studios in Abbey Road, when Elgar and Gracie Fields, then thirty-four, happened to be making records on the same day. An impromptu meeting between the two was arranged by W. L. Streeton, the artists' manager. Streeton has recalled, 'They were both extremely natural, and friendly and gentle with each other. He complimented her on her vocal range and command of styles, and then chatted to one or two of the orchestra before we left; of course they were quite overawed.'[14]

In memory of Queen Alexandra, who had died in 1925, Elgar set to music an ode by the new Poet Laureate, John Masefield, and received a letter on 8 June from Sir Clive Wigram (private secretary to George V), to say, 'The King has asked me to send his and the Queen's warm congratulations to you on the musical setting of the Poet Laureate's Ode. Their Majesties were much impressed by the beauty of the music, and consider it is in every way worthy of you and of the Master of the King's Musick.' The ode, *So Many True Princesses Who Have Gone*, scored for choir and military band, was performed at the unveiling of a memorial to Queen Alexandra at Marlborough House on 9 June, and the king decided he would like to possess the original score, 'signed by yourself', Elgar was told, 'so that the work by the Master of the King's Musick may be preserved in the records at Windsor Castle'. When Elgar eventually sent off the manuscript he explained to Sir Clive Wigram, 'I fear it is in rather a sad condition for the reason that copies had to be made for the performance and for this purpose it has necessarily passed

13. Only two of Polly's six children had children, Vincent and Roland. Vincent had one son, Martin, who has never benefited from the Elgar Estate as his father was not mentioned in Elgar's Will. Roland had four children, David, Susanne, Paul and Mark Grafton, all of whom currently benefit. Elgar's brother Frank had one son, also called Frank, who died only a year after Elgar; he had four daughters, Margaret, Mary, Catherine and Hilary Elgar, who also benefit.

14. *Elgar on Record* by Jerrold Northrop Moore.

through many hands since I penned it.' When Elgar suggested to Gaisberg that the ode, which lasted four and a half minutes, might be recorded he was told that there were 'so many complications in the way and the cost would be so prohibitive that with great regret we are forced to give up the idea'. Elgar's may have been a name to conjure with, but Gaisberg was clearly first and foremost a businessman.

A more promising business proposition which the company lined up for 1932 was a recording of the Violin Concerto to be conducted by the seventy-five-year-old Elgar and performed by the fifteen-year-old American, Yehudi Menuhin. From start to finish (the recording was followed by a visit to Paris the following year for the old man and the young boy to perform the concerto together in public) the collaboration brought great personal and musical pleasure to Elgar's last days. 'The boy has already mastered the technical difficulties and is most enthusiastic over the work,' Gaisberg assured Elgar on 7 June. 'He is looking forward to meeting you tremendously. I think you will be pleased and amazed at his genius.'

Yehudi and his father were to stay in style at Grosvenor House, and it was to their rooms on Park Lane that the composer went on 12 July to meet them, and to run through the concerto accompanied on the piano by Ivor Newton, who recalled, 'We played right through the concerto except for the tuttis ... Menuhin and Elgar discussed the music like equals, but with great courtesy and lack of self-consciousness on the boy's part.' Newton says he was amazed at Menuhin's maturity of outlook and his ability to raise points for discussion without ever sounding like anything but a master violinist discussing a work with a composer for whom he had unbounded respect. Most of the time, Elgar apparently sat back in a chair with his eyes closed, listening intently, 'but it was easy to see the impression that Yehudi had made on him'.[15]

It was indeed. Elgar wrote the next day to Bernard Shaw, 'I am recording the Violin Concerto tomorrow and Friday with Yehudi Menuhin – wonderful boy.' Four days after the recording session, he wrote to Gaisberg, 'I hope our work pleases you: we did our best: of course, *Yehudi* is wonderful and will be splendid.' He wrote again on 18 August, telling Gaisberg, 'The *tone* of that wonderful boy is marvellous', and becoming impatient five days later, he wrote on a postcard, 'Send me the *other* set of records of the Concerto *as soon as you can* – there's a dear.'

Writing forty-five years later in his autobiography,[16] Yehudi Menuhin gave an account of the recording session that gives full credit to Elgar's contribution

15. *Elgar on Record* by Jerrold Northrop Moore.
16. *Unfinished Journey* (Macdonald & Jane, 1977).

to what turned out to be a truly great recording of the Violin Concerto, a recording which in some respects has never been surpassed. 'At the recording studio,' Menuhin writes, 'Elgar was a figure of great dignity but without a shred of self-importance. I had never seen anyone conduct less, or show less determination to impose himself. All was ease and equanimity, almost as if his presence and movements were superfluous ... The orchestra surrendered itself to his invisible authority with joy, confidence and devotion.'

In November, to coincide with release of the records, Elgar and Menuhin repeated their duet at the Albert Hall, in a concert, says Menuhin, 'to make a 16-year-old boy at once proud and humble'. Beecham conducted Menuhin in the first half in concertos by Bach and Mozart, and after the interval, Elgar, 'propped on a red velvet stool', conducted his own concerto. To perform three concertos in one concert was for Menuhin no mean achievement, even allowing for the energy and enthusiasm of youth, and Elgar again found his playing 'wonderful'. However, in a letter to Gaisberg written on 25 November, in connection with the proposed performance in Paris, he expressed doubts about going over to conduct the work himself. 'I fear,' he said, 'the press and the public would not consider me good enough company for such a great artist in France,' a remark which smacks more of an intended compliment to the latest light of his eye ('Your friendship has given me a new zest in life,' he told Yehudi) than of any serious desire to withdraw.

It did not in fact take much to persuade Elgar to go to France in May 1933 to conduct the concerto, for the trip offered an opportunity not only to visit Paris again but to see his 'old friend' and stricken compatriot, Frederick Delius, who lived at Grez-sur-Loing. Elgar learned in April, with evident relief ('the best news is that you will go to Paris'), that Gaisberg was to accompany him as well as make all the arrangements, and these included plans for Elgar to undertake his first flight in an aeroplane. He and Gaisberg and Elgar's manservant Richard Mountford took off from Croydon at 3.30 p.m. on 29 May, arriving in Paris shortly after five o'clock, where Gaisberg had rooms booked at the Hotel Royal Monceau in the Avenue Hoch. Before he flew, Elgar wrote to Bernard Shaw, not too seriously perhaps, to say, 'I somehow feel I shall not return,' and before he got into the aeroplane he posed on the steps for photographs. He completed a crossword puzzle during the journey, and wrote to tell Adela Schuster that according to the insurance people, the risk was 'at the same rate as railway travelling'. It was also 'wonderful to avoid changes, oily-smelling boats and the hundred other troubles of the channel crossing'.

Fred Gaisberg, who gave an account of the journey in his book *Music on Record*, tells us that Elgar celebrated his first night in Paris with a 'fine dinner'.

There was a rehearsal next morning, with the Symphony Orchestra of Paris, and luncheon at the Menuhins' house in St Cloud. Madame Menuhin had prepared a Palestinian dish of boned fish moulded into a loaf and boiled for an hour, which apparently found favour with Elgar, for he asked for a second helping. Before undertaking the forty-mile pilgrimage to see Delius, Elgar wisely had a rest, and when the Menuhins' new Buick broke down they had to hail a taxi.

It was well after five o'clock when they arrived at Delius's 'simple, two-storied, whitewashed farmhouse'. Delius received Elgar 'in a long room with a low ceiling, and three old-fashioned windows looking out on a pretty rose garden'. Gaisberg also noted that all the furnishings were 'dowdy and rather grimy with use, such as might be found in a Bayswater boarding-house'. Whether Gaisberg had ever seen the inside of a Bayswater boarding-house may be doubted. He is on more interesting ground when he tells us the way in which Elgar seemed to overcome at once any possibility of embarrassment on account of Delius's paralysed condition, initiating an animated conversation that ranged over music, literature and the state of the Florida orange industry. Dowdy though Gaisberg may have reckoned the home, at his request Mrs Delius produced 'a great stock of sandwiches, made of homemade bread and first-class ham', and Delius rose to the occasion by opening a bottle of champagne in Elgar's honour. There is no doubt, from subsequent comments made by Elgar when he returned home (to Gaisberg he wrote, 'Our visit to Delius was a great event to me'), that he found it a memorable and moving experience.

The concert was held next day, and Gaisberg's young niece, Isabella Wallich, was deputed to accompany Elgar in a car to the concert hall. Elgar, she has said in a radio broadcast, was shaking all over and held her hand throughout the journey. Not realizing that Elgar should have been taken to the artists' entrance, Isabella steered him to the main door where they were turned away because they had no tickets. By the time they turned up behind the platform the Menuhins had almost given them up for lost. But, says Gaisberg, the concert was 'a brilliant repetition of the London performance', which he tempers by adding, 'The Concerto was received with enthusiasm, but one felt that it had not made the impression that was its due.' It is true that the French have never taken to Elgar in the way the Germans have, but Gaisberg's account should perhaps be treated with caution; he also tells us that Elgar, on his return to Croydon, was motored to Billy Reed's house where a bottle of wine was opened, 'to drink to Elgar's 76th birthday and the bestowal upon him of the Order of Merit by the King'. Elgar had of course received the OM in 1911, and Gaisberg had confused it with Elgar's latest honour, the advancement from KCVO to Knight Grand Cross of the Royal Victorian Order; to the American Gaisberg, one British honour must have been much like another. This was in fact the last of the many honours Elgar received, and for an artist it was an unprecedented mark of royal favour.

CHAPTER SEVEN

'Billy, This is the End'

———❦————————————————————❧———

1932–34

The last years of Elgar's life were bedevilled by final and desperate attempts at serious composition. The last sketches for a piano concerto have been dated 1932; the first sketches went back to 1909 and he had attempted to pull the work together in 1914, 1917 and 1926, often by trying to make use of material left over from other compositions. His heart never really seems to have been in the concerto, and the only movement he eventually came close to finishing at the end of his life was the slow movement, ultimately completed and scored by Percy Young and played at the Royal Festival Hall on 30 January 1956 by Elgar's friend Harriet Cohen.

The search for a suitable operatic libretto had occupied him spasmodically over many years, resulting in abandoned suggestions from a number of friends, and at one time Elgar even asked Bernard Shaw to prepare a libretto for him. In 1919 Elgar had written in a postscript to a letter to Walford Davies, 'Oh! about the opera – I have never found a subject I cared about – I wanted something heroic and noble but I am only offered blood and lust in the way of libretti.' Eventually, and very near the end of his life, Elgar hit upon what seems a most unlikely text, Ben Jonson's *The Devil is an Ass*. His friend Sir Barry Jackson, founder of the Birmingham Repertory Theatre and one of the organizers of the Malvern Festival, at first tried to dissuade Elgar, but on second thoughts he produced a draft libretto, and it fired the old man's imagination. Reed tells us that Elgar immediately set to work on the libretto with a mass of alterations and amendments of his own, the work growing until there was a pile of manuscript on his desk. The plot involved a character called Wittipol who was to disguise himself as a Spanish lady, a teacher of deportment, in order to woo Frances, the ward of Fitzdotrell, and so the opera gained the title *The Spanish Lady*. The sketches show a preponderance of dances: a Saraband was resurrected from a sketchbook dating back to 1878, a new Bourrée was completed, and a Country Dance and a rather hop-skip-and-jump Burlesco are also in performable shape. Reed recalled, too, playing through with Elgar a Spanish Dance and a Bolero.

Some 180 fragments for the opera are said to have come to light, and it is evident that working on them in his last years brought Elgar a lot of pleasure. According to Reed, he would explain 'with a wealth of detail' everything that was to happen on the stage, 'at the particular bar we were trying over'. He even drew a plan of the stage, showing all the properties and exactly where the characters were to stand. 'But,' says Reed, 'if I am ever asked what it was all about I shall have to confess that I have not the slightest idea, and never had.' Reed attributes Elgar's abandonment of work on the opera to a project that was much more controversial, and even in a way tragic: a commission to write a third symphony.

In 1932, says Fred Gaisberg, Elgar played to him 'a fine love duet set for soprano and tenor', intended for *The Spanish Lady*, 'parts of a piano concerto' and 'a beautiful slow movement and an intriguing scherzo for a Third Symphony', and he adds, 'his brain was intensely alert, and at the end of his life seemed suddenly to have acquired a creative urge that would not let him rest'. Indeed, in the same year Elgar was still fussing over the First Symphony; in a letter dated 22 November to Adrian Boult he wrote, 'I do not want to worry you unduly but perhaps one of your assistants could see to the following matter, *if* you approve of my suggestion. In the first Symphony there are some passages which I have never got to my liking. In the passage beginning four bars before ⁣30⁣ (and occurring twice more) I want an echo effect ...' Precisely when the creative urge that would not let him rest got to grips with a new symphony is impossible to say, for Elgar was constantly looking through sketchbooks and making notes, but in view of his acceptance of a commission for the work it is necessary to unravel the history.

There must have been talk in positive terms about a symphony prior to August 1932, for on 4 August that year Walter Legge, editor of the Gramophone Company's magazine the *Voice*, exercised his youthful if misguided initiative by approaching Elgar in the following vein: 'I hope you will forgive me for writing to you on this topic, but I have heard, on what I believe to be very reliable authority, that you have practically completed a third symphony. Is there any truth in this rumour? If you can tell me, I should be delighted to make use of the information, not only in The Voice but in the general press. Moreover, our mutual friend Ernest Newman is very anxious to know whether there is any truth in the news, which I passed on to him for what it is worth.'

Legge's 'very reliable authority' was most likely Fred Gaisberg. Newman was at the time music critic of the *Sunday Times*. Before Legge had even solicited, never mind received, confirmation about something he admitted was only a rumour, he had passed on to Newman a possible scoop and was all geared up to issuing a general press release. Under the circumstances, Elgar's enigmatic reply was unlikely to dampen the impending avalanche of interest. 'Dear Mr Legge,' he wrote, 'Many thanks for your letter: there is nothing to say about the mythical Symphony for some time, – probably a long time, – possibly no time, – never.' What was Legge expected to make of that? It was not a denial that a new symphony was a possibility, and Legge clearly did not read it as such, for the rumour gathered momentum, coming to the surface one month later at the Three Choirs Festival. On the prospectus for Worcester that year were *The Dream of Gerontius*, *The Music Makers*, the First Symphony, *For the Fallen* and the *Severn Suite*, yet at a public gathering during the festival Elgar apparently let slip one of his childish remarks to the effect that no one wanted his music now, the implication being that there would be no point in finishing a third symphony. The idea that a new symphony was virtually complete and was denied to the world because no one wanted it struck someone present so forcefully, either a *Daily Mail* reporter or someone sharp enough to tip off the *Daily Mail*, that next day the paper carried a story demanding a performance for the new symphony.

Elgar's old friend and champion Sir Landon Ronald by now had a finger in a number of musical pies; he had become a director of the Gramophone Company, he was head of the Guildhall School of Music and, most pertinent of all, he was chairman of the BBC's Music Advisory Committee. A man of enormous energy and enthusiasm, he saw the chance of a major coup for the BBC, and in consultation with Bernard Shaw he suggested to its chairman, Sir John Reith, that the BBC should make sure of getting the glory for patronizing Elgar's Third Symphony by encouraging him to complete it with the offer of a large and therefore almost irresistible commission. The result was an offer of £1,000, with the additional promise of quarterly payments of £250 'during such time as the composer may be engaged upon the proposed musical work or for a period of one year whichever is the shorter'. The prospect of picking up £2,000 if he took a year to produce the symphony, to a man who had just signed a last Will and Testament asserting the 'sudden collapse of everything artistic and commercial', must have restored his faith in miracles. On 9 December he accepted.

On what basis did Elgar accept the commission? Had he contracted to produce the full score of a work already so nearly completed in outline as to be virtually written, or was he to begin a new symphony from scratch (always allowing for the existence of sketches and fragments)? Unless large portions of the score have been destroyed – and this seems most unlikely – the answer, surely, is the latter. If that was the case, and the general impression was that a symphony was all but written and just required scoring, was he being dishonest? The BBC made no investigations of its own. Adrian Boult, the BBC's Director of Music, was under the clear impression that 'another Symphony is coming, and coming in the autumn', as he wrote to Elgar on 15 December 1932, the day after the official announcement had been made, adding, 'I had no idea until I saw the paper this morning that it was already so far advanced.' The BBC wanted to secure a new symphony without having to pay royalties on its own broadcast or public performances, and it hoped it was on to a good investment. Reverting to the subject of the new work on 11 January 1933, Boult told Elgar, 'We now look forward with the keenest interest to the grand concert of next season, & feel confident that the third Symphony will take its place with the other two, & most proud that the BBC orchestra will be the first to produce it.'

No matter what Elgar may have said or believed, or allowed to be said or believed by others, regarding the state of composition and therefore the probable date of delivery of the score, he must have known, on receipt of Boult's letters of 15 December and 11 January, that the BBC was expecting the imminent fulfilment of the commission, and from that point onwards the onus was on him to keep to the deadline or to tell the BBC there would be a delay. If progress on the symphony was such that Elgar knew – and judging by what survives, he must have known – that there was no hope of producing a fully orchestrated symphonic work in time to meet the expectations of the people who had commissioned it, he had a clear duty to say so. Not only did he fail to say so, having been given two openings by Boult, but at the time he accepted the commission he had already, blatantly, covered his tracks. He would, he had told Sir John Reith, always treasure the remembrance of his kindness and consideration, *'whatever happens'*. Those words he underlined himself, and they were not the words of a man who had reason to be confident that he would produce the finished work within a reasonable period of time. They were the words of a man who was saying, 'On your own head be it.' When Gaisberg wrote to Elgar on 15 December, having, like Boult, read of the commission in the papers that morning, he was already pressing for the work to be recorded, 'immediately before or after the inaugural performance', and Elgar responded the next day, in a letter more concerned with other matters, with the cryptic note, 'I shall be glad to do the Prelude etc when you are ready: as to Sym. III – ?'

Knowing that the BBC was confident that the work was about to materialize, he must have felt under intolerable pressure to produce it, and he does seem to have got down to work as hard and as conscientiously as he was able, allowing for his age and the fact that thirteen years had elapsed since his last major work. The pressure was boosted every thirteen weeks when a cheque for £250 would arrive in the post. On receipt of his first advance, Elgar wrote to Reith, early in 1933, to say, 'I am hoping to begin scoring the work very shortly. I am satisfied with the progress made by the "sketch" and I hope that the "fabric" of the music is as good as anything I have done.' He added, perhaps significantly, 'But naturally there are moments when one feels uncertain. However, I am doing the best I can and up to the present the symphony is the *strongest* thing I have put on paper.' Whether Elgar meant to convey modest concern about the quality of his work, or a hint that work was progressing but slowly, he was now in a hopeless situation. Almost anything he said or wrote could only serve to increase pressure of one kind or another. This particular letter encouraged Owen Mase, Adrian Boult's assistant, to write in April to say that the BBC would like to perform the symphony on 18 October, and he asked, just as directly, 'I wonder if you could tell me whether it will be finished in time?' He pointed out that parts and score would have to be ready by the end of September at the latest, 'so that the fullest rehearsal and preparation could be given'. According to Humphrey Burton, former Head of Music and Arts, BBC Television, Elgar's reply to that vital letter has apparently been removed from the BBC's archives.[1] We can deduce however that Elgar at this point came clean and said there was no chance of meeting the autumn deadline, agreeing to produce the symphony instead in time for performance in May 1934, because on 2 May 1933 Mase wrote to Elgar to say, 'I am very glad we may go ahead and announce the Symphony for the May Festival 1934.'

Even that promise was a foolhardy one. Elgar was obliged to break off work on the symphony in October, because of ill-health, and judging by the quantity of score in existence at that time (he never worked on it again), any hope of completion even by May 1934 must have been a dismal one when he agreed to the new date.

On 17 August, Elgar and the pianist Harriet Cohen had tea with Gaisberg in London, and recalling the event in *Music on Record*, Gaisberg says, 'Elgar joyfully announced to us that his Third Symphony was practically complete, a Piano Concerto was nearly finished, and he was half way through an opera. I really think vanity kept him going.' Although a definite date had been agreed between Elgar and Boult's assistant for a performance of the projected symphony, Gaisberg was writing to Elgar the day after taking tea with him not only to pester him about recording the work but to say, 'I am looking forward . . . to hearing from Dr Boult about the date set for the concert.' There seems to have been a decided lack of communication between Gaisberg and Boult, or between Boult and Mase. In any case, Elgar knew the date: May

1. *Journal of the Royal Society of Arts*, March 1979.

1934. Why had he not told Gaisberg? In a letter written the same day, and which therefore presumably crossed in the post with Gaisberg's letter, Elgar wrote, 'I saw Dr Adrian Boult last night & passed on your suggestion about recording the incipient Sym III. [Elgar and Gaisberg had evidently discussed the matter over tea.] He seemed delighted at the idea & we shall hear more of it – whether you will ever hear more of Sym III or E.E. remains to be seen. I delicately put the matter.'

'I delicately put the matter.' What did that mean? Not only had Elgar been obliged to arrange a new delivery date for the manuscript, a date he seems to have been unwilling to divulge to Gaisberg, but he was now entangled in plans to record the symphony, plans which he tells Gaisberg 'we shall hear more about' while in the same breath warning him he may never hear anything more of the symphony. No one seems to have realized the muddle the old man was in, and 'I delicately put the matter' was surely a plea to all these good, well-intentioned friends who were so desperately striving to get him to write one last masterpiece to leave him in peace, or at any rate not to be too cross or disappointed if the masterpiece never materialized.

That Elgar was at work on the symphony is not in doubt. Reed says the material had been in his mind for years, but that during 1933 a clear vision was forming, and he would 'write a portion of the finale, or the middle section of the second movement, and then work at the development of the first movement'. He adds, 'It did not seem at all odd to him to begin things in the middle, or to switch off suddenly from one movement to another. It is evident that he had the whole conception in his mind in a more or less nebulous condition.' Elgar told Reed that he was not going to cast it in the same form as the two earlier symphonies; it was to be more simple in construction and design. 'He was going to revert to the old-fashioned repeat in the exposition of the first movement with a *prima* and *seconda volta*. The second movement was to be of a light character with contrasts, but not quick; it was to be a slow-moving kind of scherzo.'

Reed also tells us that Elgar wrote out the main themes on a single stave for him to play on the violin while Elgar filled in the harmonies on the piano. One day the two of them played what Reed described as 'a great deal' of the work to Bernard Shaw and his wife when they came to tea. Conscientious as all this activity sounds, it still does not seem to tally with Elgar's assertion to Reith so early in 1933 that he was 'hoping to begin scoring the work very shortly', especially when Reed also tells us that the last movement was to be fiery and rugged but he could never find out how it was to end, and that he could never induce Elgar to begin playing the slow movement at the beginning. 'We always started either at the middle section,' he wrote, 'or what I imagined would be about the six or eighth bar.' Whenever they reached a point where the coda might begin he would 'leave off suddenly and abruptly ... and say, "Enough of this. Let us go and take the dogs on the common." He would be very restless and ill at ease, and would not discuss the symphony any more, and it would be quite a while before he became calm and resumed his normal good spirits.' Reed tells us that the main theme for the second movement, an Allegretto, was 'very light and rather wistful', a simple little tune that Elgar loved, and would play again and again. It is all too easy to imagine him getting diverted by pleasantries of this nature when he should have been concentrating on working out the overall form and forcing himself to orchestrate the work.

Reed must have realized what state the symphony was in. Other visitors during the summer of 1933 were under no illusions, among them Basil Maine, who has left a vivid account of progress from exactly this period. 'When he played parts of the work to me on the piano he relied partly on the sketches (so disjointed and disordered as to be a kind of jigsaw puzzle), partly on memory, partly I imagine on extemporization. During the improvised (or memorized) passages, it was possible to think that one was beginning to share Elgar's vision, but the experience was so clouded and so fleeting that it could not possibly be re-captured by means of the sketches alone.'[2] These remarks take on an even greater significance in the light of attempts made after Elgar's death to reconstruct the symphony from his sketches.

Although he had a chill in April, which prevented him attending a dinner in honour of Bruno Walter, Elgar seems to have been in good health during 1933, rising and bathing each morning at seven o'clock and enjoying a good appetite. His musical appreciation was undimmed, and in old age he acquired the endearing habit of admiring his own work from a distance, almost as if someone else had written it, remarking to Gaisberg, for example, about the *Serenade* for strings, 'What grand music, what a wonderful melody.' Conscious perhaps that he was a local as well as a national celebrity, he enjoyed taking visitors on conducted tours of Worcester, pointing out to them the landmarks of his youth. He paid regular visits to Alice's grave at Little Malvern, and he seems, like many old people, to have become dependent on his friends for company. Having had Gaisberg to stay in August, he was writing to him on 20 September to ask him to stay again, saying, 'It is years since you were here.'

On 18 May the Worcester Schools Music Festival gave the first performance of a new unison song, *The Woodland Stream*, and Elgar also composed at this time a little orchestral tribute to one of his dogs, *Mina*. He was becoming

2. *Basil Maine on Music* (Westhouse, 1945).

anxious about events on the continent, writing to Adela Schuster on 17 March to say, 'I am in a maze regarding events in Germany – what are they doing? In this morning's paper it is said that the greatest conductor Bruno Walter and, stranger still, Einstein are ostracised: are we all mad? The Jews have always been my best and kindest friends.'[3]

On 16 May a charity concert was held at the Wigmore Hall for Elgar's seventy-sixth birthday, at which the three late chamber works were performed, and after Lady Maud Warrender had written a letter personally to the king, both the king and queen lent their patronage to the event. Harriet Cohen paid all the expenses, and proceeds went to the Musicians' Benevolent Fund.

In August, Elgar was invited by Henry Wood to conduct the Second Symphony at the Queen's Hall. Before the concert he was treated by Gaisberg to 'a light dinner and a bottle of claret' at the Langham Hotel, and on their way to the concert (the Queen's Hall was round the corner from the hotel), they encountered 'an itinerant fiddler' playing *Salut d'Amour*. According to Gaisberg, Elgar asked the violinist if he knew what he was playing, and when the man informed him it was *Salut d'Amour* by Elgar, Elgar gave him half-a-crown and said, 'Take this, it's more than Elgar ever made out of it.' The story has every sign of being apocryphal, as indeed have many others told about Elgar. For example, Gaisberg relates that at a performance of *The Dream of Gerontius* in Leeds, Elgar was sitting in a box as guest of honour, and one of the local dignitaries, sitting next to Elgar and 'ignorant of his identity', nudged him and said, 'Who's the composer of this awful stuff?' 'I think it's a fellow called Elgar,' Elgar replies. 'Come on,' says the Yorkshireman. 'Let's beat it and have a drink before the pubs are closed.' The story has a nice north country ring to it, but it is hard to believe that the dignitary concerned had been placed next to Elgar without being told who he was.

Reed tells one story, illustrating the composer's wit, which is so good that one may be allowed to hope it is true. Apparently after complimenting Elgar on his overture *Cockaigne*, a jocular admirer went on to say, 'But I always thought cocaine was an anaesthetic. Let's hope the overture won't have that effect on its hearers. If it does, why not call it chloroform?' To which Elgar responded without a moment's hesitation, 'Ether will do.'

In September, Elgar paid his last visit to the Three Choirs Festival, held in 1933 in Hereford. A viola arrangement of the Cello Concerto was given its first performance on 6 September with Lionel Tertis as the soloist and

3. When Bruno Walter eventually left Austria following Hitler's invasion, Adrian Boult generously offered to step down from his post at the BBC in order that Walter might hold it for as long as he wished. The suggestion was vetoed by Sir Hugh Allen on the grounds that it would not be appropriate for a senior musical post at the BBC to be held by a foreigner.

Elgar conducting. A month later, however, he had to go into a nursing home in Worcester for what he thought would be an operation for a gastric condition. On 7 October, the day he was due to go into the nursing home, he did what undoubtedly he thought to be the honourable thing, for legally it was quite unnecessary, and wrote a letter to Sir John Reith. 'I am extremely sorry to have to tell you that everything is held up for the present,' he announced. 'I am not at all sure how things will turn out and have made arrangements that in case the Symphony does not materialise the sums you have paid on account shall be returned. This catastrophe came without warning as I was in the midst of scoring the work. Perhaps,' he added, 'it will not be necessary to refer publicly to the Symphony in any way at present; we will wait and see what happens to me.'

Elgar had by this time received his entire advance 'grant', as his generous BBC contract described it, of £1,000, and the statement that he was in the midst of scoring the work could only have reassured Reith that the work was well on the way and was on schedule for production in May the next year. Elgar of course knew that it was still on the drawing board, and he must have felt a great sense of relief on receiving from Reith an assurance that he would show his letter to no one but Boult.

Elgar's offer to repay the £1,000 advance was, after some irrelevant soul-searching on the part of the BBC, never taken up; in a memorandum to his legal adviser, Mr Jardine Brown, Sir John Reith wrote, a week after Elgar had died, that he was told by Sir Landon Ronald that Elgar had 'not left much money and that his daughter, Mrs Blake, would be inconvenienced if she had to return the money, her husband apparently not making much of things'.

'I am not well and have lumbago,' Elgar had written to Gaisberg on 22 September; he had told Reith he was having a gastric operation, and three weeks after the operation, Carice was referring to sciatica. 'The pain was going on,' she reported to the Gramophone Company on 26 October, on a postcard, '& nothing seems to stop it. Yesterday & today though it has really been much less; & he has had some real sleep – & enjoyed a few records – So I *hope* – hardly daring to breathe – that the sciatica is subsiding.'

Elgar had suffered from attacks of lumbago for many years, and during his fatal illness it seems that much of his pain was caused by pressure on the sciatic nerve. By November it was apparent to his friends at least that the pressure was in fact being caused by a malignant tumour, and on 10 November Landon Ronald, reporting that Elgar was rambling and often bursting into tears, appears to have believed there was little chance of recovery. His condition was not, however, considered so serious that Reed need be summoned by telegram, and Mary Clifford, Elgar's secretary, merely wrote asking him to pay a visit. As soon as Elgar saw Reed he 'broke down and wept piteously'. Reed held his hand for a long time until he became calmer, when Elgar said, 'Don't take any notice. I was afraid that when I saw you I should make a fool of myself.' Elgar's doctor, Moore Ede, had agreed to a consultation on 12 November with Lord Horder, a senior physician at St Bartholomew's Hospital whose patients included King George V, and between them they had come to the conclusion that Elgar had cancer. Reed, who was Elgar's 'nearest and most intimate friend, and must therefore be told the truth', was informed of this by Dr Ede, who gave Elgar from six to twelve months to live. On 13 November, Elgar saw a report in a newspaper that he was not progressing satisfactorily, and as Horder had been to see him the day before he naturally became suspicious about his condition.

He had every reason to be. On 20 November, Carice sent a telegram to Reed: 'Father unconscious sinking rapidly' Before losing consciousness Elgar had asked for Reed.) During the afternoon, when Reed, Carice and a nurse were present, he rallied, and Reed again held his hand. 'It was evident that he was trying very hard to speak,' Reed has recorded. 'And gradually and at long intervals the words came from him. "I want you ... to do something for me ... the symphony all bits and pieces ... no one would understand ... no one ... no one."'

Reed says that 'a look of great anguish came over his face as he said this', and his voice died away with exhaustion. Reed then leant over Elgar and said, 'What can I do for you? Try to tell me. I will do anything for you; you know that.'

Again there was a long silence, but 'a more peaceful expression came into his face'. Before long, 'he drew me down again and said, "Don't let anyone tinker with it ... no one could understand ... no one must tinker with it."'

Reed then gave Elgar an assurance that no one would ever tamper with the unfinished symphony in any way, 'or attempt to construct what would have been a most unsatisfactory work'. A little later, Elgar said, 'in a whisper with great emotion, "I think you had better burn it."'

Reed and Carice 'exchanged glances', and Reed saw that Elgar's daughter looked, 'as I am sure I did', a little startled at this suggestion. 'Then,' says Reed, 'I felt that it was only a suggestion and not really a request, so I leaned over him and said, "I don't think it is necessary to burn it. It would be awful to do that. But Carice and I will remember that no one is to try and put it together. No one shall ever tinker with it. We promise you that."' Hearing this, 'Elgar seemed to grow more peaceful. His strugglings and efforts to speak ceased; he lay there with his eyes open, watching us.'

In the light of subsequent moves to have the unfinished symphony performed in some shape or other, it is worth noting that Reed took it upon himself to interpret a clear request from Elgar to have the score destroyed as merely 'a suggestion', and that he then gave Elgar an undertaking which he was not strictly speaking in any position to honour – he was not, for instance, an executor or trustee of his Will. If he had not satisfied himself that Elgar was, after all, content for the manuscript to remain in existence, would Reed then have burnt it after Elgar's death? It would have required some courage, although he would have been morally justified to do so, but he would then have laid himself open to blame for allowing what would have been thought a great masterpiece to go up in flames merely to satisfy the semi-conscious whims of an eccentric old man. If it is felt that Reed should not have brought pressure of any sort on Elgar to change his mind, it should be remembered that Elgar was greatly given to dramatization; Reed, perhaps taking this into account, may have been genuinely convinced that Elgar was not really serious when he asked to have the score burnt. On the other hand he must have known as well as Elgar how very far from completion the symphony was, and been aware of the possibility that Elgar might have wanted the evidence of his inability to meet the May deadline destroyed. In fairness to Reed, whatever interpretation one puts upon these events, it is reasonable to assume that under very trying circumstances he felt at the time that he was acting for the best.

After Elgar's death, Reed gathered up and collated every scrap of score that appeared to represent work on the Third Symphony, and writing many years later he recalled that the first movement, marked Allegro Molto Maestoso, was to plunge at once into a definite statement of the principal subject (this would have been in true Elgarian mould), a theme of rugged and sweeping character in 12/8 time, sounding 'as if it had always been going on, as the sound of the sea or the wind in the trees – inevitable music'. The main theme for the second movement, an Allegretto, was 'very light and rather wistful', the simple little theme that Elgar loved and which he and Reed played over and over again on the piano and violin. Of the third movement, an Adagio, the only part apparently completed was a 'broad, dignified and very expressive melody of 18 bars'. Reed says that Elgar wrote out this melody for violin, and exhorted Reed to 'tear his heart out' every time he played it, 'so much was he overcome by its emotional significance'. The last movement was to open majestically, and Elgar left an introductory four bars in full score.

Reed has provided a full description of the unfinished Third Symphony in *Elgar As I Knew Him*, as well as a valuable insight into Elgar's general method of composition. The odd mixture of sketches, motifs and fragments in full score that survive illustrate Elgar's lateral approach; he rarely started anything at the beginning but worked at a theme and brought it to a climax, for then, as he said, he knew to what he was leading. Reed says: 'Like Beethoven, he allowed an idea which may have occurred to him as a short phrase to germinate and transform and throw out branches.' Elgar was entirely self-taught as a composer. He had told Reed at their first meeting that he knew nothing about harmony or counterpoint and he once remarked of a music critic that the man knew more about music than he did himself. After a performance of *The Dream of Gerontius* in Lincoln Cathedral he said to Reed, rubbing his hands with glee, 'Billy, I believe there is a lot of double counterpoint, or whatever they call it, in that.' Reed says that Elgar was proud – and justly so – of his skill in laying out his music for the orchestra, knowing unerringly what he wanted in the way of orchestral or choral tone, balance and colour. 'I do not think he ever altered or modified one single note of anything he had once set down in the score,' Reed tells us. 'Meyerbeer's plan of writing alternative scorings in different coloured inks to find out how they sounded was a favourite subject of derision with Elgar. He could not understand the need for any experiments in orchestration. Nothing in his own work ever surprised him when he heard it coming from the orchestra, or choir and orchestra, for the first time; he just *knew* how it should sound, and was never disappointed.' Elgar may have been self-taught, but not for nothing had he learnt his craft as an orchestral player.

Sir Adrian Boult has said that had Elgar completed the Third Symphony, 'it would in a way have been retarded, compressed, more enclosed than the two previous symphonies. When I was at the BBC we had a terrible time fighting off people who wanted to disregard Elgar's instructions and tinker with it. Bantock wrote at one time and said he would like to try and complete it, but there was not enough written down to amplify. In any event, I think a man's wishes made on his death-bed should be respected, and Elgar was determined the sketches should be left alone.'[4]

After Elgar's death, some of the sketches were published in the *Listener*, even though the BBC had made an agreement with Carice to see that 'none of the old manuscripts (of the symphony) shall ever be published in whole or in part and that they will not permit any person whatever to have access to the said manuscripts for the purpose of finishing or completing any alteration'. Speaking to a meeting of the Royal Society of Arts on 13 December 1978, Humphrey Burton said he believed the time had come for this provision to be set aside, 'at least to the extent of arranging for a new, independent assessment of the Third Symphony manuscripts and sketches'. Ten years

4. In conversation with the author.

previously, BBC Radio Music Talks had decided to make a programme in which the sketches would be 'orchestrated, organised into some kind of coherence and performed under the baton of Sir Adrian Boult by the BBC Symphony Orchestra'.[5] Carice, after 'considerable hesitation', had accepted the BBC's argument in favour of a single performance which would be the equivalent of the publication in the *Listener* of some of the sketches. At that time Boult presumably had no qualms about disregarding Elgar's death-bed wishes.

A recording studio was booked, and 'the BBC's chosen musicologist' went ahead with his musical reconstruction, 'to the point that the orchestral score of Elgar's Third Symphony was sent off in order for the individual parts to be copied out'. Alas for the enterprise, the parts then went for checking to a retired BBC music executive and composer, 'who felt most strongly that the BBC was breaking faith with its legal undertaking to the Elgar Estate'. In spite of the fact that Carice had released the BBC from its original obligations, the corporation's lawyers had second thoughts about the legality of the proposed programme. Sir Adrian Boult, too, had second thoughts, and decided not to conduct, so the whole project folded.

In 1978, however, the BBC's lawyers had third thoughts, and the trustees of the Elgar Estate gave permission to BBC Television 'for the performance of the sketches for the Symphony to be included in a television programme on the basis that they are performed on the piano. No orchestration or completion of the sketches will be allowed.' In his talk to the Royal Society of Arts, Mr Burton said, 'It may well be necessary to ask the trustees for permission to perform the sketches in the violin and piano version which Fred Gaisberg and others so enjoyed in 1933,' an idea which failed to find favour with Mr Wulstan Atkins, Elgar's godson and chairman of the trustees, who told the meeting, 'I would personally strongly object to any attempt to play the fragments on any instrument or instruments other than a piano since Elgar's orchestration was essentially his own, and this would be "tinkering with the fragments", which is the one thing Elgar most wanted to avoid.' Burton's suggestion did not amount to a desire to orchestrate the fragments, and Elgar himself had been perfectly happy listening to the sketches on piano and violin, but at all events even this plan seems to have collapsed. Since Mr Burton gave his talk, the BBC has done more research, and discovered that 'whatever Elgar may have told the BBC, he had not got very far with the Third Symphony'. Proposals for a 'performance of the sketches' have been abandoned.[6]

5. *Journal of the Royal Society of Arts*, March 1979.
6. Letter of 11 June 1980 from Mr Humphrey Burton to the author.

Elgar's final reference to the Third Symphony was made when, lying ill in bed, he wrote a few bars of music, almost certainly the last music he ever put on paper; when Reed came to visit him one day, Elgar handed the scrap of paper to his friend, and with tears streaming down his cheeks he said, 'Billy, this is the end.' Reed tells us that Elgar would not explain whether he meant it was the end of the Adagio or the end of the last movement, that is to say, the end of the symphony. It seems not to have occurred to Reed that Elgar may simply have been saying, 'This is the end of my music, the end of my life.'

On 24 November 1933, four days after Carice had cabled Billy Reed to say that her father was 'sinking rapidly', Sir Granville Bantock took it upon himself to call on Sir John Reith at the BBC to inform him that Elgar was most unlikely to live for more than a day or two, and to ask Sir John to approach the Dean of Westminster, William Foxley Norris, with a view, as Reith put it in a letter to the dean later that day, 'to asking whether you would consider an Abbey burial for Elgar'.[7] Almost unbelievably, Reith, after passing on the information from Bantock that Elgar was leaving instructions that he wished to be buried quietly at Malvern, went on to say that the musicians on whose behalf Bantock had approached him thought that 'in a case of this sort national considerations ... should override such a request'.

In his letter to the dean, Reith mentioned the possibility that objections to the plan – a plan Elgar's interfering friends were trying to implement for the disposal of his body without his consent and before he was even dead – might be raised by the Roman Catholic authorities. Replying to Reith on 28 November, Foxley Norris said, 'There seems to be no [dou]bt that Elgar is a Roman and if this is so, I am afraid I could not offer burial in the Abbey for two reasons.

'1. That the Romans would, I should think, certainly forbid it, and I don't want to put the Abbey in that position, and

'2. That there can be no burials now here without cremation and they would not allow that.

'I am afraid, therefore, that it is out of the question.'

The dean went on to say that Elgar's position in the world of art was such that no doubt he might offer the abbey 'for the first part of the Serv[ice]' if he was to be buried according to his own wish, in the country, but he was not prepared to do even that if there would be Roman Catholic objection.[8]

The following day Reith acknowledged the dean's letter, saying he would

7. Westminster Abbey Muniments 61909.
8. Westminster Abbey Muniments 61910A.

'privately explain it, or at any rate bits of it, to Sir Granville Bantock'. He was however unable to do so in time to prevent Bantock from going that very day, 29 November, not only over his own head but over the dean's. Without waiting to see what response Reith had obtained from Norris, Bantock wrote to the prime minister, Ramsay MacDonald, to try to enlist his 'sanction and approval' for Elgar's burial in the abbey.[9]

Elgar's physical and emotional stamina were to prove stronger now that he was dying than they had sometimes appeared during his lifetime, and Bantock's efforts were not only presumptuous but premature. On 6 December Elgar had rallied sufficiently to thank Bernard Shaw for sending him a play and a preface. 'I am still in the deepest pain,' he told Shaw, but the next day he was dictating a letter to Gaisberg to ask, 'quite *privately*, between *ourselves*', whether he had a photographer at his disposal who would come down to the nursing home in Worcester and 'take photographs of me *in this room*'. The photographer duly arrived with Gaisberg on 12 December. 'During the visit,' Gaisberg recorded, 'I was struck at the great improvement in Sir E. His brain was clear; he was interested and alert.' Gaisberg had taken him as a gift a record of Yehudi Menuhin and his thirteen-year-old sister Hephzibah playing the Mozart Sonata in A minor. 'The gramophone,' Gaisberg noted, 'remains his favourite distraction.'

One day Troyte Griffith went to see Elgar in the nursing home, and they listened to Elgar's String Quartet. After the slow movement, Griffith said, 'Surely that is as fine as a movement by Beethoven.' Elgar replied, 'Yes, it is, and there is something in it that has never been done before.' When Griffith asked what that was, he received the irritating sort of reply Elgar could always be expected to reserve for a non-musician: 'Nothing you would understand, merely an arrangement of notes.'[10]

So marked was Elgar's improvement that rumours spread to the effect that he had left the nursing home, and Adrian Boult was even under the impression that he was again commuting between the London flat and Worcestershire. 'It is splendid to hear ... that you are now getting well again,' he wrote to Elgar on 16 December. 'As I see no lights in your flat tonight I expect you are at Malvern for the weekend.' Elgar replied from the nursing home to say, 'I fear my friends are unduly optimistic; the announcement of my return home was a mistake and I fear it will be a considerable time before this can happen.' It was Elgar, however, who was being unduly pessimistic, for on 1 January 1934 he was allowed home.

It seems likely that Elgar was allowed home not because the doctors thought

9. Westminster Abbey Muniments 61912B.
10. Notes by Troyte Griffith at Elgar's Birthplace.

he was cured but because they knew he was dying and they thought he would wish to die at Marl Bank. Only eight days after his return from the nursing home, Carice was writing to Gaisberg to say, 'We have had a terrible few days of pain & morphia. I cannot see how it is to go on like this – it's such agony & yet he is so strong in himself. It is a tragedy.' Desperately ill and in dreadful pain though her father was, in the same letter Carice was agreeing to a somewhat bizarre plan to link up a recording session in London with Elgar's bedroom. Dr Ede had seen 'no objection medically to your wonderful proposal', Carice told Gaisberg. 'The only fear is that he might be in pain when you have arranged it – but we think probably he would pull himself together & be able to listen – & that it would do more good than anything as it would interest him & make him feel he was in things more.' Tactfully, she asked Gaisberg to write direct to Elgar about the idea, '& not mention that you have told me or asked the Dr – it does please him to be in things. I can see it irks him if arrangements (which one cannot help) come through me – & in this case there is no need.'

Incredible though it may seem, when writing to Elgar suggesting the recording session, Gaisberg shifted the responsibility for initiating it to the man mortally stricken with cancer. 'Needless to say,' he wrote, 'we could not carry this out unless we had a direct request from you to do so, appearing as if it was inspired by yourself alone, because, should the result be a set-back in your recovery, the press and public would blame it on us. In this letter, I enclose a letter giving the idea, which you could sign if you feel so disposed ...' In other words, it was to appear as if Elgar, while lying ill in bed, had been so egocentric as to propose an expensive recording session involving the installation of telephone lines, loudspeakers and microphones.

In many ways an innocent to the end, Elgar seems only to have expressed delight at the whole enterprise, and the session was fixed for 22 January. That morning he was barely conscious. Gaisberg however had planned the arrangements like a military operation, and the business of 'immediately proceeding to Sir Edward Elgar's house ... commencing installing the equipment ... lunch being taken on the train ... Post Office lines being available from 3 to 5 pm ... the microphone and loudspeaker for Sir Edward Elgar being moved into his room at 3.45 pm' were inexorably set in motion. On arriving at Marl Bank, Gaisberg went to see Elgar. 'He began many conversations, but his voice seemed to fade and he dozed off. I was much concerned for fear he would not rouse himself in time for our recording. He recognised me but could not concentrate. I was told by Mrs Blake that he had had frequent injections of morphia, but it was principally the toxic poisoning from the wound that was making him so drowsy.'

Elgar in fact regained full consciousness late in the afternoon, and with an amazing display of courage, and in a bedroom crowded out by Fred Gaisberg and the engineers, Sir Ivor Atkins, Elgar's niece Madeleine Grafton, his secretary Miss Mary Clifford, his manservant, his doctor and a maid, he attended in minute detail to the recording session, criticizing certain passages, talking cheerfully to the orchestral players, led by Billy Reed, and even remarking to Gaisberg, at the opening of the Triumphal March from *Caractacus*, 'I say, Fred, isn't that a gorgeous melody. Who could have written such a beautiful melody?' Carice wrote the next day to reassure Gaisberg that 'Father is none the worse in any way from yesterday afternoon. He is still very muddled, but when clear he thinks of it all with great pleasure, and I am sure enjoyed it ... I am so glad he was able to do it.'

The most tantalizing enigma of Elgar's whole enigmatic career was to result from a visit he received in February from Ernest Newman, certain details of which Newman decided to reveal many years later, in an exceptionally irresponsible article in the *Sunday Times*. According to Newman, Elgar 'made a single short remark about himself', which Newman had never disclosed to anyone and had no intention of ever disclosing, 'for it would lend itself too easily to the crudest of misinterpretations'. Having whetted his readers' appetites, Newman then went on to scatter a few vague clues by adding, 'It explains a good deal in him that has always been obscure or puzzling to us; it has a particular bearing, I am convinced, on that passion of his for public mysteryfication of which the most remarkable outward expressions were his two "enigmas" – that of the Variations and that of the "Soul" enshrined in the violin concerto.'[11] Newman returned to the creation of his own enigma when he wrote to Gerald Abraham a letter quoted in the *Listener* on 23 July 1959: 'Elgar's distressing remark,' he told Dr Abraham, 'consisted of only five words, but the scope they would give to a "reading" of him is infinite, so I am determined to keep them to myself.' With studied arrogance he added, 'They are too tragic for the ear of the mob.'

If Newman was determined to keep Elgar's five distressing words to himself, he would have done Elgar a greater service by refraining altogether from drawing attention to the incident since all he succeeded in doing was to provoke speculation. In any case Elgar was by that time being heavily drugged with morphia to relieve his pain and was, according to his daughter, 'very muddled'.

It may be of interest to note that Newman was apparently the sole witness of another side of Elgar's character. Again writing in the *Sunday Times*, on 23 October 1955, he recalled his first meeting with Elgar, in

11. *Sunday Times*, 6 November 1955.

Liverpool in 1901, when he was thirty-three: 'He gave me even then the impression of an exceptionally nervous, self-divided and secretly unhappy man; in the light of all we came to know of him in later life, I can see now that he was at that time rather bewildered and nervous at the half-realisation that his days of spiritual privacy – always so dear to him – were probably coming to an end; while no doubt gratified by his rapidly growing fame he was in his heart of hearts afraid of the future. I remember distinctly a dinner ... at which Mrs Elgar tactfully steered the conversation away from the topic of suicide that had suddenly arisen; she whispered to me that Edward was always talking of making an end of himself.'

Elgar may well have suffered from the kind of depression that leads to thoughts of suicide, but as Newman does not date the dinner party we cannot easily judge how well he knew the Elgars at the time and therefore how much store we can set by his account. Elgar was knighted in 1904, and if Alice was still 'Mrs Elgar' they cannot have known each other long. Moreover, Newman was a journalist, and Alice would have needed to be very sure of his discretion before disclosing such a personal matter, especially one so violently in opposition not only to the teaching of the church to which both she and Elgar belonged but to the laws of the state which at that time regarded attempted suicide as a criminal offence. There is no corroborative evidence that Elgar was 'always talking of making an end of himself': of the three most intimate friends of Elgar who wrote memoirs – Dorabella, Rosa Burley and Billy Reed – none gives the slightest hint that his depression was that serious, and, had it been, it would have been a condition almost impossible to hide from friends and therefore one that would in all probability have been reported and discussed among them. Either Alice or Newman exaggerated the case; and Alice's entire life was devoted to boosting her husband's morale, enlarging his reputation and seeing his detractors off with a flea in their ear.

On 28 January, only six days after the recording session, Gaisberg and Reed went down to Marl Bank with sample pressings of the new records, and while they were there Elgar produced from under his pillow the manuscript of the little orchestral piece he had written the previous year, called *Mina*. He scribbled a dedication and gave it to Gaisberg. Perhaps it was his way of thanking him for arranging the recording session in his bedroom, and this time it was Gaisberg's turn to burst into tears. He recovered himself sufficiently on returning to London to have the score recorded immediately. 'Everyone is amazed at its freshness and beauty,' he told Carice on 9 February. 'It is really a charming little work.' And by 13 February he was able to produce his final surprise for Elgar, posting a copy of the new record for him to play. It arrived safely, and two days later Carice wrote to Gaisberg to say, 'I had the opportunity of playing the Mina record to Father today. He wants me to tell you that he much enjoyed hearing it – & thinks it so kind of you to have done it.' There followed a string of constructive criticisms which testify to the considerable emotional courage Elgar was able to summon up in his last days. 'He hopes you will not mind his saying,' Carice wrote, 'that it is too fast – he knows the time was not marked – & it wants more stress on the first note of the opening part. The next tune should be much softer & quieter.' After passing on further detailed comments she added, 'He is so sorry to make all these criticisms – & hopes you may have an opportunity of making another record – he does not wish this one published as it stands.'

So far as music was concerned, that was Elgar's last wish, and no doubt he was pleased to learn that it had been carried out. Gaisberg replied on 20 February to Carice's letter, saying he had taken due note and would carry out the changes as directed at the first opportunity. 'It was wonderful to think that he had a lucid moment and could so clearly express his criticisms,' he wrote, adding what was undeniably true, 'It seems almost a miracle.' Three days later, on 23 February, Billy Reed received a telegram from Carice: 'End came most peacefully 7.45 this morning please tell Gaisberg.'

Perhaps the most celebrated artist in England had died, and in *The Times* he rated a fourth leader. 'No man,' it ran, 'was ever more loved by the comparatively few men and women who really came near to him.' *The Times*'s obituary itself contained this revealing remark: 'He . . . often yearned to get out of the limelight at the very moment when he deliberately walked into it.' Sir Ivor Atkins must have voiced the feelings of most musicians of his time when he said, 'He had thought deeply and had suffered deeply, and his music speaks fearlessly of these experiences of the human heart. And there, to my mind, lies his greatness. He was true to, and belonged to, the great line of composers of whom I need only instance Brahms, who were not ashamed of human feelings and who were content to be the poets of human emotion.'

Elgar left no instructions in his Will for his funeral, but Billy Reed tells us that he had asked Carice for a private one, and this verbal request seems to be borne out by Bantock's knowledge of it. We know that in 1920 Elgar had asked Troyte Griffith to try to secure the burial plot next to Alice's, and as Elgar was eventually interred there it seems that Troyte succeeded; Fred Gaisberg however tells us that at a later date Elgar expressed a wish to be cremated. In *Edward Elgar: His Life and Music*, a book read in proof by Carice, Diana McVeagh is at pains to stress that Elgar died a Catholic; she says that he received Extreme Unction, and that an offer of burial in Westminster Abbey had to be refused because he was a Catholic, although, as the abbey records show, no offer of burial there was ever in fact extended. Many of Elgar's friends clearly knew of his wish to be cremated, for on the day Elgar died a request from Hugh Allen, Granville Bantock, Adrian Boult, Walford Davies, John McEwen (principal of the Royal Academy of Music), Landon Ronald and Stanley Roper (organist at the Chapel Royal), 'representing the musicians of England', was sent to the Dean of Westminster asking him to allow Elgar's ashes to be buried in the abbey. Before he had even received this petition (made, incidentally, without consultation with Carice) the dean had consented on the telephone to the importunate Bantock to a memorial service 'if desired', but *not* (and the dean underlined the word 'not' in a note he later made at the top of the request for burial of the ashes) 'burial in Abbey'.[12] Bantock had already been on the telephone to Sir John Reith asking for a decision about an abbey burial, and Reith had telegraphed the dean to tell him this. The day of Elgar's death was indeed alive with the buzz of telephone wires. The dean responded to Reith's telegram with another saying, 'Memorial but not burial. Writing.'[13] The offer finally filtered past all this muddle of misplaced enthusiasm and crossed wires to Elgar's next of kin, and Carice telegraphed the dean on the day after Elgar's death to say that her father had 'always and emphatically expressed his wishes that there should be no memorial service'. She went on to say she felt that regretfully she should not accede to his suggestion.[14]

Billy Reed informs us that Ivor Atkins, even before the funeral had taken place, was planning a memorial service to be held in Worcester Cathedral, and in the event the dean and chapter moved with exceptional speed and arranged a memorial service for 2 March. Carice must have received news of this just after turning down the Dean of Westminster's offer, for she sent a second telegram to him on 24 February to say 'Since wiring have heard that Dean of Worcester will hold memorial service in Worcester Cathedral therefore I cannot withhold my consent to your holding a service [if] so desired.'[15] The Dean of Worcester had presumably announced the memorial service without waiting to ascertain the family's wishes (no one else was bothering to do so), and under the pressure of events Carice just caved in. A final offer from Foxley Norris – 'Abbey available for memorial service if desired'[16] – was dispatched simultaneously to Bantock and Carice later the same day, but for some reason came to nothing.[17]

12. Westminster Abbey Muniments 61914.
13. Westminster Abbey Muniments 61916.
14. Typed copy of a telegram badly damaged in the bombing of Westminster Abbey Deanery.
15. Typed copy of a telegram badly damaged in the bombing of Westminster Abbey Deanery.
16. Westminster Abbey Muniments 61917.
17. Elgar was eventually commemorated in Westminster Abbey with a memorial tablet in the floor of the north choir aisle. At the instigation of Sir Adrian Boult it was unveiled on 1 June 1972 by the prime minister, the Rt Hon. Edward Heath, and dedicated by the dean at that time, the Very Reverend Eric Abbott.

A Low Requiem Mass was said on 26 February at St George's Church in Worcester, where Elgar and his father had played the organ, and on the same cold, snowy day he was laid to rest alongside Alice in the little churchyard at St Wulstan's in Little Malvern. It was, just as Elgar seems to have wanted it to be, a private service attended only by members of the family and close friends, among whom were Ivor Atkins, Landon Ronald, Troyte Griffith, Billy Reed, Elgar's secretary and his manservant. Also there was Elgar's oldest friend, Hubert Leicester, the childhood companion who had later described him as a 'miserable looking lad, with legs like drumsticks', the boy with whom Elgar liked to remember that he had walked to school 'always to the brightly-lit west ... at our backs "the unthrift sun shot vital gold", filling Payne's Meadows with glory and illuminating for two small boys a world to conquer and to love'. It was the tragedy of Elgar's tormented life that while he succeeded in conquering the world he never learned to love it.

Select Bibliography

Burley, Rosa, and Frank C. Carruthers, *Edward Elgar: The Record of a Friendship* (Barrie & Jenkins, 1972)

Elgar, Sir Edward, *A Future for English Music and Other Lectures*, ed. Percy M. Young (Dennis Dobson, 1968)

My Friends Pictured Within: The Enigma Variations (Novello, 1946)

Ensor, Sir Robert, *England 1870–1914* (Clarendon Press, 1970)

Kennedy, Michael, *Elgar: Orchestral Music* (BBC Publications, 1970)

Portrait of Elgar (Oxford University Press, 1968)

McVeagh, Diana M., *Edward Elgar: His Life and Music* (J. M. Dent, 1950)

Maine, Basil, *Elgar: His Life and Works* (Bell & Sons, 1933)

Moore, Jerrold Northrop, *Elgar: A Life in Photographs* (Oxford University Press, 1972)

Elgar on Record: The Composer and the Gramophone (Oxford University Press, 1975)

(ed.) *Music and Friends: Letters to Sir Adrian Boult* (Hamish Hamilton, 1979)

New Grove Dictionary of Music and Musicians, The, Sixth Edition (Macmillan, 1980)

Parrott, Ian, *Elgar* (J. M. Dent, 1971)

Powell, Mrs Richard, *Edward Elgar: Memories of a Variation* (Remploy, 1937)

Priestley, J. B., *The Edwardians* (Sphere Books, 1972)

Reed, William H., *Elgar* (J. M. Dent, 1939)

Elgar As I Knew Him (Gollancz, 1936)

Young, Percy M., *Alice Elgar: Enigma of a Victorian Lady* (Dennis Dobson, 1943)

Elgar: OM (Collins, 1955)

(ed.) *Letters of Edward Elgar* (Geoffrey Bles, 1956)

(ed.) *Letters to Nimrod from Edward Elgar* (Dennis Dobson, 1963)

Index